Spain 1812–1996

Spain
1812–1996

MODERN HISTORY FOR MODERN LANGUAGES

Christopher J. Ross

A member of the Hodder Headline Group
LONDON

Co-published in the United States of America by
Oxford University Press Inc., New York

First published in Great Britain in 2000 by
Arnold, a member of the Hodder Headline Group
338 Euston Road, London NW1 3BH

http://www.arnoldpublishers.com

Co-published in the United States of America by
Oxford University Press Inc.,
198 Madison Avenue, New York, NY10016

British Library Cataloguing in Publicatiion Data
A catalogue record for this book is available from the British Library

Library of Congress Cataloging-in-Publication Data
A catalog record for this book is available from the Library of Congress

ISBN 0 340 74112 0 (hb)
ISBN 0 340 74113 9 (pb)

1 2 3 4 5 6 7 8 9 10

Production Editor: Wendy Rooke
Production Controller: Iain McWilliams
Cover Design: Terry Griffiths

Typeset in 9.25 on 13 Lucida by Phoenix Photosetting, Chatham, Kent
Printed and bound in Great Britain by MPG Books Ltd, Bodmin, Cornwall

What do you think about this book? Or any other Arnold title?
Please send your comments to feedback.arnold@hodder.co.uk

For Tony

Contents

Preface

It is perhaps easiest, and best, to begin by saying what this book is not. It is neither a detailed, chronological account of events in Spain, nor an attempt to provide new insights into their historical significance. The latter, in particular, it could not be, because I am not a trained historian. Nor is the book aimed primarily at students of history. Instead, its intention is to help students, in the widest sense, of contemporary Spain to recognise and understand the historical references that come up so frequently in contacts with the country and in reading about it. It is also intended to be accessible to them, regardless of whether they are currently studying other aspects of modern history, or have done so in the past.

One obvious prerequisite for understanding is information. However, I have taken the view that the provision of facts – stating dates, describing events, naming names – should not be the book's main concern. I have tried to concentrate instead on giving an overview of developments and the relationships between them. In doing so, I am well aware of laying myself open to charges of superficiality and over-simplification. All the more so as the book's focus is almost entirely on politics and on one of its major components, economics; social and cultural aspects are touched on only in passing. I can but hope that the generalisations involved are on balance more enlightening than misleading and, above all, that the book might encourage and allow readers to go more deeply into subjects which, inevitably, are covered only briefly here.

Any history book of finite length faces the problem of limits – of where to begin and where to end. Many courses on modern Spanish history, I know, concentrate mainly or wholly on the twentieth century. However, I felt that the best way of grasping the country's political development in the modern era was to consider the last two centuries as a unit, bound together by a single theme: the arduous but ultimately successful struggle to establish democratic institutions and practices. In that sense, the year 1812 provides an obvious starting point, with the appearance of Spain's first constitution. As the endpoint I have chosen 1996, because the general election held in that year completed a full cycle of alternation in power from Right to Left and back again, under free democratic conditions, for the first time in the country's history.

The book begins with a prologue which gives an outline picture of what Spain was like in 1812, and why. The main text consists of ten chapters, arranged chronologically, with the level of detail increasing significantly as time progresses. Internally, the chapters are divided into thematic sections. Each begins with a paragraph outlining the main contemporary developments in the wider world which impinged on those in Spain, for the benefit of readers who have not previously studied modern western history. Each is followed by one or more 'exhibits', contemporary Spanish texts relating to the themes covered in the chapter, and accompanied by a number of questions designed to raise discussion on them. Following the last chapter, an 'afterword' attempts to draw out some themes of relevance to current events.

The overview approach notwithstanding, some concepts and institutions either crop up recurrently or are particularly important during a particular period. A brief summary of their main features and complete evolution, not restricted to the period of the particular chapter in which they are included, have been highlighted in special 'inserts'. They are given in their Spanish form, with an English equivalent. Throughout I have tried to use natural English terminology; where reference is made to specifically Spanish concepts I have tried to render them in a way which transmits the meaning rather than the appearance of the words (e.g. 'clans' rather than 'families' for the groups that jostled for influence under the Franco regime, and were known in Spanish as *familias*). Where words appear in single inverted commas they are a direct literal translation of the Spanish (e.g. 'social concertation' for *concertación social*). Bracketed Spanish terms are intended to give an indication of usage in context; there is no suggestion that they are the sole Spanish equivalent to the preceding English word or phrase.

I have included relatively frequent cross-references, of the form '(pxxx)', since otherwise the thematic structure would require an unreasonable amount of repetition. No direct references to other works are included in the text, however, as I believe they serve little purpose in a book of this sort. I make no claims of originality, and any given statement could be checked or followed up in a number of the sources cited in the 'Further Reading' section. Here, again, I have only attempted to scratch the surface, and to indicate works that should be reasonably accessible to non-historians. Anyone who subsequently takes a serious academic interest in some aspect of the period discussed will find them a useful starting point for further bibliographic searching.

I owe a number of debts of gratitude to the various authors whose works I have consulted. I should also like to thank Elena Seymenliyska for coming up with the original idea for the book, and for her advice during its gestation, and to thank Mag. Rafael de la Dueña, of the Instituto Cervantes in Vienna, for his help in locating appropriate exhibits. I am deeply grateful to my parents and brother, who in their various ways planted and nurtured an interest in history that has given me enormous pleasure, and ultimately allowed me to undertake the task of writing this book. Most of all, though, I am indebted to my wife Ulli for her encouragement and support, and for putting up with the emotional ups and downs of the book's production while living through an altogether more fundamental and demanding type of gestation period.

Christopher J. Ross, Vienna, December 1999

Chronology of main events

1812   Constitution of Cadiz issued
1814   Ferdinand VII restores absolute rule
1820   Riego's declaration forces Ferdinand to recognise Constitution
1823   Absolute rule re-imposed
1833   Outbreak of First Carlist War; moderate liberals called to government
1840   Carlist War ends; Progressives stage revolution
1843   Moderate rule restored
1854   Progressives stage revolution
1856   Liberal Union assumes power
1868   'Glorious Revolution' deposes Isabella II
1873   First Republic declared
1874   Monarchy restored in the person of Alfonso XII
1895   Formation of Basque Nationalist Party (PNV)
1898   Defeat in war with USA leads to loss of Cuba and most other colonies
1909   Unrest in Barcelona culminates in the 'Tragic Week'
1914   Catalan regional government established
1917   Protests by various groups lead to severe crisis
1918   Formation and collapse of national government
1923   General Primo de Rivera seizes power
1930   Primo de Rivera resigns
1931   King Alfonso XIII flees the country; Second Republic declared
1933   Right-wing government elected
1934   Attempted left-wing revolution fails disastrously
1936   Popular Front government elected; attempted right-wing coup leads to outbreak of civil war
1939   General Franco wins civil war, establishes dictatorship
1946   UN recommends international boycott of Spain
1953   Agreements signed with Vatican and USA; end of Spain's isolation
1959   Stabilisation Plan marks change of economic strategy
1962   Spain refused admission to European Economic Community
1968   ETA begins campaign of violence
1973   ETA assassinates Admiral Carrero Blanco
1975   Franco dies, Juan Carlos I crowned king
1977   Democratic general election is held, won by centrist UCD
1978   Adoption of new constitution
1979   Devolution granted to Catalonia and the Basque Country

1981   Military extremists attempt coup
1982   Socialist government elected
1983   Initial devolution process completed, with creation of 17 regions
1986   Spain enters European Community; Socialist government re-elected
1988   Main trade unions stage general strike
1989   Socialist government re-elected
1992   Government adopts convergence plan to meet Maastricht criteria
1993   Socialist government re-elected, but requires support from Catalan CiU
1994   Further round of devolution completed
1995   GAL affair results in arrest of former Interior Minister
1996   People's Party wins election, forms government with support of Catalan CiU

Prologue

The course of Spain's history was determined, to an astonishing degree, by one relatively brief period. In little over 50 years, the country was transformed from a collection of relatively insignificant statelets into Europe's leading power, and the centre of a transcontinental empire. The gross mismatch between this new status and Spain's limited resources meant that her imperial glory was short-lived, and followed by a rapid decline – relative to her European neighbours – that was not reversed until the recent past. Hence the crucial importance of that fateful half-century and of its key moment, the most famous date in Spanish history.

The first significance of 1492 is that it marks the end of the 'Reconquest' (*Reconquista*), the almost eight-centuries-long process of expelling the Moors from the Iberian Peninsula. For much of that time large tracts of what is now Spain were under Muslim rule, especially in the south. Yet the lasting impact of Arab occupation was relatively slight. More important were the effects of the Reconquest itself on the various kingdoms of the gradually expanding Christian north; Portugal, Castile, Navarre and Aragon.

One enduring effect of occupation was the high value accorded in Spain, as in other societies frequently at war, to military activities and prowess; another was the tendency to grant extensive rights over newly recovered territory to local communities or powerful nobles. Perhaps most important of all, as it progressed the Reconquest became less a matter of regaining land and more a religious affair, a Crusade comparable – and explicitly compared – to the attempts to recover the Holy Land from Muslim rule. As a result, the inhabitants and rulers of Christian Spain came to see themselves as having a particularly close relationship with the Catholic Church.

These features were most marked in Castile, which by the fifteenth century was the only Christian kingdom with a Moorish frontier. Already the strongest Iberian power, Castile's influence was further extended when Ferdinand, husband of its reigning Queen Isabella I, succeeded to the throne of Aragon, thus uniting the two kingdoms under Castilian leadership. From this strengthened base the 'Catholic Monarchs' launched the campaign that enabled them, in January 1492, to capture the last Moorish stronghold of Granada. With the exception of Navarre, which was not incorporated until 1515, a united Spain had been established within its modern boundaries.

Before the momentous year was out the young kingdom was presented with a dazzling challenge and opportunity. In December, Columbus returned from his first voyage under Isabella's sponsorship to announce the discovery of the 'Indies', which as it transpired were, in fact, the Americas. Over the next half century he and his successors were to establish a vast Spanish Empire whose mineral riches – above all, silver – were shipped in vast quantities to the motherland.

Spain's imperial power was by no means limited to the New World. In 1519, Ferdinand's grandson and successor as King of Spain, Charles I, inherited from his other grandfather a collection of territories sprawling from the Netherlands to Italy – the family possessions of the Hapsburgs. While these made him the most powerful man in Christian Europe, they also brought him numerous and powerful enemies. Charles was engaged in almost constant struggle throughout his reign, as a defender of Christendom against the Turks, of Catholicism against the newly-emerged threat of Protestantism, and of the Hapsburg lands against the rising power of France.

Although Charles's son, Philip II, did not inherit the last of these in their entirety, Spain's position as Europe's leading power, and her sense of a special link with the Church, meant that his commitments remained as great as his father's. The effects on what was essentially a poor country, with few natural resources, were devastating. The costs of constant war soaked up the flow of American treasure, saddling it with debts that were to burden it for centuries, and leaving nothing over for the country's development.

The primacy of foreign affairs also prevented much-needed reform at home, where the former kingdoms of Castile, Aragon and Navarre, like the colonies and the European possessions, were governed as distinct entities. Moreover, the various Aragonese territories – Catalonia, Valencia and Aragon itself – and also the Basque provinces, including Navarre, were effectively exempted from taxation and military service, so that the burden of these fell almost entirely on Castile. Conversely, the merchants of Barcelona and Valencia were excluded from trade with the Americas, which remained the preserve of Castile. However, since that region was lacking in commercial expertise, the main beneficiaries of the American treasure were Italian and German bankers.

These conditions precipitated a rapid decline in Spanish fortunes during the seventeenth century, a process paralleled by the degeneration of the Hapsburg line, whose last representative – Charles II – died childless in 1700. His death triggered off the War of Succession, in which Spain was reduced to the status of battleground and booty for the European powers. It was ended in 1713 by the Treaty of Utrecht, under which Gibraltar was ceded to Britain. The Treaty's main effect, however, was to place a representative of the French Bourbon dynasty on the vacant Spanish throne, in the person of Philip V.

Although Spain was permitted to retain her American Empire, she was stripped of all her European possessions. By removing the temptation to play the role of European power that had so overstretched her limited resources, these provisions contributed to a modest revival in the country's fortunes. This process was helped along by Philip's reforms, brought together in the New Structure (*Nueva Planta*) decrees, which abolished the privileges of the former Aragonese territories, and of Catalonia in particular. Henceforth the whole of Spain was to be run on the King's behalf by a single council of ministers – the 'Council of Castile'.

These measures were a foretaste of the Spanish Bourbons' intention to install the system of absolute monarchy (*absolutismo*) already established by their French cousins. This differed from earlier, feudal forms of rule in that the King's authority was untrammelled by the rights of particular social groups, institutions or regions. However, the Bourbons enjoyed limited success in Spain. This was partly due to the country's terrain, which made it much harder to centralise administration. But their plans also met stubborn resistance from those who stood to lose power and influence, especially the nobles and the Church. And, above all, the royal authorities' chronic poverty severely limited the Bourbons' capacity to impose their rule.

Later in the century Spain was touched by another form of French influence – the intellectual revolution known as the Enlightenment (*Ilustración*). Its main impact was felt after 1759, when Charles III came to the throne. Able and energetic, he was strongly influenced by the enlightened despotism (*absolutismo ilustrado*) then in vogue among Europe's monarchs, and attempted to apply its lessons in Spain. He encouraged agricultural improvement, through irrigation programmes and the settlement of sparsely populated areas. Crafts and primitive industry were promoted by government funding and the relaxation of restrictions to trade, such as internal customs duties.

Once again, a lack of resources restricted the impact of Charles' measures. He was not helped by the fact that the new thinking was associated with a country against which Spain had spent the better part of two centuries at war; its adherents were widely despised as 'Frenchified' (*afrancesados*). Moreover, despite taking steps to restrict the Church's power – most controversially, by expelling the Jesuits from Spain and her colonies in 1767 – he could not break its hold over much of the population. The Church controlled most of what passed for an education system, and was well placed to resist tooth and nail the new philosophical and scientific ideas with which Europe was abuzz.

Thus, as the eighteenth century drew to a close, the '**old order**' that was about to be shaken by the French Revolution was far from fully developed in Spain. Not only the Church, but most of the landowning aristocracy and the mass of the people were deeply conservative, and tied firmly to traditional ideas and practices. The state apparatus was

---

antiguo régimen

old order

The name *ancien régime*, associated above all with France, was given in retrospect to the structures characteristic of late eighteenth-century Europe. Its main features were: politically, the system of absolute monarchy, under which individuals were subjects without rights of their own; socially, a strict hierarchy dominated by the court and aristocracy; and economically, extensive intervention by the royal authorities into the workings of an embryonic market. In Spain it also encompassed a number of features left over from earlier periods, including the nobles' rights of jurisdiction over their tenants (*señoríos*), the system of entail, which meant that much land could not be bought or sold (p9) and the **traditional privileges** (p13) still retained by a number of areas.

---

weak and there were few signs of the modern economic development that was starting to take place elsewhere in western Europe. The fact that Spain was also militarily insignificant confirmed its status as a backwater, increasingly cut off from events to the north.

Spain's isolation was abruptly interrupted by the 1789 Revolution and the subsequent wars between France's new rulers and their enemies. Too weak to resist her neighbour, she was drawn into a series of costly campaigns on France's side; in 1805 almost her entire fleet was destroyed at Trafalgar. Three years later Napoleon Bonaparte, by now Emperor of France, decided he needed direct control over Spain in order to invade Britain's ally, Portugal. His troops occupied much of northern Spain, and in May 1808 he forced King Charles IV and his son Ferdinand to renounce their claims to the Spanish throne, which he awarded to his brother Joseph, thereby triggering the 'War of Independence' – known to English-speakers as the Peninsular War.

The War lasted until 1813, when the last French troops were driven out of Spain. During that time they controlled much of the country, or at least the larger towns, the main routes and the surrounding districts. In the occupied areas they imposed the changes of their own Revolution, removing restrictions on the use of land and property, and the privileges enjoyed by Church and aristocracy. Such reforms earned the French a degree of support, especially from government officials influenced by Enlightenment ideas. But only a tiny minority were 'Frenchified'; the vast majority of Spaniards bitterly opposed French occupation. To a considerable extent, the War was the first genuinely national experience in Spanish history.

The mass of the people saw the War in very traditional terms, considering that its purpose was to place their rightful King, Ferdinand – 'Our Heart's Desire' (*El Deseado*), as he became known – on his father's throne. As well as monarchism, however, the War also served to reinforce support for the Church, whose clergy often played a leading role in organising and sustaining resistance. At the same time, there was a redoubled hatred of all things French – a not unnatural response to the occupiers' sometimes gruesome methods, which were often repaid in kind. These three factors – Church, King and visceral anti-French feeling – came to form the basis of a primitive and deeply conservative patriotism.

Another important aspect of the War was the nature of the fighting. After their regular army had suffered several crushing defeats, the Spaniards wisely left conventional warfare to the British forces that had landed in Portugal. They concentrated instead on guerrilla warfare (*guerra de guerrillas*), with irregular, locally-based bands using their knowledge of the terrain to harry the superior French forces. This had the effect of establishing a tradition and experience of such techniques among the civilian population. It also reconfirmed the strong local loyalties to individual regions, districts and even villages, which Spain's geography and history had always encouraged.

The regionalist tendency was reinforced in another way, too. With their master gone, most local representatives of the old royal authorities held back from organising resistance to the French. The task fell instead to *ad hoc* local committees (*juntas*) which, with the French in control of most main roads, operated more or less autonomously, under the leadership of prominent figures in local society. To the extent that the role fell to the landowning nobility, the emergence of the committees served to reinforce not only local loyalties but also the status of traditional institutions.

In some cases, however, precisely the opposite occurred. In many towns in the south and south-east, where the French presence was weakest, direction of the committees was seized by merchants and early manufacturers, who represented the newer commercial forces in society. As such they were especially susceptible to the revolutionary ideas brought by the French, including the notion that a country should not be governed by the whim of a hereditary monarch but by the will of its people, of the nation as a whole. And among a populace that had been left largely to fight for its own liberation, that had a wider appeal too.

In 1810 this idea of national sovereignty inspired local committees around the country to send representatives to an assembly. It met in Cadiz, which, protected by a British fleet, had become the effective capital of unoccupied Spain. Two years later the impromptu Parliament completed drawing up a blueprint for the country's future government: the Cadiz Constitution.

CHAPTER 1

Liberals and generals (1812–1868)

Throughout continental Europe the final defeat of revolutionary France in 1815 led to re-establishment of the old order. Its key characteristics were the absolute power of the monarch and his chosen ministers, and wide-ranging legal restrictions on economic activity. As a result, absolute rule conflicted with the interests of the growing commercial middle classes, who regarded with envy the political and economic freedoms enjoyed by their British counterparts, and in particular their right to own and enclose land. This *bourgeoisie* formed the core of the movement for change known as liberalism, whose most dramatic moments came in the various revolutions of 1830 and 1848. Its progress was halting but real, and by the 1860s most western European states had in place constitutions formally limiting absolute rule, and establishing some democratic rights as well as economic freedoms. These developments went hand-in-hand with the beginnings of industrialisation similar to that already experienced in Britain. Having thus largely achieved their main, economic aims, liberals tended to lose their reformist zeal and increasingly allied with more conservative forces in society, in order to resist destabilising pressures for further political change.

The Constitution approved at Cadiz in 1812 placed Spain at the head of the Europe-wide movement for political and economic reform known as liberalism. However, it faced formidable obstacles in Spain, and made only halting progress there up to the middle of the century. Curiously, by then the country's government was firmly in the hands of men who regarded themselves as liberals. The reasons for this paradox were, first, the changes that had occurred in Spanish liberalism since 1812 and, second, the chronic instability that had been the country's most striking feature in the interim. While these circumstances had given liberals their chance, they had also led to the emergence of the Army as the most powerful institution in Spain, giving rise to a highly distinctive form of politics dominated by its commanders.

A surfeit of constitutions

For its architects, the first men to whom the term 'liberal' was applied, the Cadiz Constitution proved a pyrrhic victory. Its real impact was strictly limited; of the 22 years up to its repeal it was in force for only five. In the meantime, liberals had divided into those who remained true to its radical principles, and others who had come to take a more conservative view. Once events conspired to bring liberals into government these differences were

liberalismo
....
the (Spanish) liberal
movement

_____

Although liberal ideas found
expression early in Spain, the
country's liberal movement
remained weak due to the slow
pace of economic development
and the limited impact made by
the Enlightenment (p3). Even so,
and with the exception of the First
Republic (pp27–9), liberals formed
Spain's government from the
1830s to 1923. During that time
they were constantly divided
between radicals, who favoured
wide-ranging democratic reforms,
and conservatives anxious to
consolidate their gains by alliance
with the institutions of the **old
order** (p4). Although theoretically
based on constitutional principles
their rule depended, first, on
alliances with Army leaders
(pp18–21) and, after 1876, on a
form of sham democracy
(pp29–32), so that the liberal
values of rationality and tolerance
were often suppressed. They lived
on, however, and eventually found
expression in the reforms carried
out under the Second Republic
(pp67–9) and during the 1980s
(p143).
See also: **Moderados** (p10);
Progresistas (p11); **Unión
Liberal** (p20); **Partido
Conservador** (p30); **Partido
Liberal** (p31)

expressed in a flurry of further constitutions,
which fatally undermined the meaning of constitutional rule.

In 1812 Spain was an unlikely candidate
to be **the liberal movement**'s birthplace.
Compared to other parts of western Europe,
the usual breeding ground of liberal ideas –
the emergent commercial middle class – was
small. But the circumstances of the War of
Independence had a twofold effect on the
parliament meeting in Cadiz (p5). The representatives came disproportionately from the
southern towns, where the social foundation
of liberalism was strongest, and the tone of
debate was set by the notion that the War was
a national liberation struggle. The result was a
document that embodied liberal principles in
a remarkably advanced form for the time and,
above all, for the country.

Thus the Constitution of Cadiz guaranteed
a wide range of individual and collective freedoms. Although the monarch would remain
head of state, his powers and those of his
appointed ministers were to be greatly constrained. In effect the Parliament (_Cortes_) would
become the most powerful institution in Spain.
It was to consist of a single chamber, elected
partly by universal suffrage and partly on a
property-based franchise, i.e. by landowners.
In addition, the Constitution abolished the
right of nobility and Church to hold land in per-
petuity, as well as other privileges enjoyed by
them and by particular localities.

These features made the constitution a
model, particularly in southern Europe.
However, they were out of tune with a country
where the mass of the people and powerful
institutions remained deeply conservative (pp3–4). This became clear as soon as the French
had been driven out and Ferdinand VII was restored to the throne. For just one year later,
in 1814, he was able to re-impose absolute rule without any significant resistance. The
Constitution was set aside, and many of its architects persecuted or forced into exile.
This chastening experience served to dampen their radical ardour considerably.

In 1820 these 'men of 1812' (_doceañistas_) got a second chance, when Ferdinand was
forced to reintroduce constitutional rule (pp15–16). During the 'three years of the

Constitution' (*trienio constitucional*) that followed they approved the economic reforms which were their main goal, including the **disentailment** of Church lands. That done, their main concern was to ensure that they had the stability necessary to enjoy their gains. This aim, however, was threatened by persistent unrest (p12). They therefore sought a compromise with the King, and offered to water down the Constitution's political provisions by establishing a second, non-elected house of Parliament and reducing parliamentary controls on government. By doing so the 'men of 1812' alienated most of their former supporters, so that when Ferdinand spurned their approach they were left completely isolated.

As a result, the initiative passed to a group of more radical liberals. These less well-off 'hotheads' (*exaltados*) bitterly resented the

> ### *desamortización*
> #### disentailment
>
> A key aim of Spanish liberals, disentailment involved abolishing the practices of entailment and mortmain (*manos muertas*) which prevented much land from being traded, in particular the nobility's hereditary estates, common land and land in the hands of the Church, especially monasteries and convents. It was intended by idealistic liberals to create a class of landowning small farmers, but in practice most disentailed land was purchased by the already well-off, who included many leading liberals.

wealth of the Church and nobility. Their support came from the provincial towns, from journalists – press freedom had given rise to a newspaper boom – and from the horde of 'post-seekers' (*pretendientes*), whose perennial hope was that a change in government would bring them an official job. Their programme was based on achieving greater political freedoms, and especially on the introduction of a wider property-franchise that would give them the vote. That demand, and the intemperate way it was expressed, provoked unrest among their own supporters as well as among those who thought reform had already gone too far. The result was a wave of minor insurrections (p16) – exactly the sort of instability which the 'men of 1812' so dreaded.

In 1823 the instability was ended, but not in the way the 'men of 1812' would have wished. Instead, a French army, sponsored by the main European powers, invaded Spain and restored absolute rule once again. Reform was halted, and measures taken during the preceding three years reversed. The effects were disastrous, as Spain's administration was simply too antiquated for contemporary needs. Yet despite the obvious need for change, and the government's discredit due to the loss of most of Spain's American colonies in 1828, the liberals remained impotent. When they attempted an invasion of their own in 1830 it was a pitiful failure.

Three years later, however, events again conspired to bring them to power, when on Ferdinand's death the reactionary Carlist movement rose in revolt (p12). His widow Maria Cristina, acting as Regent, found herself with little support, and was therefore obliged to hand over the conduct of the subsequent civil war and the government in general to a group of leading liberals, who became known as '**Moderates**'. These successors of the 'men of 1812' continued to believe that the old order needed drastic reform and, in particular, that the monarch's power would have to be curtailed. They also believed that it should pass not to the nation as a whole, but to that section of the populace which was in a position to use it intelligently – in other words, to people like them, the owners of substantial property. These ideas formed the basis of what, in all but name, was Spain's second constitution.

This Royal Statute, enacted in 1834, evaded the question of sovereignty (i.e. the ultimate source of authority) by assigning it 'jointly' to Crown and Parliament. In practice, however, the balance was tilted strongly in the monarchy's favour, since it retained the right to appoint and dismiss all ministers – who were largely freed from parliamentary control – and to summon and dissolve parliament itself. It was decided that Parliament was to have two houses: the upper one would consist of the hereditary aristocracy and appointees of the monarch; the lower one would be elected, but on a high-qualification property-franchise. In practice, under one per cent of the population were eligible to vote.

Despite – or because of – these limited concessions, Maria Cristina and her supporters (*cristinos*) remained dangerously isolated, facing not only the Carlist revolt, but also repeated uprisings by **Progressives**, as the more radical liberals were now known. Their pressure forced the Regent to appoint as prime minister Juan Alvarez Mendizábal, a financier whose master-plan was to disentail a further tranche of Church and common lands. Its aim was to solve the government's appalling financial problems while also pacifying at least some of the Progressives, by allowing them to share in the carve-up of disentailed land. Its failure on both counts left Mendizábal no alternative but to meet the political demands of his Progressive sponsors.

Together they pushed through a new Constitution, under which the electorate was greatly extended by a lowering of the property qualification. And, while Maria Cristina would still appoint the second chamber, she would have to do so from lists of candidates drawn up by the voters. Local authorities were also to be elected, and would be placed in control of the militia, the volunteer force set up in 1820–23 as radical liberalism's own defence force. To the disgust of the most radical Progressives, however, many provisions of the 1834 Statute were retained, including the upper house, the monarch's right to nominate the prime minister, and the government's relative independence from parliamentary control.

In principle, the 1837 Constitution still represented an important step towards democracy, but coming so soon after the Royal Statute, its practical effect was precisely the opposite. For it undermined the basic democ-

---

Moderados

Moderates

A loose grouping which emerged in the mid-1830s, the Moderates included the most conservative elements of the Spanish **liberal movement** – the wealthiest of the new commercial and industrial classes – together with some more enlightened supporters of the **old order** (p4); 'Frenchified' bureaucrats (p4) and the landowning aristocracy. They favoured a form of democracy so limited as barely to merit the name, and in many ways their rule – from 1843 to 1854 – was closer to being that of a military dictatorship (pp18–19). Thereafter they broke up into factions before disappearing altogether in the 1860s.

See also: **Unión Liberal** (p20); **Partido Conservador** (p30)

ratic precept that all political players must abide by the rules of the game, as set out in the existing constitutional order. In effect, the Progressives were stating that they were only prepared to play by their own rules. Since the Moderates took exactly the same view in reverse, constitutional rule in any real sense was impossible, as soon became evident.

Ironically, the first election held under the Progressive Constitution, in 1838, was won by the Moderates. Their opponents assumed, with some justification, that they would now reimpose the Royal Statute, whose terms virtually assured them of a parliamentary majority. These fears led the Progressives to launch the 1840 Revolution (pp16–17) – against a government elected under their Constitution – which briefly returned them to power. But in 1843 they were ousted in turn by a counter-revolution that allowed the Moderates to do precisely what the Progressives had sought to prevent: impose new rules that were tailored to their own interests.

The Moderates' 1845 Constitution reversed most of the changes made in 1837. The monarch recovered various privileges, including the right of appointing the upper house of parliament. The militia and local councils were brought under central control, and trial by jury was abolished for cases involving the press – an indication of the importance journalism had assumed in spreading radical ideas. Most crucially, the property franchise was again raised, reducing the electorate to a tiny clique of well-off males. Little remained of the democratic political principles of 1812, yet even so the new Constitution could not guarantee a parliamentary majority for the Moderates, who routinely violated it in order to retain power (pp18–19). At the same time, the still important forces in Spanish society who rejected liberalism in any form continued to believe that it went too far.

> ### *Progresistas*
> #### Progressives
>
> Another loose grouping, set up in 1836, the Progressives were the more radical wing of the **liberal movement**. Their main popular support came from the lower middle classes of the provincial towns, especially in the south and east. They aimed to establish a relatively democratic form of rule, with a large electorate (although not universal suffrage, even for males) and the elimination of aristocratic privileges and Church influence. They were only in power for brief periods in the late 1830s and following the Revolutions of 1840, 1854 and 1868, but during their time in office they were responsible for much reforming legislation. After 1870 they split into two factions, neither of which survived the First Republic of 1873–74 (pp27–9). See also: ***Unión Liberal*** (p20); ***Partido Liberal*** (p31)

The forces of reaction

The strength of opposition to liberal ideas in Spain was evident from an early stage, in the broad support for restoration of absolute rule that was expressed in 1814 and 1823. Later it was gradually undermined by economic and social change, but the slow pace of modernisation meant that reactionary feeling remained much more powerful in Spain than elsewhere in western Europe. At popular level it was strongest in areas which had traditionally enjoyed special privileges. But it also enjoyed the backing of groups and institutions – above all the Church – whose interests were similarly threatened by liberal reforms.

The Church's resistance to liberalism was partly a reaction to the secular, rationalist ideas with which the movement was associated. But it also had more material roots, as became apparent during the 'three years of the Constitution', when liberal governments showed themselves ready to accept Catholicism as Spain's sole official religion. The real threat was their sell-off of monastic land (p9), which provoked the Church into encouraging a series of rural uprisings. It also welcomed the French invasion of 1823, an operation joined by many Spanish volunteers.

Significantly, though, even the King's restoration did not satisfy some conservatives. Due to the parlous state of the country's finances, Ferdinand was forced to allow his ministers to pursue policies similar to the enlightened despotism of the previous century (p3), which involved a certain rationalisation of the country's administration and economy. Moreover, a number of those responsible for the crisis had served the French occupiers during the War of Independence, behaviour which, like their reforms, was anathema to the particular type of conservative patriotism bred by the War (p4).

The resultant reactionary frustration boiled over in a series of minor uprisings, which often enjoyed the backing of local clergy.

The main demands were for the restoration of Church influence, chiefly through the re-establishment of the Inquisition, the purging of liberals from the Army, and the reversal of even the most timid reforms, some of which had begun well before 1812, in particular, the very limited degree of general education. It was a programme designed to take Spain back to the seventeenth century, and it was espoused by the King's brother, Carlos, on whom reactionary hopes came to focus. They were shattered by the so-called 'Pragmatic Sanction', under which Ferdinand bequeathed the throne to his infant daughter Isabella. Carlos and his supporters refused to accept the decision, and on Ferdinand's death in 1833 they rose in revolt.

The philosophy of the **Carlists** was summed up in the motto 'God, King and **old laws**' (*Dios, rey y fueros*), bringing together the three key supports of the old order – with religion in the place of honour. They enjoyed the backing of the Pope, and had solid support from rural areas in the north, where Church

---

Carlismo

Carlist movement

Advocates of a return to the **old order** (p4), the Carlists (*carlistas*) came together in 1833 to support the claim of 'Charles V', as they called him, to the throne of his dead brother, Ferdinand VII. Their main support came from the Church, the rural parts of the Basque Country, Navarre, Aragon and inland Catalonia. The Carlists rose in revolt against the Spanish authorities on three occasions, in 1833–40, 1846–49 and 1872–76, but were unsuccessful on each occasion. After the third defeat their movement split, with a faction known as the 'Integralists' abandoning the claim of Charles's heirs to the throne in favour of even more reactionary demands in other areas, especially regarding the Church's status. The movement was later reunited as **Traditionalism** (p82).

See also: *monarquistas* (p74)

influence was strong and liberal attacks on local privileges were fiercely resented. But they found minimal backing in the towns, or in the southern and eastern countryside, and little from the aristocracy, many of whom had benefited directly from sales of Church land. Nor did they receive any external military aid to match that which the government received from France and Britain.

Even so, the defeat of the Carlists in the 'Seven Years War', as the First Carlist War used to be known, was not readily accomplished. The terrain in their northern strongholds – where the rural peasantry retained the traditions of guerrilla warfare learnt during the War of Independence (pp4–5) – was difficult, and the government generals often incompetent. As a result, the insurgents were able to defy a superior number of regular forces for a prolonged period, and in their heartland, on the borders of the Basque Country and Navarre, Charles was even able to establish what amounted to a mini-state.

Charles established his 'court' in the small Navarrese town of Estella, the larger towns and cities remaining loyal to the government. Despite two sieges, the Carlists were unable to capture their great objective, the Basque capital Bilbao; the failure was compounded by the loss of Zumalacárregui, their most astute commander. In desperation, long-range forays were made into government-held territory, the most famous of them being the Royal Expedition of 1837, which was led by Charles himself. It was finally defeated before Madrid by General Espartero, whose more methodical leadership at last began to achieve inroads into the Carlist heartlands.

The decisive breakthrough came in 1839. Conscious that victory was impossible, the Carlist General Maroto agreed to the Convention of Vergara, by which his forces surrendered to Espartero. In return, he and his fellow officers were allowed to join the regular army without loss of rank, and the Basque and Navarrese 'old laws' were guaranteed. Since that had always been the main concern of the small farmers who formed the backbone of the Carlist forces, they no longer had any reason to fight on. Without their support, the rebellion was over within a year.

The Carlist movement survived defeat, but it was severely weakened. It lived on in Navarre and the Basque provinces, which lost some of their privileges in 1841 for supporting a conservative uprising (p17), and in inland Catalonia, where fighting broke out again between 1846 and 1849. But although it was sometimes dubbed the 'Second Carlist War', it was really just glorified banditry. By then, too, gradual social and

---

fueros

traditional local privileges; old laws

Under the **old order** (p4), many towns and districts in Spain enjoyed traditional privileges, such as exemption from taxes or military service. By the 1830s most had been abolished, as much in the interests of administrative efficiency as from liberal principles. However, the Basque provinces and Navarre retained substantial rights, including the freedom to levy their own customs duty. This effectively excluded them from the single market which the rest of Spain now composed. Partially suppressed in 1841, these 'old laws' – as they were known in Basque – were abolished after the final defeat of the **Carlist movement** in 1876. See also: *concierto económico* (p32)

economic progress had cost Carlism most of the little influential backing it had enjoyed, and the movement split into squabbling factions.

Yet, opposition to liberal reforms remained strong, above all from the Church, whose wealth and influence were further threatened by the Progressives' 1837 Constitution. For, while it reaffirmed Catholicism's privileged status *vis-à-vis* all other creeds, it also asserted the state's authority over the Church in all temporal matters. The unrest that culminated in the Revolution of 1840 was also characterised by growing anticlerical feeling, made evident in attacks on Church personnel and property.

While relations with liberalism's radical wing were steadily deteriorating, they were improving with the Moderates who, after they regained power in 1843, showed themselves more concerned with maintaining order than in pressing for further reform (pp18–19). This new closeness led in 1851 to the signing of a Concordat, or agreement, between the Spanish government and the Vatican. Under its terms, the Pope recognised Isabella as Spain's legitimate Queen, and the Church retrospectively approved sales of disentailed land. In return, the Spanish state agreed to provide financial support for the secular clergy, i.e. parish priests, as opposed to monks and nuns. Moreover, the Concordat's unclear wording also allowed the re-establishment in Spain of monastic orders which had been expelled from the country during 1820–23 (p9).

The 1851 Concordat both reflected a revival in the Church's social influence and gave that process a further boost, in particular by allowing the teaching orders to resume their activities. Catholicism had always retained wide allegiance, especially among the older aristocracy, and the peasantry of the northern countryside. For many Moderates, now confirmed in their possession of disentailed land, the Church acquired a fresh attraction, as a defender of social order against the popular unrest which was their greatest fear.

Queen Isabella, and her court in general, were also strongly affected by the resurgence of religiosity. Her husband openly sympathised with the idea of reuniting their family with the Carlist line through marriage in order better to resist the advance of liberal ideas. Indeed, by the 1860s the court had rejoined the Church hierarchy as a focus of reaction which, along with such eminent backers, also retained a degree of popular support. But for the moment at least, despite the existence of supposedly constitutional rule, it lacked the ability to carry out what had become the usual means of changing government: a military uprising.

Insurrections, civilian and military

The struggle between liberals and their opponents in Spain was carried on against a background of extraordinary unrest. Indeed, during the 35 years from 1808 insurrections were so common that the entire period is sometimes seen as one long 'Spanish Revolution'. They took the form of civilian uprisings, military revolts or, most frequently, a combination of the two. But from 1840 on the military element became the more important, as the Army and its leaders came to dominate politics.

The persistence and extent of unrest in Spain had its roots in the War of Independence (pp4–5). With the collapse of central authority at that time, Spaniards became accustomed to the assumption of power by self-appointed local committees. Moreover, much of the civilian population acquired experience of guerrilla warfare. Within the Army, the War discredited the old officer class and brought to the fore a new breed of commanders, many of whom were ex-guerrillas. Their loyalties were not to the crown but to the country, and in the absence of a monarch, and even a national government, they tended to see the Army – and themselves – as Spain's true representatives.

The heritage of these factors was very apparent in the years that followed, when insurrections against both absolute and constitutional rule became commonplace. But while reactionaries also resorted to revolt (p12), most of its proponents were liberals of the more radical variety, unhappy at the slow pace of reform in Madrid, or at one of the periodic reversals of that process. Their '**revolutions**' tended to follow a pattern that reflected the central dilemma of the liberal movement as a whole, caught between the conflicting desires for change and order.

Revolutions usually began as an outburst of protest in provincial capitals or smaller towns, and were typically fed by discontent at the hated sales taxes (*consumos*) or the conscription of men to serve in the Army. In the second phase, leading local radicals would form revolutionary 'committees' (*juntas*), and attempt to channel the uprising into effective pressure on the authorities in Madrid. Finally – assuming that events got so far – a new government installed on the back of the uprising would attempt to bring unrest under control. However, while there were innumerable instances of such radical uprisings, the vast majority were suppressed earlier rather than later. Their main effect was thus to create an overwhelming dread of revolution among the better-off, whose property – and sometimes lives – tended to be the main victims in the first stages of disorder.

Equally unsuccessful were the earliest **military declarations** (*pronunciamientos*), directed against the absolute rule re-imposed in 1814 (p8). In 1820, however, Major Rafael de Riego succeeded in restoring the liberals to power. His rising began in Cadiz, among

---

revolución

revolution; uprising; insurrection

In nineteenth-century Spain, the term 'revolution' was used in several different senses. Popularly and by their protagonists, every minor radical insurrection was described as such, irrespective of whether it brought about any change in the way the country was run. It was applied more meaningfully to the uprisings which brought the **Progressives** to power in 1840, 1854 and 1868, but more rarely to the subsequent counter-insurrections by which the **Moderates** regained it on each occasion. In a broader sense it represented the aspiration both of the Republicans and the workers' movement. However, while for the former 'revolution' implied abolition of the monarchy and democratic political reform, for the latter it involved much more far-reaching changes in Spain's economy and society. Finally, the term was even used by some conservatives '**regenerationists**' (p40) to describe the imposition of changes designed precisely to maintain the existing social order (p41).

See also: **PSOE** (p47); *anarquismo* (p48), *anarcosindicalismo* (p48); *Partido Republicano Radical* (p50)

disgruntled troops waiting to embark for the colonial war in Latin America. The crucial factor in his success was the 'negative declaration' of Army leaders who refused to put it down. Civilian politicians played little part until success was assured, thereby sowing the first seeds of contempt for themselves among even liberally-minded soldiers. Yet Riego's declaration was not a military coup, in the sense that it intended to install a purely military government. Its purpose was to help like-minded civilians to power.

Riego's action set the pattern for the many military revolts – mostly failures – of the next two decades. The first came in 1822, when officers in the elite guards regiment attempted to overturn the then liberal government, but otherwise conservative military revolts remained rare. Some were staged by relatively junior officers, as in 1836, when a group of sergeants who mutinied at the summer palace of La Granja forced the Queen to reinstate Mendizábal as prime minister (p10). Then, as in the following year, military intervention combined with civilian unrest to maintain the more radical liberals in power.

These two uprisings took place against the backdrop of the First Carlist War (p13), whose effects fundamentally changed the relationship between military and civilian insurgency. With the government facing bankruptcy, the troops involved were paid irregularly at best, so that discontent in the ranks became endemic – and was now being directed at the liberal politicians who formed the government. The politicians effectively left the war's conduct in the hands of the leading generals, thus strengthening the latter's conviction that they were the people's true representatives. The effects were soon seen, in the most dramatic upheaval to date.

The Revolution of 1840 began as a civilian affair, an attempt by the Progressives to pre-empt the repeal of their 1837 Constitution (pp10–11). When the government failed to put down their protests, the Regent Maria Cristina appealed over its head to General Espartero (p13). But, instead of coming to her aid, he put himself at the head of the uprising, allying with the Progressives and orchestrating demonstrations of popular support for himself. His enormous prestige, and continuing Progressive unrest, left Maria Cristina

---

pronunciamiento
(military) declaration

A characteristically Spanish form of military revolt, declarations tended to follow a pattern. A typical declaration began with the action that gave it its name; the reading of a statement of grievances by officers to their troops, as an appeal for support. If successful, this would be followed by risings at other barracks, and by a march on Madrid to force a change of government. Senior officers who did not support a declaration but refused to suppress it were said to have carried out a 'negative declaration'. In time, declarations came to be seen within the Army as a legitimate form of protest, with their own etiquette; for instance, that those involved in an unsuccessful revolt should be dealt with leniently. During the period 1812–40 most declarations were made in support of liberal reforms. Thereafter they gradually became more reactionary, a process that culminated in the revolts of 1923 and 1936, both of which imposed right-wing military dictatorships.

with no option but to appoint Espartero Prime Minister; she surrendered her powers as Regent to him soon after.

This assumption of power by a military leader, which was the crucial departure of the 1840 Revolution, had implications for the future. It was possible only because of Espartero's rank, which allowed him to expect obedience from the Army as a whole. The days of intervention by majors and sergeants were over: declarations had become a matter for generals. Espartero now had responsibility for the always tricky final stage of revolution; the re-establishment of order and central authority over the provinces he had himself helped to inflame.

Espartero did not handle this second task well. By failing immediately to crush continuing radical unrest he alarmed the Progressive leadership; by the brutal means he eventually employed to do so he enraged much of the party rank and file. His tendency to consult only a small group of military cronies further alienated his civilian allies; it also started grumbling in the Army, which was compounded by his failure to respond to its concerns about pay and conditions. He caused further offence by dealing harshly with some of the more conservative officers who rose against him in 1841, thus breaching the odd etiquette that had come to surround such declarations. In 1843, these various strands of discontent came together with the Moderates to stage another rising, and Espartero was driven into exile.

Once again the revolt was led by the military, this time in the person of General Narváez. Over the next decade, while maintaining the appearance of constitutional rule (pp18–19), he used the Army to ensure that the Progressives were excluded from power. Their powerlessness led them to formulate the notion that revolution was justified against a government that defied the 'will of the people'. The incumbent Moderates used that claim to brand their opponents as dangerous extremists and a threat to stability, conveniently forgetting how they themselves had come to power. What events in 1843 had shown was that the only real difference between the two groups' attitudes to a revolution was in how they would deal with its aftermath, as was demonstrated again after the next major uprising.

Because of the circumstances that preceded it (p20), the Revolution of 1854 involved dissident Moderates as well as Progressives and more radical elements, among them large numbers of the Madrid poor. It was the unprecedented unrest in the capital, where barricades were erected and entire districts temporarily lost to government control, that prompted Queen Isabella to ally with alarmed Progressive leaders. Together they appealed to Espartero, who in exile had regained much of his former popularity, to head the government and restore order. He accepted the task but, as in 1840, proved unequal to it. Unrest continued to flare up, and his government became increasingly split on how to deal with it, until in 1856 these divisions provided the excuse to dismiss him as Prime Minister.

Espartero's removal was orchestrated by General Leopoldo O'Donnell, who was now the Queen's most trusted adviser, despite having been the leading military participant in the uprising two years earlier. O'Donnell showed none of Espartero's hesitation, and rapidly crushed both the Madrid poor and the Progressive-inclined militia (p10), thus establishing himself as the country's new strongman. By demonstating his mastery of the revolutionary process, O'Donnell marked himself out as the archetype of the political generals on whom both wings of the liberal movement had come to depend.

Militarised liberalism

For the quarter-century after 1843 Spain experienced a respite from turmoil. In appearance, liberalism had triumphed; a constitution was in force and government was largely in the hands of its proponents. In reality, however, power lay with the Army and its leaders, and constitutional rule was a fiction, not least because the monarch still retained considerable powers. When, in 1854, Queen Isabella abused them, she provoked a major upheaval. But she failed to heed the warning, and eventually her activities undermined the curious system of militarised liberalism.

The stability of the so-called 'Isabelline era' rested on two foundations. On the one hand, the gradual extension of property and wealth undermined the radicalism of the lower middle classes by giving them a stake in the system. On the other, integrating the leading generals into the upper echelons of civilian life reduced the potential for military uprisings. Economically, they became heavily involved in commerce and finance: politically, they were assured of seats in the upper house of Parliament, the Senate. For much of the period the prime minister was a general.

This militarisation of politics reached its zenith in the period up to 1854, during which General Ramón Narváez ruled as the closest approximation to a dictator in nineteenth-century Spain. Martial law was imposed at the least sign of unrest, and radicals subjected to a range of repressive legislation. So effective were these methods that the Europe-wide outburst of liberal revolutions in 1848 was barely felt in liberalism's homeland. Yet Narváez regarded himself as a liberal, and not without justification; he resisted pressure to restore Church influence over public life (p14) and more than once accepted the Queen's decision to replace him, albeit by another conservative.

The military nature of Narváez's rule was also apparent in the care he took to avoid imitating his forerunner, Espartero, by losing Army support (p17). The end of the Carlist War, and the terms on which it was achieved, had made this danger more acute by creating a gross oversupply of officers (p13). To assure them of posts Narváez maintained both the Army's complement and its budget at an inflated level, brooking no interference in these matters by civilian politicians. In doing so he reinforced the Army's growing sense of itself as a caste apart from, and superior to, civil society.

At the same time, Narváez was also keen to avoid Espartero's other major error, that of alienating his civilian allies. Thus, outside the purely Army sphere, he left matters largely in the hands of his allies, the Moderate leaders (p17). Their main concern, like his, was to avoid upheaval, but they also wished to push ahead with the unfinished task of dismantling the old order, and their time in power brought a number of important reforms.

Thus substantial changes were made to the administration of justice and government. The universities were placed under central, lay control. Most importantly, Narváez's finance minister, Alejandro Mon, overhauled the entire tax system, placing it on a more rational footing. Inevitably, his measures caused resentment among those who had previously enjoyed special fiscal privileges, notably the Catalans, as did retention of the hated sales taxes under a new name. But they also ensured, at long last, that the government had an assured source of income.

At the same time, though, the Moderates were making a mockery of liberal principles. Unable to achieve a reliable majority even among the tiny elite enfranchised by their own 1845 Constitution (p11), they resorted to blatant **election-rigging** on a massive scale. Yet the fact that they, and Narváez, considered holding elections at all indicates that they saw the need for a façade of constitutional practice to help maintain stability. For the same reason, they were careful to allow their Progressive rivals enough seats to give them the appearance of a parliamentary opposition.

For a long time that status, with the associated hope that the Queen might some day call them to office, was enough for the Progressives' leaders. By and large they were similar to their Moderate counterparts, in both social origin and views. The differences were of degree, not substance: they spoke with greater vehemence in their attacks on the Church, and held a stronger attachment to free trade – and that more in blind imitation of British liberalism than because of any benefits for Spain. The real divide between the two groups was more practical. In essence, the Moderates were the party of government, while the Progressives represented those who were frustrated by their exclusion from power.

That difference was both the effect and cause of the two parties' fluid, unstable nature. Neither had a formal structure; instead they were loose alliances between the supporters of powerful individuals subject to a constant flow of defections in both directions, and provoked as much by success or failure in obtaining official posts as by conviction. In addition, the Progressives suffered a steady leakage of supporters disillusioned with the futility of parliamentary opposition. In 1849 these defectors joined with other radicals to set up the Democratic Party (*Partido Demó-crata*).

The new grouping was Republican in all but name, and rejected the sham of constitutional rule as it existed. But, however different in their philosophy, the Democrats resembled the other parties in their fluidity. They too lost a steady trickle of leading supporters to the Progressives, attracted by the prospect of a seat in Parliament. And they were constantly

> ### *fraude electoral*
> ### election-rigging
>
> First perfected by the **Moderates** between 1843 and 1854, when the electorate was tiny (p11), election-rigging was later used by all parties (pp20, 27) and involved a range of fraudulent activities. Electoral rolls would be published late, so that those omitted had no time to complain. Since votes were cast publicly, patronage and intimidation could be used to influence electors. By contrast, scrutiny of the votes was secret, so that as a last resort results could simply be falsified. The whole operation was controlled by the Interior Ministry in Madrid, which allowed the government to determine the composition of Parliament down to the identity of individual members. After the Restoration of 1876 election-rigging became part of the wider system of **political clientilism** (p33), and remained widespread as late as 1923.

split over the question of whether to co-operate with the Progressives, just as the latter were torn between continuing to play the role of parliamentary opposition and devoting their energies to revolutionary conspiracies. These divisions played no small part in maintaining Moderate domination.

Eventually, though, differences among the Moderates gave the Queen an excuse and the opportunity she needed to indulge her own reactionary tendencies (p14). In 1852 she used her prerogative to appoint as prime minister an extreme conservative Moderate with strong Church links, Juan Bravo Murrillo. His proposals for what amounted to a civilian dictatorship so alarmed generals close to both parties that they forced his dismissal. Yet even then Isabella refused to call on a mainstream Moderate, and far less on a Progressive. Her obstinacy, at a time when financial speculation had made her mother deeply unpopular, triggered off the Revolution of 1854 (p17).

During the 'two Progressive years' (*bienio progresista*) that followed, the more radical Progressives were soon sidelined. Nevertheless, a number of significant reforms were introduced, including a further tranche of disentailment (p9) and Spain's first legal framework for modern business activity. A new Constitution, providing for greater democratic rights, was also drawn up. But before it could come into effect the Progressives were once again ousted from power by the ex-Moderate General Leopoldo O'Donnell (p17), who became Prime Minister in 1858.

O'Donnell's rise to power in the wake of a Progressive revolution was reminiscent of Narváez's, and he had no more qualms about rigging elections than his predecessor. Yet his rule marked a definite step away from the old Moderates' ascendancy. For O'Donnell appreciated that times had changed. The 1854 Revolution had destroyed the Moderates as a coherent political force. And its cause had been royal intransigence rather than Progressive radicalism; indeed, by their reaction to it the Progressive leaders had confirmed that they were almost as frightened of unrest as their opponents. O'Donnell's recipe for restoring stability was therefore to create a new government party by reuniting the two main strands of the Spanish liberal elite.

> ### Unión Liberal
> ·······································
> Liberal Union
> ─────────────
> Founded in 1856 by General Leopoldo O'Donnell to support his own rule, the Union brought together the less conservative and authoritarian sections of the old **Moderates** with the less radical **Progressives**, and held power until 1863. Most of its supporters (*unionistas*) joined in the 1868 Revolution, after which, for a time, it formed part of General Prim's coalition government (p26).
> See also: **Partido Conservador** (p30); **Partido Liberal** (p31)

This **Liberal Union** got off to a promising start. Repression of both radicals and reactionaries was eased, and more intellectual freedom permitted; bizarrely, it was reflected in a vogue for the teachings of a minor German philosopher, Krause, which became an important influence in the universities. Moreover, the Union's pragmatic policies contributed to a burst of economic development, centred on a railway boom, and a corresponding rise in prosperity. In the 1860s, however, a sharp economic downturn set in. Suddenly, the divisions of wealth that had widened rapidly during the foregoing prosperity seemed much more grave, aggravating the ever-present discontent of the poor. Faced with its first crisis, the Union crumbled into warring factions, and in 1863 O'Donnell was forced to resign.

The more radical Progressives who had been excluded from the Union now expected the Queen to call them to power. When she failed to do so their leaders, civilian and military, **boycotted official politics** and joined the Democrats in plotting to overthrow her by means of a revolution. However, oblivious to the fact that she was undermining her own throne, the Queen appointed a succession of prime ministers close to her own increasingly reactionary views (p14). In 1867 the last of them, Luis González Bravo, forced those generals who had remained loyal to the Liberal Union into exile. By doing so he removed the Queen's last political support, condemning both her and the system of militarised liberalism to oblivion.

> *retraimiento*
> ....
> boycott of official politics
>
> A tactic intended to expose the lack of support enjoyed by the government, and so prepare the ground for a 'justified' revolution (p17), a boycott involved refusing to take part in the farce of rigged elections, or to act out the role of parliamentary opposition. It was first practised by the **Progressives** during periods of **Moderate** ascendancy, but after the Revolution of 1868 it was employed against them by the supporters of the **Liberal Union**, and in 1874 by all the monarchist parties against the Republicans (p27).

Exhibit 1.1: Manifesto issued by the Saragossa *Junta provisional* (1840)

A typical statement issued by civilian revolutionaries

> La ciudad de Zaragoza acaba de levantar el pendón de la resistencia legal contra un poder que ha quebrantado la Constitución política del Estado, y que ha sometido la España a la dirección de manos extranjeras.
>
> [. . . E]l Ayuntamiento de Zaragoza se reunió ayer tarde en sesión extraordinaria y acordó [. . .] que una Junta provisional reasumiese en sus manos la autoridad pública y la dirección de los negocios de gobierno. Con este objeto, y a fin de que la madurez de la liberación correspondiera más ostensiblemente a la grandiosidad de la empresa, creyó oportuno el cuerpo municipal convocar a su sesión de este día una reunión de ciudadanos que, por su posición personal y por la confianza que mereciesen al país, contribuyeran con sus consejos al acierto que para casos tan graves conviene procurar a toda costa. [. . .]
>
> De esperar es que la justa ansiedad del público calme con una determinación de esta naturaleza, que bastará por sí sola para poner al abrigo de cualquier conflicto las personas y los bienes de todos los ciudadanos pacíficos; de creer es, asimismo, que la confianza que le inspiran a todos los buenos patricios del Aragón las personas que componen la Junta de gobierno proporcione en breve el restablecimiento de la Constitución política del Estado en todas sus partes y con todas sus leales y legítimas consecuencias.

Source: Fernández Clemente, E. (1975) *Aragón contemporánea (1833–1936)*. Madrid: Siglo XXI.

Exhibit 1.2: General O'Donnell's *Manifiesto de Manzanares* (1854)

One of the most famous military declarations

Españoles: La entusiasta acogida que va encontrando en los pueblos el Ejército liberal; el esfuerzo de los soldados que le componen, tan heróicamente mostrado en los campos de Vicálvaro; el aplauso con que en todas partes ha sido recibida la noticia de nuestro patriótico alzamiento, aseguran desde ahora el triunfo de la libertad y de las leyes que hemos jurado defender. Dentro de pocos días, la mayor parte de las provincias habrán sacudido el yugo de los tiranos; el Ejército entero habrá venido a ponerse bajo nuestras banderas, que son las leales; la nación disfrutará los beneficios del régimen representativo, por el cual ha derramado hasta ahora tanta sangre inútil y ha soportado tan costosos sacrificios. Día es, pues, de decir lo que estamos resueltos a hacer en el de la victoria. Nosotros queremos la conservación del trono, pero sin camarilla que lo deshonre; queremos la práctica rigurosa de las leyes fundamentales, mejorándolas, sobre todo la electoral y la de imprenta; queremos la rebaja de los impuestos, fundada en una estricta economía; queremos que se respeten en los empleos militares y civiles la antigüedad y los merecimientos; queremos arrancar los pueblos a la centralización que los devora, dándoles la independencia local necesaria para que conserven y aumenten sus intereses propios, y como garantía de todo esto queremos y plantearemos, bajo sólidas bases, la Milicia Nacional. Tales son nuestros intentos, que expresamos francamente, sin imponerlos por eso a la nación. Las Juntas de gobierno que deben irse constituyendo en las provincias libres; las Cortes generales que luego se reúnan; la misma nación, en fin, fijará las bases definitivas de la regeneración liberal a que aspiramos. Nosotros tenemos consagradas a la voluntad nacional nuestras espadas, y no las envainaremos hasta que ella esté cumplida.

Source: Artola, M. (1991) *Partidos y programas políticos 1808–1936: Tomo II.* Madrid: Alianza.

Topics

■ What notion of legality and legitimacy emerges from Exhibits 1.1 and 1.2? In other words, how do the revolutionaries justify their actions, and what conception do they appear to have of the role and status of laws?

■ What, judging by Exhibit 1.1, appear to be the main concerns of the Saragossa revolutionaries?

■ What social and political interests are reflected in the demands set out in O'Donnell's declaration (Exhibit 1.2)? How compatible are they with each other? How do they relate to O'Donnell's later career?

■ Why was Spain so unstable for so much of the period 1812–1868?

■ What was 'politics' in Spain at that time? Who did it involve? With what issues was it concerned?

CHAPTER 2

Out of chaos, stability? (1868–1898)

Beginning with the creation of modern Italy and Germany, the nineteenth century's final third represented a golden age for European liberalism. In alliance with elements of the old ruling classes, especially the landowning nobility, continental liberals succeeded in establishing a framework for capitalist economic activity and in harnessing the state's power to promote economic development. The result was a second wave of industrialisation in which steel, chemicals and electricity replaced coal and textiles as the key sectors. Meanwhile discontent among the lower classes was dampened down by growing prosperity and by the absence of wars, other than the campaigns involved in extending colonial rule to Africa, which were considered to be relatively cheap in terms of European lives. As a result, governments felt sufficiently confident to extend parliamentary government and the – male – franchise, thereby incorporating a growing proportion of the population into political life. Education, too, was massively expanded, so that by the end of the century universal schooling, to primary level at least, had become the norm.

The 1868 Revolution was an attempt to restore the relative calm of the Isabelline era by removing the element that had disrupted it: the Queen. However, it soon transpired that, in doing so, the revolutionaries had also removed militarised liberalism's cornerstone. Consequently, far from restoring normality, the Revolution set Spain on a downward slide into the worst disorder for half a century, culminating in two further military interventions. The experience had a salutary effect on Spain's political elite. Appalled at the chaos they had triggered off, they devised new political arrangements that not only brought a lengthy period without overt unrest but seemingly also embodied liberal ideas in a relatively advanced form. But appearances were deceptive, and beneath the glossy political surface things were very different.

The 'revolutionary years'

Although the 'Glorious Revolution' itself was a rapid affair, it was only the beginning of what are commonly termed the 'six revolutionary years' (*sexenio revolucionario*). Its victorious leaders faced not only the usual task of suppressing their more radical followers, but also that of filling the vacant throne. Their disagreements over how to do so compounded unrest in the country. They also rendered the new king's position untenable, thereby making a republic inevitable – and with it yet more chaos.

The speedy success of the 'September Revolution', as the 1868 Revolution was also known, reflected almost universal discontent at a time when economic downturn had hit the profits of the rich and the always precarious living standards of the poor alike. Most of the political elite had been alienated by Queen Isabella's behaviour, which had driven virtually all liberals, not only Progressives but even the more moderate Liberal Unionists, out of political life (p21). It was therefore possible to build a broad alliance incorporating both these groups, as well as many Democrats (p19), with the objective of deposing the Queen.

The architect of this 'September Coalition' was General Juan Prim, a leading Progressive. On 19 September, at Cadiz, he organised a military declaration (p16), which was soon followed by other uprisings across the south and east. Before the month was out the meagre forces loyal to Isabella had been defeated by General Serrano at Alcolea, and the Queen herself forced into exile. The Revolution had triumphed and, with Prim installed as Prime Minister, the coalition set about drawing up a new Constitution.

The 1869 Constitution incorporated a number of long-cherished Progressive aims. Known as the 'liberal conquests', they included universal male suffrage, religious freedom, trial by jury, and freedom of association and the press. However, the new Constitution also stipulated that Spain should remain a monarchy, a decision that infuriated the Coalition's more radical supporters. They promptly established a Republican Party, and set about channelling the popular discontent that was already growing against Prim's government.

One cause of dissatisfaction was the suppression of the local 'revolutionary committees' (*juntas revolucionarias*) which had as usual sprung up in the uprising's wake (p15). But the main cause lay on the other side of the Atlantic, in Cuba, where a revolt against Spanish rule had broken out within a month of the 1868 Revolution itself. The poorly trained and equipped Spanish forces sent to suppress the revolt suffered severe casualties, mainly from tropical disease. The Cuban War also made it impossible to abolish the *quinta* system of conscription, as Prim had promised, or to fulfil his other main pledge, which was to reduce taxation. All these effects fell disproportionately on the poor who, understandably, directed their anger against their new masters.

Cuba also increased the tensions within the September Coalition. The Progressives who led the government were broadly sympathetic to the revolt, and sought to end it by concessions. But their policy enraged the Unionists, who regarded Cuba as the last precious remnant of Spain's imperial past. But what really undermined Unionist backing for Prim was the question of a new king. For the 1869 Constitution retained not only the monarchy but also its considerable privileges, including the right to appoint the prime minister. Mindful of previous experience, both the main coalition parties were anxious for a king with views close to their own.

The Unionists had a candidate to hand; Isabella's brother-in-law, the French Duke of Montpensier. But the Progressives feared that crowning another Bourbon would mean a return to the system which had locked them out of power. They accordingly scoured

Europe for a willing alternative of suitably aristocratic lineage – a process which did nothing for Spain's prestige, or that of its new rulers. It ended when Prim secured the agreement of Amadeus, Duke of Savoy, and pushed through his appointment as Spain's new king in December 1870.

Prim's protégé worried Unionists for the same reasons that made him attractive to Progressives. Amadeus's father was the first king of a newly united Italy, whose constitution was much too democratic for Unionists' tastes. Furthermore, as staunch Catholics, many were gravely affronted by the new kingdom's take-over of the Papal States, which had long been ruled by the Church. Once events confirmed their fear that Amadeus would favour the Progressives, the Unionists turned their exclusion into a self-fulfilling prophecy by boycotting politics (p21). Despairing of returning to power while Amadeus remained on the throne, their thoughts turned increasingly to deposing him.

Crucially, the King was left to face these difficulties without his mentor, who was assassinated in Madrid on the very day Amadeus arrived in Spain. Prim's death removed the only figure capable of imposing authority on an increasingly restless populace, and of holding together a government sufficiently broad-based to be stable. Without him even his own Progressives split, their left wing breaking away to form a separate Radical Party. The factions spent the next two years squabbling with each other in Parliament, seemingly oblivious to the popular discontent being fanned by Republican agitators. Their behaviour so disillusioned Amadeus that on 11 February 1873 he abdicated.

That same day Parliament voted to abolish the monarchy, and proclaimed Spain a republic. Only a small proportion of its members genuinely supported the step, partly because the Republican Party remained a small, if vocal, minority in the country, and partly because it continued to suffer the effects of election-rigging (p19). But there was simply no viable alternative left. In the event, as the only party wholeheartedly committed to the new form of state, the **Republicans** were voted into power, with Figueras, one of their leaders, becoming Spain's first President.

Thus was the country's fate placed in the hands of a grouping that was peculiarly volatile, due largely to its insistence on federalism as the solution to Spain's problems. In the provinces, where grievances against central government taxes were rife, the idea of devolving power struck a chord with many, especially in the lower middle classes. But it also meant that such supporters were constantly suspicious of the party's Madrid-based leadership. At the same time, the implacable opposition of many provincial Republicans to all parties loyal to the monarchy – an attitude that earned them the name of 'intransigents' – clashed with the leadership's policy of maintaining good relations with the Radicals.

It was thus a bitter blow for these compromisers (*benévolos*) when, in April, the Radicals attempted a military coup and, on its discovery, followed all the other monarchist parties in boycotting politics altogether (p21). The upshot was that the Republicans won an overwhelming victory at the May general election, on a turnout of under 40 per cent. But the lack of an opposition merely strengthened the intransigents' demands that the Republic's constitution should include very extensive devolution to

Republicanismo

Republicanism; Republican movement

With its roots in the Democratic Party of the 1850s and 1860s (p19), Republicanism grew out of the **liberal movement** (p8). The first officially republican party was founded in 1869, by dissident Democrats. It was notable for its fervent belief in federalism as the necessary accompaniment to abolition of the monarchy. These Federal Republicans, whose support came mainly from the small-town lower middle classes (shopkeepers, teachers, etc.), governed Spain during the first phase of the First Republic. After the restoration of the monarchy the movement was long in the political doldrums, until in 1908 it split into two factions: the **Radical Republicans** (p50) and the **Reformists** (p41).

See also: *Pacto de San Sebastián* (p63)

the regions. Here, too, the Republican leaders took a more moderate line, conscious of the need for a viable central government. In July Pi y Margall, who had replaced Figueras as President, presented their draft constitution to Parliament. It provoked the intransigents into insurrection.

This '**cantonalist**' revolt forced Pi to resign as President. He was replaced by Salmerón, and the movement was quickly defeated. However, that was not the case of another uprising, this time in the North. There, given renewed hope by Isabella's removal, the Carlist movement had risen again. Although the Carlists' support was no longer what it had been (pp13–14), amidst the confusion of events they were able, as in the 1830s, to take control of much of the Basque Country and Navarre (p13). Like his grandfather, the new pretender to the throne – also called Carlos – established a mini-state with its capital at Estella; over the winter of 1873–74 his forces laid siege to Bilbao.

Politically isolated, these events left the Republican leaders totally dependent on an Army increasingly disillusioned by their failure to maintain order. To retain its loyalty the government was obliged to adopt ever more authoritarian policies. These, in turn, only increased the dissatisfaction of those parts of society who had to provide the fighting men and tax revenue for the Carlist and cantonalist conflicts, as well as for the continuing Cuban War. As a result, the government was subject to constant attacks in Parliament which first forced Salmerón to resign, and then, in January 1874, defeated his replacement, Castelar.

At that point the Army stepped in. General Pavía forcibly dissolved Parliament, and a unitary – i.e. centralist – republic was estab-

cantonalismo

'cantonalist' movement

The 'cantonalists', who made up the extreme federalist wing of **Republicanism** in the 1870s, believed that provinces and their subdivisions should be allowed virtually to run their own affairs. In the summer of 1873 they attempted to set up several such 'cantons' in southern and eastern Spain, but being poorly co-ordinated, and lacking any military resources, they were soon suppressed by the Army. Only in Cartagena was the 'canton' able to hold out for any significant time. The term became a byword for the chaos of the 'six revolutionary years', and of the First Republic in particular.

lished, with Serrano as President. On paper, its governments were attempts to revive the September Coalition: in practice they were drawn from the remains of the Radicals. Ruling mainly by decree, their practice made a mockery of the 'liberal conquests' of 1869. Isolated and unpopular, despite the relief of Bilbao, their fate was sealed by failure to defeat the Carlists.

As the war entered another winter, the Army's patience again gave out. On 29 December 1874, at Sagunto, Brigadier-General Martínez Campos staged a declaration (p16) in favour of Isabella II's son, Alfonso. Within days the government had collapsed, and the First Republic with it, after less than two years of existence. Despite its brief span, the Republic remained imprinted on popular memory as a time of chaos and suffering, an image exploited by those opposed not merely to Republicanism but to change in any form.

The 'Restoration settlement'

The Sagunto declaration was no rogue affair. For some time civilian politicians – relics of the old Liberal Union, Moderate and Progressive parties – had been plotting to restore the monarchy. Indeed, by the end of 1874 no one, civilian or soldier, was prepared to resist such a step. The universal desire was for peace and stability, which over the next quarter-century was to be met to a very considerable degree by the arrangements known as the Restoration settlement.

Its architect was Antonio Cánovas del Castillo, whose efforts over the previous few years had persuaded almost all Spaniards of any influence not only that the monarchy must be restored, but that Alfonso was the legitimate and only realistic candidate. Furthermore, the settlement as a whole closely reflected his ideas. Their model was Britain, whose prosperity and freedom from internal strife were the antithesis of Spain's experience.

To Cánovas' mind the foundations of British success were, firstly, that a broad spectrum of the country's political and economic leaders had regular access to government and, secondly, that power could change hands between sections of this elite without military involvement. He noted, too, that while Britain had achieved both without having a written constitution, Spain had not, despite producing five such documents since 1812. Accordingly, although the formal basis of his settlement was a new Constitution, what it really offered was a new style of political practice.

That in turn rested on two pillars. The first of these, initially regarded by Cánovas as the more crucial, was the King. Under the 1876 Constitution Alfonso retained the power to appoint and dismiss prime ministers – his mother's abuse of which had triggered off disaster in 1868 (p21). So Cánovas devoted great efforts to imbuing in Alfonso the notion that the price of retaining his theoretically wide powers was to abstain from using them in practice. Hence his deep concern when Alfonso died suddenly in 1885. Yet Cánovas' worries turned out to be groundless. Alfonso's widow, Maria Cristina, acting as regent for her infant son, proved willing and able to apply his teaching as well as her husband had done.

In practice, the second of the two pillars – the existence of two well-disciplined political parties – proved more fundamental to Cánovas' arrangements. These 'dynastic parties' – so-called from their allegiance to the Bourbon line – were in a sense heirs of the mid-century Moderates and Progressives (pp10, 11). But essentially they were Cánovas' creation, modelled explicitly on the two great British parties of the period, whose leaders' speeches he was reputed to learn by heart.

Thus, bizarrely, as well as founding his own **Conservative Party**, Cánovas also played an important role in creating its sparring-partner, the **Liberals**. And in truth the two were more allies than rivals, since the key to peaceful alternation lay in their agreement voluntarily to abandon power to each other at regular intervals. Moreover, while out of government, each agreed to act out the part of parliamentary opposition, rather than turning to conspiracy or exposing the charade by boycotting politics (p21). The necessary discipline among the party rank and file was maintained partly by the knowledge of eventual return to office, and partly by the personal authority and political skills of Cánovas and his Liberal counterpart, Práxedes Sagasta.

These arrangements finally allowed governments to operate without the constant threat of insurrection. Thus the Conservatives, who held power for much of the Restoration's first decade, were able to reverse a number of the 'liberal conquests' of 1869 without any return to disorder. And, once the Liberals had enjoyed a sustained period of office after 1885, universal – male – suffrage and other reforms were reintroduced, again without any threat to stability. More broadly, one of the settlement's unquestionable achievements was to create a more relaxed climate, not just in political but also in social and cultural terms.

The more settled atmosphere was illustrated by the way in which the thorny issue of the Church's status was handled. In the spirit of compromise promoted by Cánovas, the 1876 Constitution made Catholicism the official state religion, but explicitly permitted the private practice of other faiths. Even that compromise proved unacceptable to a significant sector of right-wing opinion, including some in his own party. To mollify it, Cánovas consolidated the Church's virtual monopoly over school education. Typically, he did so not through new legislation but simply by failing to raise the tax income necessary to provide the state schooling required by existing law.

Partido Conservador

Conservative Party

Founded in 1875 by Antonio Cánovas del Castillo, the party's original name of 'Liberal–Conservative' reflected its roots in the **liberal movement** (p8), specifically the **Liberal Unionists** (p20) and the **Moderates** (p10). However, its philosophy was truly conservative, in the sense of opposing any challenge to traditional institutions – the monarchy, the landowning aristocracy and the Catholic Church – and the established order in general. From the 1890s the party was increasingly rent by disputes between followers of Cánovas' pragmatic approach to politics and critics of the corruption which pervaded Restoration politics. After 1909 these led to the Conservatives' effectively splitting over the 'puritan' policies of its leader, Antonio Maura (p42). Greatly weakened, it was finally destroyed by the 1923 coup.

See also: *turno pacífico* (p33)

Cánovas' inaction helped to maintain the revival of the Church's social influence among the better-off (p14), which had been further boosted by the strongly anticlerical nature of much unrest during the 'six revolutionary years'. The Liberals accepted this with surprising equanimity, partly thanks to the Constitution's guarantee of a private sphere of religious freedom, but mainly because of their opponents' political practice. Thus the Conservatives made no attempt to block the establishment of private lay schools, among them the influential 'Institute of Free Education', which provided an education system outside Church influence to those who were able to pay. They also refused to accept the Church's demands to be allowed to set up its own universities.

The religious issue also demonstrated the dynastic parties' ability to neutralise potentially disruptive elements on their fringes by incorporating them. For Cánovas' pragmatic approach reconciled all but the most reactionary right-wingers, and in 1883 the small but influential Catholic Union party joined his Conservatives. On the Left, the Liberals exercised a similar capacity for assimilation (*atraccionismo*), luring disillusioned and dispirited Republicans (p29) with the prospect of access to power and influence. Even the Republican leaders forswore any attempt to overthrow the new regime by force, and accepted its existence as a fact: some, most notably ex-President Castelar, came close to giving it their positive endorsement.

The only significant figure who refused to accept the new disposition was the former Radical leader (p27), Ruiz Zorrilla. After going into exile he launched several abortive coup attempts, but their pitiful failure served only to underline the solidity of Cánovas' arrangements. On the Right, too, any remaining military threat was extinguished when the Carlist uprising was finally crushed in 1876. Splintering into traditionalist and reformist factions, Carlism virtually disappeared for 60 years (p82). Its defeat was followed by the abolition of Basque and Navarrese traditional privileges, thus finally making Spain one single economic entity (p13). The price paid, apparently minor, was a **special financial arrangement** which effectively devolved tax-raising powers to the two areas.

Two years after the Carlists' defeat the Cuban War also came to an end, thus removing the principal cause of popular resentment. The change in popular mood was further boosted by a marked improvement in Spain's economic situation. The initial stimulus came from foreign investment in mining, itself the result of liberalising legis-

> ### *Partido Liberal*
> ### Liberal Party
>
> Founded in 1875 by Práxedes Sagasta, originally under the name of 'Fusionist Liberals', the party was broadly the successor of the **Progressives** (p11) as the more radical wing of the **liberal movement** (p8). However, its commitment to reform was strictly limited by its participation in the undemocratic arrangements to ensure **peaceful alternation in power** (p33). After 1900, except during the brief leadership of José Canalejas (p42), its main concern became to halt the resurgent influence of the Church, especially in the field of education. Although it was in government for long periods the party became increasingly factionalised, and was effectively destroyed by the 1923 coup.

concierto económico
....
special (Basque and Navarrese)
financial accord

In compensation for the
suppression of their **traditional
privileges** (p13) in 1876, special
accords were concluded with the
Basque provinces and Navarre,
under which the provincial
authorities collected taxes in their
area and paid the central
government a lump sum for the
services it provided. Franco
partially suppressed these
arrangements after he captured
the area (p87), but under the
devolution arrangements
introduced after his death (p132)
they were re-instated in full.

lation brought in during the revolutionary period. Thereafter a number of factors combined to sustain the upturn: a phylloxera epidemic decimated the French wine sector; the Bessemer process was discovered, making Basque iron ore potentially profitable for the first time; and the railways experienced a second boom.

These developments relieved to some extent the precarious conditions of the poor, and gave the small but growing middle class a strong stake in the existing order, symbolised by the aristocratic titles granted to a number of industrialists. They also gave the appearance that Spain was, at last, catching up on its neighbours socially and economically, just as the political arrangements that contributed to them were leading to advances in the political sphere. Indeed, one supporter of the Restoration settlement, pointing to the fact that Spain had universal male suffrage while only around one-fifth of British adults had the vote, dubbed Spain 'Europe's most modern monarchy'.

Towards 'the disaster'

Such a grandiose claim may have had some basis in constitutional theory. But, as Cánovas had recognised, what mattered was political practice, and there, any advances made in his settlement were more than cancelled out by other, retrograde aspects. Not only that; political backwardness had social and economic effects, which tended to hold Spain back in those spheres, too. Far from leading the field in modernisation Spain had missed out on most of its key aspects, and was drifting towards the calamitous events of 1898.

The Restoration settlement's fundamental weakness was that its apparently liberal, even democratic political arrangements were a sham. That was true first and foremost of Cánovas' boast that he had taken the Army out of politics. He always insisted that the Restoration had been the result of civilian plotting, and played down the military contribution. But in reality, Alfonso's coronation had been secured by the refusal of other generals to put down Martínez Campos' revolt (p29).

Nor thereafter did the Army cease to be the ultimate arbiter of events; it merely refrained from exercising that role, because civilian politicians were careful to observe its sensibilities. They respected the tradition established by Narváez, and kept strictly out of its internal affairs (p18). However, at the same time they left responsibility for law and order in its hands and those of the militarised Civil Guard. The real change was that, coming on top of the unnerving 'revolutionary years', the Army's pampered treatment extinguished what remained of its reforming ardour. From now on its influence was conservative, if not downright reactionary.

For the moment, though, that political stance was less damaging than the corruption at the settlement's core, the arrangements which ensured that **power alternated peacefully** between the two dynastic parties. For, just as earlier in the century, elections were a sham, with the results determined in advance by the government of the day. What was new was the scale of **political clientilism** required to ensure that outcome, with an electorate so much larger than before (p30).

The key to the operation of clientilism was local government. Mayors of individual towns and villages, and the civil governors responsible for an entire province, wielded very extensive powers that were the main source of the patronage and sanctions needed to make clientilism work. They were also

turno pacífico

peaceful alternation in power

The practice of peaceful alternation, established after the Restoration of 1876, not only enabled the **Conservative** and **Liberal Parties** (pp30, 31) to monopolise and exchange government office without the military **declarations** (p16) common before 1868, but also to do so without holding genuine elections. The success of this strategy depended on the prime minister at the time voluntarily resigning and advising the king to appoint a figure from the opposing party in his place. An election would then be held, allowing the new government to obtain a majority by the use of **clientilism**. Initially based on tacit agreement, the arrangement was formalised in 1885 by the secret Pact of El Pardo between the party leaders, Cánovas and Sagasta.

caciquismo

political clientilism

Particularly prevalent during the Restoration period, when it became a byword for corruption, clientilism was a system that allowed election results to be influenced by governments once the electorate had become too large for **election-rigging** (p19) alone to achieve that end. Its agents were local party bosses (*caciques*), drawn from the influential members of local society, such as landowners, mayors and even priests, who dispensed favours and official jobs on orders from their leaders in Madrid, as well as resorting to straightforward bribery and intimidation.

named by the central government in Madrid, which could thus keep tight control over the whole system. Its model was the one that had long been used in France, where abuses were kept in check by independent district courts. But in Spain the magistrates were also government appointees, and themselves integrated into the apparatus of clientilism.

Nor did the Conservative and Liberal Parties (pp30, 31) who ran this system bear any real resemblance to their British namesakes, whose rivalry was the political expression of the conflicting economic interests of industrialists and commercially-minded large landowners. In Spain, where industrialists remained scarce, and few landowners were interested in their estates' commercial potential, the parties remained mere cliques of politicians, concerned with no interests except their own. Rather than providing a means of transforming programmes into action they acted as channels for distributing the favours of office – jobs, contracts, honours – to their supporters whenever the system brought them back to power. In some areas a single local boss might even serve both parties at once.

The parties were the first part of Cánovas' construction in which cracks appeared. Ironically, they came from within his own Conservatives, with the emergence of a faction who regarded the corruption involved in alternation as a threat to the country's moral fibre. The leader of these 'puritans', Francisco Silvela, proposed ending the practice by loosening central control over local councils, and making them subject to genuine elections. Yet he too believed in control by the elite, and so planned an element of corporate suffrage. This gave the owners of businesses the right to have votes in that capacity, *in addition* to those they were entitled to as citizens. Fearing that this change in the voting system would exclude them permanently from local, and thus from national power, the Liberals rejected the plan out of hand. Silvela then pressed his leader to abandon alternation.

Cánovas' refusal to do so split the Conservative Party. But the division was only temporary, and normality – in Restoration terms – soon returned. Despite fading memories of the 'revolutionary years' (pp25–9), despite Cánovas' murder (p48) and Sagasta's retirement around the turn of the century, the Liberals and Conservatives continued to be held together by the promise of regular booty. And opposition to them continued to be smothered by the clientilist system, by widespread apathy and cynicism, and, when the need arose, by military repression, as with the upsurge of anarchist activity in the 1880s (p48). However, if the political cracks could be papered over, the settlement's other damaging effects could not.

Some of the difficulties resulted from Cánovas' religious compromise (pp30–1), whose terms were devised to cement the alliance between the Church and the better-off, among whom the upsurge in Church attendance was concentrated. Apart from the peasant farmers of Old Castile, the poor abandoned the Church in droves, disillusioned by its failure to denounce the appalling living and working conditions in the southern countryside and the embryonic northern industrial areas. It is hardly surprising that bitter anticlericalism should have become a major aspect of social division in Spain. And more immediately, those unable to afford a private lay education were forced to rely – at best – on hopelessly antiquated Church-run establishments.

The lack of a proper education system did not merely blight the lives of millions; it also severely constrained the country's economic development. Similarly, the centralisation of local government had worse effects than the spreading of dubious moral values: with even the most minor of decisions requiring approval from Madrid, the operation of the councils was painfully slow. Worst of all, under a fiscal system unchanged since the 1850s, taxes were ludicrously low, and their application little better than arbitrary. But reforming the system would have meant taking on influential sectors of opinion – something no government would risk – so that both central and local administration were starved of the funds they urgently needed to improve the country's physical and social infrastructure.

The inadequacy of the infrastructure was painfully clear to Castilian wheat farmers. Spain's transport system was so antiquated that, since the 1869 free trade legislation, American imports could undercut them in the vital Catalan and Basque markets. In 1885 the other mainstay of the rural economy suffered a devastating blow, when Spanish vines, too, were hit by phylloxera. Economic growth (pp31–2), based on rising rural incomes which were in turn founded on the wine trade's rapid expansion, was reversed. For the masses, in particular, the accompanying rise in prosperity was brought to an abrupt halt.

If farming remained so important to the economy it was because industrialisation was so limited. Apart from the mines and railways, almost all of which were foreign-controlled, industry was confined to two sectors; textile manufacture in Catalonia, and iron and steel production in the Basque Country. Yet even in those centres the picture was less rosy than it seemed, because the technology used in both industries was outdated – a problem compounded in the Catalan case by the small size of the firms involved. As a result, both regions were threatened by more competitive European rivals.

The response of the Basque and Catalan industrialists was to join the Castilian cereal farmers in lobbying for an end to free trade. In 1891 their efforts bore fruit when the government introduced prohibitive tariffs on imported goods and produce. However, while such protectionism safeguarded the short-term profits of the three powerful groups concerned, it was extremely bad for their customers, who now had no alternative sources of supply. In the longer term protection was also disastrous for the three sectors themselves, since it removed any incentive to increase productivity or to innovate, causing Spain to fall still further behind the leading industrial countries.

That fact was brought brutally home by events in Cuba. Indeed, the country's last important colony was itself a prime example of how Spain was out of phase with the industrialised world. Even at the zenith of commercially-driven colonialism, Spain was still drawing little benefit from Cuba's economy, since it was largely controlled by American interests. When a fresh rebellion broke out on the island in 1895 the same interests orchestrated an outcry in favour of US intervention, as a result of which the battleship *Maine* was sent to the island. When it exploded in Havana harbour in February 1898, although the cause was probably an accident, public reaction left President McKinley with no option but to declare war.

Spain was hopelessly outmatched. Its fleet – as opposed to the bloated naval bureaucracy, filled on the basis of political favours – had suffered gravely from the general lack of public funds. The ships' guns were antiquated, the crew had not been trained to use them, and they had insufficient coal to steam at full speed. The results would have been comic, had they not been so tragic. In the summer of 1898 the entire navy was destroyed in a few engagements lasting a matter of hours; in the decisive engagement, which took place off Santiago de Cuba, only one American sailor died. The Philippines and Puerto Rico were lost to the USA, and Cuba, while nominally independent, became a *de facto* American dependency.

Reaction in Spain to 'the disaster', as these events soon came to be known, was as revealing as the events themselves. Conservative politicians and much of public opinion – the former blind to reality, the latter hopelessly ill-informed – went from the assumption of easy victory to numbed shock. And while the Liberals were generally quicker to foresee the appalling outcome, they cynically chose to keep their insight to themselves, for fear of losing popularity. Material backwardness, while bad enough in itself, was far from the full price of what was presented as stability but was really stagnation.

Exhibit 2.1: A voice of radical Republicanism (1870)

Extracts from an edition of a Republican paper which appeared two days before the arrival of King Amadeus in Spain, and the assassination of his mentor, General Prim

[. . .]No le bastaba a ese grande reo de lesa-revolución, que se llama *gobierno septembrista*, haber negado los derechos individuales, disputar la *Soberanía del pueblo* con la soberanía de un tirano extranjero, *inviolable, indiscutible, inamovible y hereditario*; desmoralizar la administración, desangrar a todas las clases de la sociedad, oprimir al pueblo y amordazar la prensa; era necesario algo más, y para que nada faltara a sus traiciones, a sus crímenes y perjurios, ha concluido por sancionarlos con el voto de una [Asamblea] Constituyente facciosa, que con la vergüenza y el vilipendio de la nación española, ha votado su muerte, que está reclamando su más pronta e inmediata ejecución. [. . .]

Ciudadanos españoles sin distinción de clases ni de partidos políticos: el rostro de nuestra madre la patria ha sido escupido y abofeteado, su altivez humillada y su honor difamado por un *intruso*, por un TIRANO EXTRANJERO. ¿Qué hacemos? ¿A qué aguardamos? ¿Consentiremos que *un tirano de Italia* esclavice al valeroso pueblo español, a la *España con honra, libre e* INDEPENDIENTE? [. . .]

Ciudadanos españoles: *la patria está en peligro*. Cuando el tirano extranjero coloque su inmunda planta en tierra española, que esta afrenta sea para todos la señal de exclamar con el coraje de los pueblos ultrajados:

¡AL *combate!*
¡ABAJO LO EXISTENTE!
¡VIVA EL EJÉRCITO ESPAÑOL HONRADO!
¡VIVA LA SOBERANÍA NACIONAL!
¡VIVA LA REVOLUCIÓN!

Source: El Combate, Madrid (25 December 1870).

Exhibit 2.2: Cánovas on the monarchy (1886)

Extracts from a speech to Parliament

La idea de todos los monárquicos y en todas partes, es que la monarquía, que para eso es hereditaria, porque de otra suerte sería una irrisión que hereditaria se llamase, es, por su naturaleza, perpetua. [. . .]

No hay que pensar, pues, que con esta convicción nosotros podamos aceptar ni poco ni mucho, ni de cerca ni de lejos, el principio de una evolución pacífica y falsamente apellidada legal, detrás de la cual pudiera estar la supresión de la monarquía. Nosotros concebimos una monarquía que puede errar, que puede caer; pero nosotros no podemos admitir que eso se prevea por las leyes de un país; no podemos admitir que, en las circunstancias normales de la nación, se tenga por sobreentendida en las leyes y en el régimen político, que el rey pueda ser a cada instante separado por un funcionario cualquiera, sin los beneficios siquiera de la inamovilidad, ni de los reglamentos. [. . .]

Para nosotros jamás, por ningún camino se puede llegar, por medio de la legalidad, a la supresiòn de la monarquía, a causa de que no hay legalidad sin la monarquìa, a causa de que sin la monarquía puede haber hechos, puede haber fuerza, puede haber batallas, pero no hay, ni puede haber, legalidad. [. . .]

Source: Diario de Sesiones (3 July 1886).

Topics
FOR DISCUSSION

■ How would you describe the tone of Exhibit 2.1? What sort of political climate does it conjure up?

■ What do its authors appear to want? What ideas seem to lie behind the text?

■ How does Cánovas conceive the notion of legality (Exhibit 2.2)? Are there any similarities with the conceptions illustrated in Exhibits 1.1 and 1.2?

■ What does Cánovas mean by the 'régimen político', which he implicitly places on a par with laws?

■ Bearing in mind that it enjoyed very widespread support, why did the 1868 Revolution turn out so disastrously?

■ In a sense, the Restoration period represents the 'golden age' of the Spanish liberal movement. How do its arrangements relate to the aspirations embodied in the Cadiz Constitution?

CHAPTER 3

Change frustrated (1898–1923)

As the new century began and industrialisation continued in Europe, the organised workers' movement formed in the old gathered strength. It was divided into various branches. The largest, Marxist socialism, held that economic advance would lead inevitably to the fall of capitalism and social revolution, a process some socialists sought to accelerate by working for political reform. Anarchists, whose sole interest was revolution itself, thought such activity pointless; their main strength was in Russia, the great power where industrialisation had made least headway. Common to all these groups, however, was the belief that workers' loyalties were to their class, rather than to their country. A major factor in holding them in check was thus the rise of nationalism, which in 1914 culminated in the outbreak of the First World War. In most countries, ideas of international class solidarity were forgotten as workers flocked to join up. Russia took a different path, and the communist revolution of 1917 gave renewed heart to militant workers across the world. It also provoked a virulent reaction from their opponents, the first sign of which came with Mussolini's seizure of power in Italy, in 1922.

Although its direct impact was limited – the framework of the Restoration settlement remained in place for a further quarter-century – the 'disaster' of 1898 had a profound effect on Spain. By setting off a process of national self-examination, it stimulated various forces which sought to bring about far-reaching change in the way the country was run, including a vague but widely-felt urge to 'regenerate' it. Another was the feeling of distinctiveness in certain regions which led to demands for some form of self-government. Yet a third was the workers' movement, which believed in a quite different form of salvation, through social revolution. The three were very different from each other; they were also far from homogeneous, and divided into a number of often contradictory strands. The result was their common frustration.

The 'Regenerationists'

Some Spaniards had long been aware of their country's failure to keep pace with its neighbours, politically, socially and above all economically. But the events of 1898 brought that failure into sharp relief for many, and crystallised a belief that drastic action was needed. Such 'regenerationist' thinking emanated from all the better-informed sections of society, from both within and without

regneracionismo

'regenerationist'
ideas/thinking

Although the term had already
been in use before, the events of
1898 brought the notion of
regeneration to the forefront of
public debate in Spain. Indeed,
the literary and philosophical
strand of regenerationist thinking
is associated with the group
known as the '1898 generation'
(*generación del 98*), whose most
significant members were Miguel
de Unamuno, José Ortega y
Gasset and Ramón Maeztu. The
group's ideas were diverse, and
also varied over time, so that it is
impossible to speak of a coherent
'movement'. The same is even
more true of the wide range of
regenerationist proposals put
forward for changes in political,
economic and social structures.
However, what they all had in
common was a concern about
Spain's general backwardness
(*atraso*), and a desire to eliminate
it.

the elite which had access to power under the
Restoration settlement.

Regenerationist ideas were not just
diverse; they were also downright contradictory. Thus, for Republicans, the term meant
abolishing the monarchy. Yet the young King,
Alfonso XIII, who came of age in 1902, could
also be seen as a regenerationist, given his
interest in new technology and plans for Army
reform. In fact the closest thing to a coherent
regenerationist programme was to be found in
the life and works of one man; Joaquín Costa.

At the core of Costa's work were his
extensive proposals for agricultural reform
through technical improvements, and especially for more and better irrigation, which he
attempted with some success to implement in
his native Aragon. To complement them he
advocated drastic land reform (p70). He also
argued that the large estates of the south,
notoriously underused and thus unable to
provide adequate employment, should be
broken up and sold off to create the class of
small farmers of which some early liberals had
dreamt (p9). These changes would, he felt,
release the 'live forces' stifled by the existing
arrangements.

Costa saw that these 'forces' were
excluded from influence by the practice of political clientilism (p33). To try and break
its hold, in 1899 he set up a party-cum-business association, the National League of
Producers. This soon received support from the Chambers of Commerce, who were the
representatives of small business in Spain's provincial towns. However, larger industrialists showed no desire to break their alliance with the large landowners (p35), and
without their help the League made no electoral headway. Its main achievement was to
organise a non-payment campaign against what the government of the day understood
by regeneration, tax reform (p41), which was also the prerequisite for implementation
of Costa's own plans. In the face of such contradictions, and its powerful opponents,
the League soon collapsed.

This failure convinced Costa that clientilism could not be defeated under the
existing system. To achieve that, he felt that Spain needed an 'iron surgeon' (*cirujano de
hierro*), a charismatic leader who would enjoy virtually unlimited powers for a brief
period, before returning the country to parliamentary rule. In the aftermath of 1898 a
candidate for the role appeared in the shape of General Polavieja, who had commanded
Spanish forces in the Philippines. On his return he took up Costa's attacks on the polit-

ical system, quickly attracting a mass following which forced through his appointment as Minister of War. But Polavieja's plans to modernise the Army – for him the key to regeneration – were also blocked by the government's budget reform plans (p41). Polavieja resigned in protest, and his support faded away.

Costa's other hope lay with the **Reformist Republicans**, who agreed with his emphasis on concrete, viable proposals rather than dogma. Thus, instead of just railing against Church control over the school system, as Republicans had tended to do in the past, the Reformists drew up detailed plans to change the content of education, and in particular to introduce an element of vocational training. However, like Costa, they were prevented from making further progress by the workings of clientilism (p33), and they remained a small, though influential minority.

> ### *Partido Republicano Reformista*
>
> Reformist Republican Party
>
> The Reformists were one of the two factions into which the **Republican movement** (p28) divided in 1908. They subsequently abandoned their almost exclusive concern with constitutional reform (abolition of the monarchy, federalism) in favour of formulating practical proposals for change in specific fields, particularly education. The party enjoyed little electoral success, and disappeared under the Primo dictatorship, but from it emerged many of the **Left Republicans** (p68) responsible for major reforms during the Second Republic.

Given the workings of the Restoration settlement (pp29–32), the only feasible vehicles for regenerationist ideas at this time were the two 'dynastic parties'. Ironically, it was among the Conservatives that their influence was more evident, as had already been shown in Francisco Silvela's unsuccessful attempt to reform local government (p34). Now, as leader of his party, Silvela became Prime Minister in the wake of the 1898 'disaster'. Once confronted with the appalling state of public finances that had made it inevitable (p34), their reform became his top priority.

The plans of his Finance Minister, Villaverde, met widespread opposition, including from Costa's League, because they included an element of tax reform, although in fact taxation remained very low. Their principal aim, which was to bring spending under control, was achieved by the cuts that provoked Polavieja's departure. Once they had been implemented, Villaverde's changes set the tone of Spanish budget policy for the next 70 years, making it even harder for governments to stimulate economic development.

Economics were a minor concern for Silvela's protégé and successor, the greatest and most controversial of Conservative regenerationists. Like his mentor, Antonio Maura was a 'puritan' (p34); he believed that Spain's problems were essentially moral, and that he could solve them by 'dignifying' politics. He talked of a 'revolution from above', by which he meant that the steps necessary to eliminate corruption should be taken by the existing elite, to which he belonged. What he could not, or would not see was that its position depended on the very corruption he sought to eliminate.

In 1902 Maura received an early warning of the contradictions inherent in his ideas. As Interior Minister, he insisted on reducing the government's use of clientilist tactics (p33) in that year's election, which resulted in significant Republican gains in the larger cities. He was undeterred, and three years later, on becoming Prime Minister, he renewed his efforts to clean up politics with a fresh attempt at local government reform. However, like Silvela, he did not intend that free local elections should break the hold of the better-off on local politics, and therefore repeated his proposal for a form of corporate suffrage (p34). Once again the plans were frustrated by the Liberals, who could see more clearly than Maura the danger they posed to the two parties' common interests (p30).

Not that Maura was blind to the threat of the new forces emerging in society. Indeed, he made no secret of the fact that his 'revolution from above' was intended primarily to pre-empt one 'from below', by the workers' movement. In 1908 his fears of such an outcome led him to introduce a number of repressive measures, including restrictions on the right of free association. The Liberals saw their chance, and joined the Republicans in a 'Bloc of the Left' to run a campaign against the new measures, under the slogan 'Maura, No!'

To Maura, the Liberals' abandonment of the tacit alliance between the 'dynastic parties' was tantamount to treason. He offered his resignation to the King, demanding the chance to manufacture a vote of confidence in fresh elections. But Alfonso, worried by the re-entry of Republicanism into mainstream politics, now saw Maura as the biggest threat to stability. He accordingly accepted the resignation offer, and handed power over to the Liberals. Many of Maura's Conservative colleagues backed the King's action, leaving their former leader an embittered and isolated figure (p50).

Up to this time the Liberal Party, which now returned to power, had shown little interest in regeneration. As the heir of the liberal movement's radical wing, its theoretical priority had been the constitutional reforms of the 1880s (p30) – although by that time the arrangements which allowed the party to carry them out had rendered them meaningless! Since then, preserving those arrangements intact had been the Liberals' over-riding concern. Their differences with the Conservatives had been reduced to hysterical attacks on the revival of Church influence – partly because the Church posed a minor threat to the relative tolerance of Restoration society, but mainly because anti-clericalism was an easy means of attracting popular support (p34).

This situation only began to change under the leadership of José Canalejas. After he was appointed Prime Minister in 1910, Canalejas sidelined the religious issue by introducing the 'Padlock Act' (*Ley del Candado*) which, while seeming to place restrictions on the monastic orders that were the main focus of popular concern, effectively left their situation unchanged. That opened the way for him to push through a second, more progressive tax reform, which for the first time hit rental incomes, and so acted as an incentive to more productive investments. He also overhauled local government finance and abolished the rich's right to buy themselves out of military service. His further plans included a scheme for rural land reform that would allow underused estates to be expropriated from their owners.

Canalejas fell victim to an assassin in 1912 (p49), before his programme could be fully implemented. However, his death was not the end of efforts to put regenerationist ideas into practice. Eduardo Dato, Maura's successor as Conservative leader, brought in

Spain's first industrial relations and social security legislation, before he too was assassinated in 1921 (p49). And the Liberal governments of the early 1920s were influenced by the ideas of the Reformist Republicans. But with Canalejas gone and Maura isolated, the only concerted attempt at regenerating Spain lasted for just a few months in 1918 (p52). Meanwhile, as the country continued to stagnate, the backwardness against which the regenerationists railed was increasing all the time.

Regionalists and nationalists

The extent of economic backwardness was far from uniform across Spain. By the 1890s Catalonia and the Basque Country, in particular, had undergone a considerable degree of industrialisation. In each case the experience gave rise to demands for self-government. But, just as the industrialisation processes and the historical backgrounds were very different, so too were Basque and Catalan regionalists – or, as many would see themselves, nationalists.

Regionalism first made its appearance in Catalonia, where feelings of distinctive identity had deep roots, since for two centuries after the creation of a united Spain the region had enjoyed extensive self-government. Even after the loss of autonomy in 1714 (p3), when Catalan ceased to be used officially, the language remained strong in daily use and literature, and in the latter part of the nineteenth century it experienced a renaissance (*renaixença*). Its leading figure, Vicent Almirall, was also the first man to give Catalan regionalism (*catalanismo*) a political dimension.

In 1892 Almirall's ideas were set out by his disciple, Enric Prat de la Riba, in what effectively became the movement's programme. These 'Manresa Principles' (*Bases de Manresa*) were steeped in Catalan history, and showed the influence of federal republicanism in the region (pp27–8). As well as calls for Catalan to become the region's official language there were demands for devolution within a federal Spain. These also reflected a newer concern voiced by Almirall: that Catalonia's development had been delayed by the backwardness of Spain as a whole, and by having to provide a disproportionate share of taxes from which it saw little return. The appearance of this grievance indicated the close links between regionalism and Catalan industry.

Industrialisation in Catalonia was a gradual process, and a natural development of Barcelona's tradition as a major port and commercial centre. It was founded on the textile industry, whose leaders' great concern in the later nineteenth century was to mount a successful campaign for import protection (p35). Although Catalan culture was important to the textile magnates, it did not spur them to political action. However, the events of 1898 persuaded them that their longer-term interests could only be protected by a fundamental change in the way Spain was run.

The industrialists' first hope when they began to look for a political leader to represent them was General Polavieja (pp40–1), who had expressed sympathy for their views. When this hope proved vain, they decided to take up Almirall's strategy of a separate Catalan party, and sponsored the foundation of the **Regionalist League**. Their financial and political clout enabled them to break the shackles of clientelism (p33), and within a few months the party had made sweeping gains at the 1901 general

Lliga Regionalista

(Catalan) Regionalist League

Formed in 1901 with the support of local business interests, the League demanded home rule for Catalonia, while also seeking to influence the policies pursued by central governments through lobbying. The leading industrialist, Françesc Cambó, was responsible for fostering the necessary contacts in Madrid; the League's other main figure, Enric Prat de la Riba, was its head within Catalonia. Until the 1920s it was by far the largest Catalan regionalist party, but thereafter it was overtaken by other, more radical groupings (p53), and ceased to be a significant force after 1923.

election. In 1906 the League brought together a broad alliance of political forces, known as Catalan Solidarity, which won an even more dramatic victory the following year.

These electoral successes further increased the magnates' leverage over Madrid, and helped them to persuade the government to impose yet higher import tariffs in 1906. In 1914 they obtained another concession when a Catalan regional government, the *Mancomunitat*, was established. Run by the League, with Prat as its first head, it enabled the industrialists to implement what amounted to a form of conservative economic regeneration in Catalonia, with considerable success.

To a large extent the League had now achieved its aims. Its demands for self-government went no further than devolution, partly because of history but above all because it responded to the industrialists' present needs. They wanted to control their own affairs, but they knew that their businesses depended on the Spanish market. They also realised that the home market would grow only if the country as a whole prospered. Hence their desire not just to remain a part of Spain, but to influence its development, and hence their rejection of any thought of independence.

Such moderation and rationality sat oddly with another aspect of the Manresa Principles, which Prat in particular tended to play up during election campaigns: their stress on a fundamental clash of interests between the 'artificial' Spanish state and the Catalan fatherland (*patria*). The indirectly elected *Mancomunitat*, with its relatively limited powers, scarcely looked like a national assembly. Its existence also accentuated a second contradiction, between the League's policies in power and its claim to represent Catalonia as a whole.

It became clear that, as on Barcelona city council, the League's first priority in regional government was to protect the textile magnates' commercial interests. Little attention was paid to social policy or the conditions of the poor, and the result, especially in Barcelona, was an increase in the already high level of social tension. But when this tension erupted in unrest, the League's leaders saw only a threat to their own property, and consistently backed a policy of outright repression. As a result, they alienated much of the mass support for regionalism which their early successes had shown to exist.

The lack of popular backing for regionalism in the Basque Country was one difference between the situations in the two regions. A more fundamental one was that, while Catalan regionalism represented an attempt to seize the benefits of industrialisation for

Catalonia, or for some Catalans, its Basque counterpart was essentially a rejection of industrialisation *per se*. It was also a reaction to a very different experience, since in the Basque Country – or more precisely, in and around Bilbao – industrialisation was anything but gradual. Instead it was a rapid and traumatic process, which transformed what was essentially an administrative and market town and its rural hinterland into a centre of large-scale heavy industry in a little over 20 years.

The historical and cultural background to these changes was also quite different. By the 1890s the Basque language (*euskera*), whose literary tradition was minimal, had died out in much of the region, particularly in the Bilbao area. Nor had the Basque Country ever formed an administrative unit, though it is true that many Basques had a strong sense of local loyalty, as they had shown in their support for the Carlist movement (p12). But their feelings focused on the area's constituent provinces, with which its traditional privileges were associated (p13).

These factors strongly influenced early Basque regionalism, whose followers shared the fiercely conservative Catholicism typical of the Carlists, and regarded cultural issues as strictly secondary. As members of Bilbao's traditional social elite, they resented the tide of industrial development that had undermined their status, and, Canute-like, they dreamed of turning it back. Their bitterness found expression in a political philosophy that often seemed more like a religious creed.

Their leader was Sabino Arana, to whom the very concept of a 'Basque Country' can be attributed. Initially he was only concerned with Bilbao and its province, Vizcaya, but under the influence of Catalan ideas he conceived the idea of a Basque nation. This was defined, according to Arana, not by cultural but by racial distinctiveness, and its 'homeland' of *Euzkadi* (now usually written *Euskadi*) took in Alava, Guipuzcoa, Navarre and parts of south-western France, as well as Vizcaya.

Around these dubious notions Arana wove a complex web of nationalist mythology. Its main themes were the Basques' unique rela-

---

Partido Nacionalista Vasco (PNV)

Basque Nationalist Party

Founded in 1895 by Sabino Arana, the PNV's main aim has always been Basque self-government, although it has remained ambivalent as to whether by that it means complete independence. Heavily influenced by traditional Catholicism, for a long time the party's programme was socially conservative, with a strong egalitarian streak; it has close links with the trade union Basque Workers' Solidarity (STV). By the 1920s it had established deep roots throughout Basque society, symbolised by the network of local PNV clubs (*batzokis*). This enabled it to survive attempts by Primo de Rivera and, above all, Franco to stamp out Basque national feeling (p96); indeed, it emerged from the Franco period greatly strengthened. Since the restoration of democracy it has been the Basque Country's largest party, running the regional government set up in 1980, first on its own, later as the dominant partner in coalitions. In recent years, with the emergence of new parties (pp147–8), it has lost its hegemony over the nationalist movement.

See also: *Frente Popular* (p76); *Euskadi ta Askatasuna* (p115)

tionship to the Church and their tradition of primitive democracy, embodied in the provincial privileges abolished in 1876 (p31). Restoration of these 'old laws' was the platform of another of Arana's creations, the **Basque Nationalist Party** (PNV). As a national goal it sounded modest, but since it would have meant separating the Basque Country from Spain economically (p13), it was quite unacceptable to any Madrid administration. To its own followers the PNV talked openly of 'independence', an aim much more in tune with its diatribes against the Spanish 'immigrants' (*maketos*) who flocked to the industries it hated.

Up to 1923 the PNV, in stark contrast to the Catalan League, had minimal impact on Spanish politics. Its ideas held scant attraction for Basque industrialists and financiers, most of whom had good links with politicians in Madrid and controlled the provincial councils which, under the 1876 settlement, enjoyed considerable financial autonomy (p32). More broadly, the party's quasi-racist rhetoric alienated industrial workers, including most indigenous ones, and the region's intellectuals. Outside Bilbao regionalists remained a small minority.

That fact, however, does not mean they had failed. Arguably isolation – from immigrants, from the modern world in general – was precisely what they sought. It allowed them to create a 'community', bound together by a dense network of associations, some social, and some designed to provide mutual support for particular groups, especially the small farmers who became the movement's bedrock. At the heart of this society-within-a-society was the PNV, giving it deeper roots across a wider social spectrum than any other party in Spain. Therein lay Basque regionalism's deceptive strength.

Like its Catalan cousin, the PNV was helped considerably by the fact that Spain had missed out on developments which were used elsewhere to fuel national feeling, especially universal education and mass participation in the political system. Economically, Spain only became a single market in 1876. Instead of engaging in the race for new colonies, it lost the remnants of Empire. And, for all the benefits, neutrality in the First World War also meant that it never experienced the surge of social solidarity felt by belligerent nations. For all these reasons, Spaniards largely lacked a strong sense of common identity to counter the competing claims, not just of regionalism but also of class loyalty.

The workers' movement

If Spain's economic backwardness was partly responsible for regionalism, it also meant that the country's industrial working class was small, and its workers' movement correspondingly weak. Particularly affected was the movement's Marxist branch. As in Russia, socialism was surpassed in both support and activity by anarchism, whose ideas were better suited to a country where poverty was concentrated on the land, and which also established a strong presence in Spain's premier industrial centre.

Marxism was represented in Spain by the **Spanish Socialist Party** (PSOE), and its sister trade union, the General Workers' Union (p59). Their founder was Pablo Iglesias, who dominated the Spanish socialist movement (*socialismo español*) until his death in 1925. He also embodied its strengths and weaknesses. A tireless organiser, he was renowned for a strict rectitude very different from the morally relaxed attitudes of most politicians. But he was no original thinker, and his party did not have the intellectual wing common elsewhere. As a result, the PSOE's ideas remained a mere rehash of basic Marxist theory, taken almost entirely from the work of French socialists without due allowance for the massive differences between the two countries.

Iglesias defined his party's task as building up class loyalty among industrial workers in preparation for a revolution that would come only once Spain had properly modernised. This pessimistic philosophy met with an understandably limited response. It was best received among those who enjoyed some status and security, such as Madrid printers like Iglesias himself, and workers in the mines and factories of Asturias and the Basque Country, where trade union activity gave a focus for socialist organisation. In Catalonia, on the other hand, where its Madrid-centred leadership was resented, the PSOE made little headway, while the potential for rural or middle-class support was mainly ignored.

While some intellectuals, including Unamuno (p40), were among the influx of members experienced by the party in the wake of 1898, the main cause was workers' resentment against the Cuban War (p35). Once that was over support fell away again, leading Iglesias to relax his refusal to co-operate with any middle-class party (*indiferencia*). In 1909 he formed a loose alliance (*conjunción*) with the Reformist Republicans (p41), thanks to which – and to opposition to the new war in Morocco (p58) – he was elected the party's first MP. In the crisis year of 1917 the PSOE even joined the broad campaign for political reform (p51). But its failure led to the Socialists becoming disillusioned with co-operation, and in 1919 they broke off the Republican alliance.

Partido Socialista Obrero Español (PSOE)

Spanish Socialist Party

Founded in 1879, initially under the title *Partido Democrático Socialista Español*, the PSOE was long typified by a cautious approach to its declared aim of social **revolution** – which it held could only come after Spain had experienced industrialisation and genuine political reform – and by the belief that socialism was a matter purely for the working class (*obrerismo*). Prior to 1923 the party enjoyed very little electoral success; its main achievement was to build up, in its strongholds of Madrid, Asturias and the Basque Country, a party organisation based on the local socialist clubs (*casas del pueblo*). Under the Second Republic, however, despite being plagued by disputes between advocates of continuing moderation and supporters of immediate revolution (pp75–6), the PSOE became Spain's largest party. Banned by the Franco regime, the PSOE took little part in opposing it. Even so, on the restoration of democracy in 1975 it re-emerged as the largest party of the Left, winning power at the general election of 1982, dominating Spanish politics through the 1980s and governing alone until defeated in 1996. During that time its policies continued the trend begun in opposition towards the political centre, and the party also underwent a number of fundamental changes (pp143–6).
See also: **Frente Popular** (p76); **Partido Comunista de España** (p86); **felipismo** (p145)

anarquismo

anarchism; (Spanish) anarchist movement

Based on the idea that humans' natural habitat is an economically self-sufficient community modelled on a traditional rural village, pure anarchists hold that all decisions should be taken by direct and equal participation. All forms of imposed authority, internal or external to the commune, are anathema to them, and they reject any idea of political organisation, such as parties. The **revolution** (p15) which ushers in the anarchist utopia will, they believe, occur spontaneously, the only form of preparation countenanced by some anarchists being 'propaganda by deed', that is, acts of terrorism against established institutions and the rich.

See also: **anarcosindicalismo** (p48); **collectivisation** (p85); **militia** (p85)

Iglesias promptly lost his seat, and the PSOE was left with the loyalty of its core supporters and a sturdy, but very patchy organisation as its only assets.

All this time **Spanish anarchism** had been playing hare to the Socialist tortoise, its mercurial progress reflecting the power and naivety of its ideas. They had greatest impact in the impoverished rural south, where day-labourers scraped a precarious existence on vast estates (*latifundios*), as well as in Aragon and the east. The dominant concern of this rural anarchism was that the land should be handed over to, and divided up among those who worked it (*reparto de la tierra*), and in the early 1880s several estates were violently seized from their owners. The authorities' brutal response dampened down that expression of anarchist unrest. When it resurfaced in the 1890s it took the form of terrorism, whose victims included Cánovas (p29). But without an organised structure its capabilities did not extend beyond acts of random violence.

Where anarchist ideas acquired greater significance was in and around Spain's largest and most dynamic city, Barcelona. As a great port, it was the entry point for new ideas, including more sophisticated versions of the anarchist creed. At the same time, its industrial growth attracted a steady stream of workers from rural areas where anarchism had already established a hold. The region's textile firms were often small enough to make their operation as communes seem feasible, and, at the same time, the confrontational attitudes of Catalan employers meant that workers desperately needed some means of defending their interests.

These factors meant that in Catalonia anarchist ideas had far more impact than Socialist ones, particularly in the form of **anarcho-syndicalism**. In 1907 its supporters set up an organisation known as Workers' Solidarity (*Solidaridad Obrera*). Four years later it was succeeded by the **National**

anarcosindicalismo

anarcho-syndicalism; anarcho-syndicalist movement

A development of pure **anarchism**, anarcho-syndicalism differs from it in the belief that workers should organise in trade unions (*sindicatos*) and engage in industrial agitation as the means of bringing about social **revolution**, in the form of a general strike.

See also: **CNT** (p49)

Labour Confederation (CNT), which quickly became by far the largest workers' organisation in Spain. The CNT's ranks included rural anarchists, although they were often suspicious of its tendency to focus on industrial issues rather then land redistribution. Equally some CNT supporters, both urban and rural, placed less faith in trade union activity than in terrorism; in 1912 they claimed a second Prime Minister in Canalejas (p42). Not surprisingly, splits were endemic in the CNT.

The CNT's relations with the Socialists were also stormy, even though the two movements did sometimes co-operate, as during the crisis of 1917 (p51). Generally, though, the PSOE's emphasis on organisation seemed too 'Prussian' (i.e. authoritarian) to anarcho-syndicalists, who also rejected the Socialists' readiness to negotiate with employers; for them, every industrial dispute was a potential revolution. For their part, the Socialists regarded anarchists of all types as irresponsible woolly-thinkers whose activities only served to hold back Spain's development, and thus its revolution too. The failure of a general strike to spark such an uprising in 1909 (p50) tended to confirm their analysis.

In Spain, as elsewhere, the Russian Revolution led to a further split in the already divided workers' movement, with the creation of a Spanish Communist Party (p86). But the

> ### *Confederación Nacional del Trabajo (CNT)*
> ....
> National Labour Confederation
> ──────────────────────────
> Founded in 1911 as the umbrella organisation of Spanish **anarco-sindicalismo**, in the absence of an anarchist party, the CNT effectively operated as the political representative of Spanish **anarchism** in general. Its history was a series of dramatic fluctuations, influxes of support and outbursts of activity alternating with savage repression and declining membership. The CNT reached its greatest strength around 1919, but thereafter suffered defeat in its 'social war' with Catalan employers (p52), and persecution under Primo's dictatorship (p59). During the Second Republic and the Civil War it again achieved mass support, but its loose structure was incapable of surviving more severe repression under the Franco regime, and only fragments survived into the post-1975 democratic era.
> See also: **Frente Popular** (p76); **Partido Comunista de España** (p86)

initial impact was small, since the new party attracted few recruits. Much more important was the effect of events in Russia on the movement's existing components: coming in a country every bit as backward as Spain, and in the wake of another failed general strike (p51), the Revolution undermined the arguments of both Socialists and anarcho-syndicalists. Conversely, it gave a boost to the advocates of direct action, who launched a new offensive. In 1921 the anarchists claimed a third Prime Minister in Dato (p43). But their main targets were the rich of Barcelona, the main setting for the final act in the drama of Spanish liberalism.

The end of liberal Spain

Given that none of the ideas on how to improve Spain's condition in the wake of 1898 could be properly realised, the Restoration settlement remained in place. But its key mechanism had ceased to function, and the country was stagnating. It was also wracked by tensions, not just between the opponents of change and its proponents, but also among the latter. The differences were most intense in Barcelona, where they repeatedly burst into the open. But although they shook the crumbling institutions built by the Spanish liberal movement, they did not bring it down.

The settlement's breakdown began in 1909, with Maura's rejection of the alternation mechanism on which it was founded (p42). Thereafter it never functioned consistently. Governments lasted only months on average, and in the absence of agreement within and between the parties, the King's right to designate a prime minister became decisive. Maura himself, although still nominally a Conservative, used his formidable appeal to build up a personal following, chiefly among the better-off young. This 'Maurist movement' (*maurismo*) was the first mass organisation of the Spanish right. Yet its leader refused either to turn it into a political party, or to use it as a base to seize power as Costa's 'iron surgeon' (p40), and so remained impotent.

Partido Republicano Radical

Radical Republican Party

Not to be confused with the Radicals of the 1870s (p27), the Radical Republican Party was one of the two factions into which the **Republican movement** (p28) divided in 1908. Offering no programme as such, its supporters concentrated on vague references to **revolution** and on virulent attacks against Catalan regionalism, the rich and existing institutions – the Church even more than the monarchy. Their main asset was the following for their leader, Alejandro Lerroux, in Barcelona. The party had run the city council several times, demonstrating a capacity for corruption to match that of the dominant dynastic parties (p30). During the Second Republic it emerged as a national political force (p68), heading a number of governments (pp72–3) before suddenly collapsing in 1935 (p74).

See also: **Pacto de San Sebastián** (p63)

In 1909, too, trouble first flared in Barcelona. The city's status as the cockpit of Spain derived from the fact that it was the point where the country's most dynamic political forces converged and clashed. It was the home of the Regionalist League (p43), which was both the representative of Catalan regionalism and the most effective vehicle of conservative regenerationist ideas (p44). It was also the stronghold of the anarcho-syndicalist CNT (p49), and of the **Radical Republican Party**, whose leader Alejandro Lerroux was a formidable populist and rabble-rouser with a faithful following among the city's lower middle classes and the poorest of its poor. In 1909 the tensions between the three exploded into violence.

The violence was triggered – while the political elite was still in turmoil following Maura's bombshell – by the call-up of reservists to fight in the colonial campaign in Morocco (p58). Agitation against the war had already brought together a Republican–Socialist alliance (p47), which now began preparations for a massive protest. But its plans were pre-empted by the anarcho-syndicalists of Workers' Solidarity (p48), who on 26 July declared a general strike in Barcelona. Thus began the notorious 'Tragic Week'.

For days the city was in chaos, effectively

cut off. Inflamed by the anticlerical rhetoric of Lerroux and the anarchists, mobs sacked Church buildings and attacked priests and nuns. After initial hesitation, the authorities' restored order by force. Many of the rioters received long prison sentences but Lerroux, their main instigator, escaped in time to avoid punishment. One man was executed; Francisco Ferrer, the organiser of the 'Modern Schools', which provided free education heavily influenced by anarchist and other libertarian ideas. His death provoked widespread protests at home and abroad, and became a potent symbol of government repression.

Eight years on came a graver crisis. The background was the First World War, which affected Spain considerably, even though it remained neutral. One reason for this was that the country's sympathies were broadly divided, between a pro-German Right and pro-French Left. Another was that neutrality allowed some industrialists to make massive profits by exporting to the combatant countries. This grossly distorted the economy; prices soared, and outside the boom sectors wages failed hopelessly to keep pace.

One group badly hit were the middle ranks of the home-based Army, already disgruntled at the quicker promotion of colleagues serving in Morocco. In the summer of 1917 some officers set up local Defence Committees (*Juntas de Defensa*). Their demands were parochial but, couched in the language of 'regeneration' (p40), with talk of army 'reform' and 'modernisation', they struck a chord with the public and turned the Committees' supporters (*junteros*) into standard-bearers of its discontent.

While the government was struggling to deal with what had become a tricky problem, it stirred up another. In trying to assuage popular resentment by a tax on war profits, it provoked the ire of industrialists, prominent among them a number of Catalans. Cambó, effective leader of the Regionalist League (p44), decided that the time had come for Catalonia to take the lead in changing Spain as a whole. He called an unofficial 'National Assembly' to draw up a new constitution, which he hoped to impose on the Madrid politicians.

Surprisingly, his idea was backed by both wings of the workers' movement, who had already been pushed by the economic situation into cooperation with each other. But Maura refused to back the pro-Assembly movement (*movimiento asambleísta*), and the Committees also kept their distance, unwilling to cooperate with Catalan regionalists. Cambó's plan thus rested on an uneasy alliance between the conservative League and the revolutionary Left.

On 19 July the Assembly met in Barcelona, only to be broken up by the police. The following month the frustration of ordinary trade unionists forced their unwilling leaders into another general strike. This time there was much more violence than in 1909, and before it was crushed there were pitched battles between strikers and police and attacks on employers' property. These, in particular, seemed to make a profound impression on Cambó, since when the government predictably rejected the proposals drawn up by his Assembly in Madrid, at the end of October, he caved in at once. Abandoning his allies and their demands for far-reaching democratic reform, he agreed to join a makeshift coalition with second-rank Liberal and Conservative leaders instead.

It was a gamble, and in the short term it paid off. But the new government only lasted into the early months of 1918, provoking the King to threaten abdication. This prospect forced the dynastic parties to close ranks. Even Maura was called in from the cold, as the only politician the Defence Committees trusted, to head a 'National Government'. For a short time this looked like a real vehicle for 'regenerationist' ideas (p40). Its driving force was Cambó who, as Minister for Development (*Fomento*), applied the economic policies pioneered by his party in regional government (p44), with considerable success. But, as in Catalonia, he ignored social problems, with fatal results.

In October the coalition's Liberal members, always suspicious of regionalism, used that omission as the excuse to withdraw support for Cambó's policies. Shortly afterwards, their intrigues forced Maura to resign, and the National Government was dead. None of its successors was remotely capable of taking the decisive measures that were so badly needed. Moreover, in their weakness they repeatedly ignored Parliament and passed legislation by decree; censorship was also widespread. The democratic facade of Spanish liberalism was ripped away to reveal the authoritarian reality beneath.

Meanwhile, the end of the First World War brought Spain's uneven boom to a juddering halt. Mismanaged by government and industrialists alike, who paid no heed to much-needed investment, it left the economy in a worse state than ever. Unable to compete despite high tariffs, many firms were forced to close, making thousands of workers redundant. The Asturian coal mines and the shipbuilding industry suffered greatly, although once again it was in Barcelona that the resultant desperation took most extreme form. In 1919 workers at the *La Canadiense* electricity company went on strike over a wage dispute. It was soon settled by government arbitration, but when the Army refused to release the arrested strikers the anarcho-syndicalists called a general strike, which was only broken after further massive arrests and the declaration of a state of war.

With industrial action now illegal, the terrorist wing of anarchism stepped up the attacks it had already begun on the Catalan business community. No longer represented by Cambó in government, the industrialists had no faith in the central authorities to protect their lives and property against terrorism. Taking matters into their own hands they set up so-called 'Free Trade Unions' – a cover for hired gunmen – and a private, paramilitary police force, the *Somatén*. They also encouraged the local army commander, General Martínez Anido, to crack down much harder on terrorists and strikers than he had been instructed to do by Madrid.

For the next four years Barcelona was outside government control, engulfed in a 'social war'. The result was never in doubt. Apart from their inferior resources, the anarchists were handicapped by internal divisions. The CNT leadership had been drawn reluctantly into the 1919 strike, and thereafter its supporters were in constant and sometimes violent dispute with the terrorists. Moreover, after their brief rapprochement, the anarchists and Socialists renewed their usual antagonism (p49).

By 1923 the anarchists had patently lost. But by then, too, the victorious Catalan elite had run into other troubles, since its political influence had been undermined by the events of 1918. In 1922 the Madrid government tried to reverse the policy of protectionist tariffs (pp43–4). Moreover, Cambó's betrayal of the Assembly movement had been the last straw for many supporters of his Regionalist League (p44), who deserted in droves to set up organisations of their own. The largest of these was Catalan Action, which demanded a Catalan republic in a loosely federal Spain. Its leader, Francisco Macià, soon became Catalonia's most popular politician, his support outstripping that of the League.

It became clear that however much the Catalan magnates were disillusioned with the existing system, they could expect little to come from its democratic reform either. Their disillusion was shared by some 'regenerationist' intellectuals, notably Maeztu (p40), who had come to see Spain's salvation in the rediscovery of its supposed 'real essence': Castilian, Catholic, and Conservative. They linked this reactionary, authoritarian nationalism to Costa's concept of an 'iron surgeon' (p40), taking Mussolini as a model.

Meantime, in July 1921, Spain had again been shaken by disaster abroad when its forces suffered a humiliating defeat at the hands of Moroccan tribesmen (p58). A parliamentary committee was set up to investigate the causes. Many had reason to fear its outcome: the Army, of whose incompetence and even corruption rumours abounded; politicians, who had ignored warnings of inadequate equipment and low morale; the King, who had allegedly encouraged the ill-fated operation. In summer 1923 the committee completed its report, which would become public once Parliament reconvened. As the country held its breath, liberal Spain was at long last laid to rest.

Exhibit 3.1: Maura's political philosophy (1917)

Extract from the Conservative politician's memoirs

Como es menester despertar a la opinión dormida, a la opinión desviada, a la opinión descreída y recelosa, hay un error que está muy en boga y que acaso sea lo más íntimo y transcendental del pensamiento del señor Cánovas del Castillo: el error de que las reformas que lastiman intereses colectivos, clases respetables, fuerzas del Estado se han de mirar con mucha circunspección y que no se puede tocar a las cosas. Si no se da con obras a la opinión algo de lo que pide, si no se ve que se la lleva por buen camino, no es fácil que se la despierte, ni se la atraiga por los organismos políticos que engendran los partidos. Por esto yo creo que *algo de violencia necesitan las reformas*: se trata de una operación de cirugía, y cuando de operar se trata el cirujano no va quitando el miembro muerto o corrompido parte por parte, sino que de una vez lo corta por donde es necesario. [. . .]

[. . . M]ás que nunca es ahora necesario restablecer aquella ya casi olvidada [. . .] confianza entre gobernantes y gobernados; y ya no hay más que un camino, que es la revolución audaz, la revolución temeraria desde el Gobierno, porque la temeridad es, no obra de nuestro albedrío, sino imposición histórica de los ajenos desaciertos. Nunca habría sido fácil la revolución desde el Gobierno, nunca habría sido recomendable, si hubiera podido dividirse la facultad y esparcirse la obra en el curso del tiempo; pero cada día que pasa, desde 1898, es mucho más escabrosa, mucho más difícil, y el éxito feliz mucho más incierto; y no está lejano el día en que ya no quede ni ese remedio.

Source: Maura, A. (1917) *Treinta y cinco años de vida pública, 1902–1913.* Madrid: Biblioteca Nueva.

Exhibit 3.2: The Tragic Week (1909)

Statement approved at a public meeting organised by the anarcho-syndicalist
Workers' Solidarity (*Solidaridad Obrera*) immediately before the events in Barcelona

Considerando que la guerra es una consecuencia fatal del régimen de producción capitalista;

Considerando, además, que, dado el sistema español de reclutamiento del ejército, sólo los obreros hacen la guerra que los burgueses declaran.

La asamblea protesta enérgicamente:

1. Contra la acción del gobierno español en Marruecos.
2. Contra los procedimientos de ciertas damas de la aristocracia, que insultaron el dolor de los reservistas, de sus mujeres y de sus hijos, dándoles medallas y escapularios, en vez de proporcionarles los medios de subsistencia que les arrebatan con la marcha del jefe de familia.
3. Contra el envío a la guerra de ciudadanos útiles a la producción y, en general, indiferentes al triunfo de la cruz sobre la media luna, cuando se podrían formar regimentos de curas y de frailes que, además de estar directamente interesados en el éxito de la religión católica, no tienen familia, ni hogar, ni son de utilidad alguna al país; y
4. Contra la actitud de los diputados republicanos que ostentando un mandato del pueblo no han aprovechado su inmunidad parlamentaria para ponerse al frente de las masas en su protesta contra la guerra.

Y compromete a la clase obrera a concentrar todas sus fuerzas, por si se hubiera de declarar la huelga general para obligar al gobierno a respetar los derechos que tienen los marroquíes a conservar intacta la independencia de su país.

Source: Ullman, J. (1972) *La semana trágica.* Barcelona.

Topics

■ What impression does Exhibit 3.1 give of Maura as a person?

■ What typical 'regenerationist' themes are identifiable in it? Which of them were to reappear in Spain's history, and in which periods?

■ What are the main grievances expressed in Exhibit 3.2? Other than Spanish workers, with whom do its authors appear to feel solidarity?

■ Are there any points of similarity between Exhibits 3.1 and 3.2?

■ What did the various forces working for change in Spain – 'regenerationists', regionalists, the workers' movement – have in common, in terms of their following and their aims? What role did Spain play in the thinking of each?

■ Why was it so hard to achieve meaningful change in Spain up to 1923?

CHAPTER 4

Change imposed (1923–1931)

The uneasy calm which settled over Spain in the summer of 1923 was broken by a familiar sort of storm. On 13 September, General Miguel Primo de Rivera staged a coup, and assumed power. His declared intentions – to restore order, and bring about the reforms so widely discussed for the last 25 years – meant that his action was generally welcomed by an exhausted country. But he failed to establish a political structure for his dictatorship and, when his reforms ran into difficulties, it fell almost as swiftly as it had risen.

Throughout Europe, the 1920s were dominated by the after-effects of World War I, and reaction against the Russian Revolution. The most dramatic effects were seen in Italy, where the Fascist Party seized power in 1922. Fascism had much in common with traditional conservatism; it was nationalist, authoritarian and anti-democratic. But there were also important differences: fascism's enthusiasm for economic development and concern with the situation of industrial workers; the cult of its leader, Mussolini; and the importance it laid on the Fascist Party itself as a means of controlling society. To not a few foreign observers these ideas seemed like interesting new departures, especially given their positive impact on Italy's backward economy. In that respect Mussolini benefited from the world economy's recovery after its post-war slump, which turned out to be brief. Indeed, it had petered out well before the 1929 Wall Street crash triggered the worst depression of modern times.

The 'Iron Surgeon'

Given the almost complete absence of opposition, Primo's coup was a virtually bloodless affair. And, though his government suspended democratic freedoms, its authority was established with little need for active repression. As a result, Primo was able to embark almost immediately on the task he had set himself – that of the 'iron surgeon' envisioned by the regenerationist thinker Costa (p40), administering drastic, emergency treatment to save his country.

Although Primo's revolt met with negligible resistance, it received no direct backing either. Two factors were crucial to its success. One was the Army's anxiety about the forthcoming results of investigations into the Moroccan War (p53). In time-honoured fashion, it staged its own 'negative declaration' and stood aside (p16). That left matters in the hands of the King. Alfonso also had cause to fear the forthcoming revelations. Additionally, he may have seen a royal dictatorship as the means finally to apply 'regenerationist' ideas (p40). Whatever the reason, he exercised his constitutional prerogative to appoint Primo his Prime Minister.

Spain's new ruler was a man of simple if contradictory beliefs. The strongest was his sense of Spanish nationalism; the 'fatherland' (*patria*) outranked traditional institutions in his scale of loyalties. His modernising tendencies were apparent in his regard for Mussolini. But Primo's basically conservative interpretation of his role as 'surgeon' was apparent in the way he fostered Church influence, and in his admiration for Maura, whose concept of 'revolution from above' (p42) he espoused.

Impulsive, with a strong sense of fairness that bordered on sentimentality, Primo approached his task in a highly personalised manner. He issued constant explanations of his actions and motives, and travelled feverishly round the country to address his people. Such direct contact with public opinion, he felt, allowed him to 'rectify' policies based on his own 'intuition' in the light of popular response. For politicians he had only contempt, sharing the increasingly prevalent Army view that they – along with 'separatism' and 'communism' – were the root of Spain's ills, which it was the soldiers' mission to cure.

Given this background, it came as no surprise that Primo's regime, at least initially, took the form of an outright military dictatorship, with the government formed by a 'Military Directorate'. Even at provincial and municipal level civilian authorities were replaced by Army officers. The 1876 Constitution was suspended, a state of siege declared and the press subjected to censorship. Although political parties were not formally banned, all senior civil servants and politicians who had previously held office were debarred, not just from administrative posts but also from directorships in firms awarded government contracts – a key source of business for many large companies.

The most serious problem facing the Directorate was the situation in **Morocco**. Here Primo showed his pragmatic streak. He did not belong to the tightly-knit group of officers involved in the fighting there, who were passionately committed to Spain's role in Africa (*africanistas*). Believing the Spanish positions to be militarily indefensible, he

---

Marruecos

Morocco

Previously confined to the garrison towns of Ceuta and Melilla, Spanish involvement in Morocco as a whole began in 1904, due to pressure to protect mining interests and the desire to prevent French control over the southern shore of the Straits of Gibraltar. Under the Franco–Moroccan Treaty of 1912 Spain was allocated a 'zone' in northern Morocco as a Protectorate, but her hold was constantly threatened by the inhospitable terrain and the resistance of local tribes. In 1921, under the leadership of Abd el Krim, they inflicted an overwhelming defeat on the Spanish 'Army of Africa' at Annual. By 1927, however, the Protectorate had been fully recovered, and it remained in Spanish hands until 1956 (p105). The strategically less valuable colony of Spanish Sahara, further to the south, was finally abandoned in 1975.

ordered a withdrawal to the coast. However, in 1925 the threat to its own interests in Morocco led France to join in operations against the local tribes, giving Primo the chance to 'rectify' his policy. He grasped it through a dramatic amphibious operation at the Bay of Alhucemas, which opened the way to complete victory.

With his internal enemies, Primo dealt more swiftly. The radical wing of Catalan regionalism (p53), which offered token resistance to his takeover, was crushed with ease. However, given his deep suspicion of anything that might threaten Spain's unity, Primo did not stop there. He banned all political expressions of regionalist feeling in both Catalonia and the Basque Country, and abolished the Catalan regional government established in 1913 (p44). The anarcho-syndicalist CNT represented a more formidable foe. But General Martínez Anido, who had been appointed Interior Minister, was given a free hand to extend the repressive policies he had used to win the 'social war' on Barcelona's streets (p52), and during 1924 the CNT's remnants were driven underground. The country was more orderly than it had been for years, if not decades.

The Socialist wing of the workers' movement offered no opposition to Primo, whom it regarded as no worse than the middle-class politicians he had ousted. Indeed, when he showed himself willing, and able, to push through reforms, the Socialists came to see him as a means of speeding capitalist development, and so the approach of their own revolution (p47). This view was especially strong in the Socialist trade union federation, the **UGT**, which enthusiastically backed reforms designed to improve working-class conditions, in particular subsidised housing and medical assistance.

But it was Primo's attempts to reduce the level of industrial conflict that led the UGT to cooperate actively with him. It not only agreed to take part in compulsory arbitration to settle labour disputes, but even became a sort of government agency responsible for operating the statutory code of practice introduced in 1926. Under the new code, arbitration powers were exercised by joint boards with equal employer and employee representation (*comités paritarios*). The latter was provided by UGT officials, while the union's leader, Francisco Largo Caballero became a sort of *de facto* labour minister.

The UGT's collaborationist line brought the union considerable dividends, allowing it to consolidate its industrial membership and establish a significant presence in the rural south. At the same time, the policy also provoked tensions within the Socialist move-

---

Unión General de Trabajadores (UGT)

General Workers' Union

The UGT was founded in 1888 as a federation of Socialist trade unions. Unlike the anarcho-syndicalist **CNT** (p49), it long saw its role as the improvement of workers' material conditions through strictly industrial activity, an attitude reflected in its cooperation with the Primo dictatorship. Under the Second Republic, when it acquired considerable influence (p75), the UGT took an increasingly militant political line that culminated in its participation in the uprising of 1934 (p76) and its revolutionary attitudes during the Civil War. The UGT was banned by the Franco regime, but after its end in 1975 the UGT reverted to moderation, before once again drifting towards militancy in the late 1980s (pp144–5).

ment as a whole, and deepened the rifts with the fledgling Communist Party (p86) and anarcho-syndicalists. However, the CNT was itself rent by feuds between moderates and extremists, who in 1927 set up the 'Iberian Anarchist Federation' (FAI) as a pure revolutionary organisation, unconcerned with trade union activity. On balance, then, one ironic result of Primo's regime was to strengthen the Socialists' position, both within the working class movement and in the country.

The measures which the UGT helped to implement enjoyed considerable success, reducing sharply the days lost to industrial conflict. They reflected the dictator's sense of social justice, also apparent in his plans for a single income tax that would hit earnings from capital as well as wages; that proposal, however, met with strong opposition from the banks, and had to be abandoned. The other factor behind Primo's economic policy was his nationalism, which led him to see issues essentially in terms of national prestige. Hence his reintroduction of import tariffs at a higher level than ever before. He saw imports as a slight on Spain's own economic capabilities, to improve which he instigated the country's first large-scale programme of state intervention.

The government's development projects took various forms. The most visible was a massive programme of infrastructure, especially roads, dams and irrigation schemes; electricity was brought to many rural areas for the first time. A number of state-run monopolies were established, sometimes in association with private interests, including the CAMPSA oil and petrol company, the national telephone company (*Telefónica*) and the powerful Water Boards (*Confederaciones Hidráulicas*), as well as a plethora of regulatory bodies to advise on, promote and control activity in a wide range of industries. Finally, to assist in financing development, Primo founded various semi-public banks, covering fields such as overseas trade, house-building and new industries.

Between 1923 and 1928 the Spanish economy showed distinct signs of improvement. Admittedly, that was partly thanks to the favourable international climate. Yet, even so, Primo's measures, social as well as economic, deserve a good deal of the credit for the upswing. Equally, when it was rudely reversed in 1928/29, some of the blame could be ascribed to the first effects of the coming world-wide depression. But the sudden and extreme nature of downturn in Spain was to a large extent caused by grave flaws inherent in those same measures.

Primo's failure, the monarchy's fall

The fact is that Primo's entire 'revolution from above' contained the seeds of its own failure. In trying to tackle the grievances of so many different groups simultaneously, he finished up by satisfying none and arousing the animosity of most. And, since his attempts at political reform were an unmitigated failure, he never gave his regime a solid basis. When the heat was turned up it simply melted away – and the King with it.

Among the first to be alienated by Primo were those intellectuals who had seen in him the realisation of their ideas (p53). One reason for this was the continuing press censorship, another Primo's tendency to intervene 'intuitively' in individual court cases, using his effectively absolute powers to right specific wrongs without thought for the wider consequences. Especially in a country with such a strong legalistic tradition, this approach soon turned admiration to scorn among the intelligentsia, and large sections of the educated classes in general.

Their indignation was heightened by Primo's effective banishment of Unamuno (p40), for protesting against one of his arbitrary interventions. Students, too, were outraged by this treatment of a highly-respected professor. They were already protesting against Primo's proposals to extend Church influence into the higher education sphere, by giving state recognition to the degrees awarded by private, Catholic universities. After Unamuno's exile their demonstrations became a permanent feature of Madrid life, and a minor but persistent irritant to the regime.

Another group whose support Primo soon lost was the Catalan business community. Its gratitude at his restoration of law and order turned to anger when he banned the use of Catalan in Church and, especially, at the suppression of devolution (p59). That step was doubly damaging to the industrialists, since it completed the swing of Catalan opinion behind demands for more far-reaching self-government (p53). Along with consolidating Socialism (p60), the other main political effect of the dictatorship was to seal the conversion of Catalan regionalism from a conservative monarchist force into a radical, republican one.

Although Catalonia was a much more serious enemy than the intellectuals, or the old politicians who had never accepted Primo – even Maura, his acknowledged inspiration, refused to back him – it was not strong enough by itself to shake the dictator's hold on power. What did eventually have that effect was Primo's scatter-gun approach to reform, which meant that every section of society that had initially backed him was sooner or later offended by one of his measures. For example, while devout Catholics welcomed his concessions to the Church, they deplored his cooperation with 'godless' socialists (p59). In the Basque Country, that worked to the benefit of regionalists (p45): elsewhere it merged with a broader conservative reaction against his regime.

The employers were never reconciled to Primo's labour legislation (p59), and those who failed to profit from the creation of state monopolies were antagonised further, as was much of the financial world. Landowners, the very bastion of conservative opinion, were outraged by Primo's attempt to introduce the mildest of land reforms (p70). And both these groups, who tended to share Primo's brand of Spanish nationalism, were disappointed by his inability to achieve either of his foreign-policy aims: the incorporation of Tangiers into Spanish Morocco (p58) and the granting of a seat on the League of Nations' Security Council.

The resultant spreading disillusion formed the background to Primo's attempts at political reform, which began in 1924 with the establishment of the Patriotic Union (UP). Partly modelled on Mussolini's Fascist Party, the UP promoted a cult of the leader, and rejected representative democracy in favour of a direct relationship between the leader and the people, for instance through the rigged referendums which were a feature of the regime. Yet Primo never intended the UP to be a genuine party, never mind a fascist one. Instead he conceived it as a 'Citizens' League', a social organisation that would allow him to tap into opinion but have no political role.

At heart Primo was a traditionalist, out of tune with fascism's modernising tendencies, and the UP's philosophy was influenced chiefly by Spanish conservatism. Only among Carlists (p12), and the personal following built up by Maura (p50), did it find a faint echo. Instead, the bulk of UP's small membership was made up of those who benefited directly from the regime, such as journalists, hangers-on and public servants – many of whom, especially at local level, had been in post before 1923. Their vested interests put paid to the 1925 Municipal Statute which had been intended to clean up local government along the lines originally proposed by Maura (p42). And more generally, too, the UP acted not as an instrument of change but as a brake on it.

At national level 1925 did bring some change with the establishment of a new government, in the form of a Civilian Directorate (*Directorio Civil*). Its members were appointed by Primo, largely from the ranks of UP. They were professional experts (*tecnócratas*), chiefly lawyers and economists, usually civil servants; their star was the young Finance Minister, José Calvo Sotelo. These new arrangements were prompted by necessity – military government having become impractical – and were intended to be temporary, pending completion of what was now Primo's main project; a new constitution.

The task of drafting the new text was given to an Advisory National Assembly (*Asamblea Nacional Consultiva*) which differed substantially from earlier constituent bodies. Whereas in the past they had been elected, albeit usually under less than free conditions, the members of Primo's Assembly were appointed by him. Moreover, its powers were limited to producing proposals for the dictator's consideration, which it did in 1928. Unsurprisingly, they pandered to his views, in particular granting the prime minister extensive new powers, including the right to nominate half the members of parliament.

At a time when the regime's popularity was waning fast, the Assembly's proposals were met by a barrage of criticism. Primo showed his political naivety, first by proposing another of his discredited referendums, and then by appointing a number of his critics to the Assembly. Naturally enough, they used their new position mainly to restate their objections, reinforcing Primo's distrust of anything that smacked of politics. His enthusiasm for a constitution rapidly faded, and the question of how Spain should be governed was left in mid-air.

In this situation of political vacuum the weaknesses in Primo's expansionist economic policies came home to roost. The original intention had been to finance them by extending the scope of income tax. When that idea was blocked by the banks (p60), Primo resorted to increased public borrowing, concealing the additional interest payments in a separate 'Extraordinary Budget'. In effect, he gambled on an economic take-off generating more revenue from existing taxes. When Spain became a victim of world depression – because of its commercial links with Latin America, one of the first areas affected – Primo lost his bet.

At home recession, combined with the inflation inevitably caused by so much public spending, had disastrous effects, especially for low earners. Abroad, the peseta came under intense pressure. For Primo the currency's value was above all a matter of national pride, and he instructed Calvo Sotelo to defend it at what was now a totally unrealistic level. That strategy merely aggravated speculation and made eventual devaluation all the more drastic, forcing the resignation of Primo's most able lieutenant.

The recession had even graver political repercussions. Primo's Socialist allies (pp59–60) grew restive at the plight of their own supporters, and devaluation was a further blow to Primo's prestige among the nationalist Right that his own rhetoric had helped to create. It was a Conservative politician, Sánchez Guerra, who first tried to channel dissent, in January 1929. Although his amateurish conspiracy was easily put down, it had an important knock-on effect. Coming on top of the proposal by the Assembly to cut his powers, its Republican overtones convinced the King that Primo had become the biggest danger to his throne, and he began to distance himself from his Prime Minister.

The last nail in the dictator's coffin was the loss of Army backing. Again it was induced by reforms that, in themselves, were perfectly sensible. To improve military efficiency Primo had insisted that promotion to the rank of general should be based not on seniority but on merit, an attack on military tradition that was bound to ruffle important feathers. On the other hand, his abolition of the Artillery Corps' special privileges was not unpopular in the rest of the Army. But any sympathy evaporated when he reacted to opposition from within the Corps by dissolving it altogether.

Primo's response to the rising tide of discontent was typically impulsive. In January 1930 he spontaneously sought the views of the various Army regional commanders (*Capitanes Generales*). When they evinced a clear lack of enthusiasm for his continuation he resigned and left the country; he died a few months later. His departure did not immediately threaten the monarchy, since although the King was tainted by his part in Primo's ascent to power (p58), and by having willingly played the dictatorship's figurehead, the continuing use of repression meant that resentment against him was so far unfocused and disorganised. But Alfonso soon contrived to change that.

Ignoring popular and even Army opinion, the King appointed another soldier to replace Primo. His choice, the aged and infirm General Berenguer, proved hopelessly indecisive, first promising to hold a general election, then failing to call it for over a year. And, while he maintained Primo's legal restrictions on political activity, little or no attempt was made to impose them in practice. His 'soft dictatorship' (*dictablanda*) was to provide perfect conditions for opposition to flourish.

It was channelled mainly by the Republican movement (p28), which had been revived by a new generation of leaders. During 1930 they conducted a campaign that destroyed the King's remaining prestige, at least among the educated classes, and in August they signed a secret agreement with other opposition groups.

This **'San Sebastion Pact'** had some

Pacto de San Sebastián

San Sebastian Pact

The Pact agreed in August 1930 in the Basque resort was a secret agreement to overthrow the monarchy. It was joined by various groups which later became known as the **Left Republicans** (p68); the **Radical Republicans** (p50); the radical Catalan regionalist Estat Català set up by Francesc Macià (p53); and several prominent defectors from the old 'dynastic parties' (p30), including Miguel Maura, son of Antonio (p41), and the ex-Liberal Niceto Alcalá Zamora.

backing from the Army, which blamed Alfonso for failing to save the Artillery Corps. A military declaration was planned for 15 December, but Colonel Galán, its commander in the Aragonese garrison-town of Jaca, jumped the gun and the conspiracy was revealed. The setback proved temporary. Galán's execution gave Republicanism a martyr and the trial of the Pact's leaders was a farce, ending in their virtual absolution. Coming from a military court, the verdict indicated how little control the royal authorities now exercised over events.

As their last throw they finally called municipal elections, for 12 April 1931. While supporters of the monarchy won most votes, they were concentrated on the land where clientilism still reigned supreme (p33). The provincial capitals, where elections had some meaning, voted massively for Republican candidates. The more responsible of the remaining monarchist politicians realised that the game was up. One of them, Count Romanones, took it upon himself to act as intermediary between the King and the opposition leaders. As a result of the contacts, Alfonso left Spain on 14 April.

Exhibit 4.1: Primo de Rivera's manifesto (1923)

Opening of Primo's 'declaration' on the morning of his coup

AL PAÍS Y AL EJÉRCITO ESPAÑOLES

Ha llegado para nosotros el momento más temido que esperado (porque hubiéramos querido vivir siempre en la legalidad y que ella rigiera sin interrupción la vida española) de recoger las ansias, de atender el clamoroso requerimiento de cuantos amando la Patria no ven para ella otra salvación que libertarla de los profesionales de la política, de los hombres que por una u otra razón nos ofrecen el cuadro de desdichas e inmoralidades que empezaron el año 98 y amenazan a España con un próximo fin trágico y deshonroso. La tupida red de la política de concupiscencias ha cogido en sus mallas, secuestrándola, hasta la voluntad real. Con frecuencia parecen pedir que gobiernen los que ellos dicen no dejan gobernar, aludiendo a los que han sido su único, aunque débil freno, y llevaron a las leyes y costumbres la poca ética sana, el tenue tinte de moral y equidad que aún tienen; pero en la realidad se avienen fáciles y contentos al turno y al reparto y entre ellos mismos designan la sucesión.

   Pues bien, ahora vamos a recabar todas las responsabilidades y a gobernar nosotros u hombres civiles que representan nuestra moral y doctrina. Basta ya de rebeldías mansas, que sin poner remedio a nada, dañan tanto y más a la disciplina que está recia y viril a que nos lanzamos por España y por el Rey.

   Este movimiento es de hombres: el que no sienta la masculinidad completamente caracterizada, que espere en un rincón, sin perturbar los días buenos que para la patria preparamos. Españoles: ¡Viva España y viva el Rey! [. . .]

Source: La Vanguardia (Barcelona), 13 September 1923.

Topics
FOR DISCUSSION

■ What insights does Exhibit 4.1 give into Primo's worldview?

■ How does Primo appear to see the role of the Army in Spain's public life? How does his view compare to that of O'Donnell (Exhibit 1.2)?

■ Could Primo have succeeded?

■ How did his situation and approach to government differ from those of Franco?

CHAPTER 5

A troubled democracy (1931–1936)

The 1930s were the decade of depression in Europe. Millions were plunged into poverty which the political and economic structures of liberal democracy seemed powerless to relieve. Many looked to the authoritarian regimes which, as it appeared from the outside, were enjoying greater success in the Soviet Union, and in Italy under fascism. In their different ways, communism and fascism were both international movements, and both strove to undermine other, democratic regimes by propaganda and by the street violence of their paramilitary gangs. Germany was especially affected, and in 1933 its conservatives attempted to forestall the threat from the Left by taking German fascism into government. Hitler and his Nazis exploited this foothold to establish their own dictatorship, eliminating democratic institutions and cracking down ruthlessly on political opponents. His rise confirmed the Left's suspicions not just of fascism but of the traditional Right, particularly given that conservatives close to the Catholic Church had imposed their own brand of authoritarian regime in Austria. The Soviet leader, Stalin, was sufficiently worried to instruct communists worldwide to change tack, and to co-operate with socialists and middle-class liberals in an all-out bid to halt fascism.

Even before King Alfonso left the country, Spain's Second Republic had been declared by popular acclaim. The country's first attempt at genuine democracy was born in very difficult circumstances, in the midst of world depression and with democracy under growing pressure throughout Europe. Insofar as it shielded Spain from the worst effects of depression, economic backwardness was now, ironically, an asset. But it could not prevent the political tension round about from seeping into Spanish affairs, especially when it resonated so strongly with internal events. For, after a period when its fate lay in the hands of its truest supporters, the Republic's politics were dominated increasingly by two aggressive and antagonistic forces whose commitment to it was questionable at best; a resurgent Right and a newly reunited Left.

The 'reforming years'

In the confusion following the King's departure a Provisional Government was formed. It was composed mainly of the Republicans who had plotted the monarchy's fall, a heterogeneous group who now became the decisive factor in determining the character of the new Republic. They were also the main driving force behind the many and wide-ranging changes of the 'two reforming years' (*bienio de reformas*) that followed.

The Provisional Government's composition was based on the 1930 San Sebastian Pact (p63). Even the one, crucial addition – the Socialist PSOE (p47) – had been represented there by two of its leading figures. All the parties involved in the Pact itself were relatively new, with the exception of the Radical Republicans (p50) – now known merely as Radicals. Their leader, Alejandro Lerroux, had been an important secondary player in sham democratic politics before 1923, and it showed, in corruption and in opportunistic attempts to exploit changes in public mood (p71). So, while his party theoretically formed the centre of the Republican bloc, it differed fundamentally from both wings, each of which was genuinely concerned with meaningful reform.

The Republican Right was a party recently formed by ex-members of the old 'dynastic parties' (p30) who had recently converted to Republicanism. Their main interest was political reform, and they had only limited support. The party's main value to its allies was to reassure the middle-classes that the Republic would not damage their interests – hence the choice of its leader, Niceto Alcalá Zamora (p63), to head the new Government.

As a result of this regrouping, the real core of Republicanism was what, in terms of ideas, constituted its left wing. The leader, and archetype, of these **Left Republicans** was Manuel Azaña. As much an intellectual as a politician, he had close links to the '1927 generation' – the new wave of literary and artistic talent whose leading figure was Federico García Lorca. For Azaña and his colleagues, cultural considerations were of prime importance. They believed strongly in the fundamental importance of education as the basis of social change, and were almost fanatically opposed to the social influence of the Church, which they regarded as the main reason for Spain's intellectual and cultural stagnation.

The first task facing the Provisional Government was to draw up a Constitution for the Republic. It was assigned to the constituent parliament (*Cortes constituyentes*) elected in June, in which the PSOE and the Radicals led the field and the government parties in conjunction won an overwhelming victory. As a result, most major issues were settled without great dispute. Spain was formally declared a Republic, its citizens were assured of a long list of rights and freedoms, and sovereignty was placed in the hands of their representatives – a single-chamber parliament to be elected by universal adult suffrage, both male and female. This house would, in turn, elect the president, whose mainly ceremonial powers would include that

---

Republicanos de izquierdas

Left Republicans

The Left Republicans were a loose grouping of several small parties during the Second Republic. They inherited the concern for practical reform of the **Reformist Republicans** (p41), from which most had emerged, but also the anticlericalism associated with the historic **Republican movement**. The group's main components were the Radical Socialists (*Partido Republicano Radical Socialista*) led by Marcelino Domingo, the Galician Republicans (ORGA) of Casares Quiroga, and Manuel Azaña's short-lived 'Republican Action', later replaced by the confusingly named 'Republican Left' (p76), also led by Azaña.
See also: *Frente Popular* (p76)

of formally appointing a prime minister – now assumed, wrongly as it turned out (p72), to be a formality.

Where compromise proved impossible was over the religious issue, since the Left Republicans, the third largest grouping in Parliament, joined the Socialists in taking a hard anticlerical line. Consequently Article 26 of the new Constitution not only decreed freedom of worship for all creeds, but also broke all links between Church and state, including the government subvention of clerical salaries (p14). The Church's position became that of a voluntary association, subject to the law and to taxation, but with some special disadvantages, including a ban on involvement in education.

Article 26 was to become the focus of widespread conservative opposition to the government (p71). For the moment, however, its main impact was within the government itself, whose more right-wing members, including Alcalá Zamora, resigned in protest at its provisions. Yet the differences were patched up and, once the Constitution had been approved in December, Alcalá Zamora was elected the Republic's first president. He was replaced as Prime Minister by Azaña, under whom the government set about implementing a series of ambitious reforms.

In some areas the government built on measures introduced by Primo de Rivera, whose system of joint industrial relations boards (p59) was retained and extended, albeit under a new name (*jurados mixtos*). Similarly, the Socialist Prieto continued Primo's programme of infrastructure investment (p60), to good effect. He could do so thanks to an overhaul of public finances that massively increased government income by tightening up tax collection and administration – and incidentally showed how inefficient they had been previously. Taxes remained low, with the top rate on income under eight per cent. This approach had the benefit of avoiding offence to the better-off, but also meant that funds for reform were restricted.

In other respects, such as social policy, the Republic made a sharp break with the past, notably in the legalisation of divorce. The most significant initiatives came in education. A large-scale school-building programme was begun, aimed at bringing education to the masses for the first time. Teacher training was also greatly expanded. In line with Left Republican ideas, too, was the attempt to bring cultural experience to impoverished rural areas, through such initiatives as the establishment of libraries, and the provision of subsidies for Lorca's travelling theatre company, '*La Barraca*'.

Another innovation was the government's policy towards the regions, or more precisely Catalonia, where the regionalist leader Macià (p53) had declared an independent republic on Alfonso's departure, and had to be persuaded to back down by the Provisional Government. His payoff came in 1932, when a regional government (*Generalitat*) was established with much wider powers than its predecessor (p44). Regional autonomy was now underpinned by a Catalan parliament, and at the first election Macià's new party, **Catalan Republican Left**, won an easy victory. While this sealed Catalonia's support for the Republic, at the same time it awakened concerns among Spanish conservatives that their country was starting to break up.

Right-wing concern was also aroused by Azaña's military reforms. These were designed to create a modern Army, which inevitably meant reducing the excessive number of officers and making promotion more dependent on ability. They should also

Esquerra Republicana de Catalunya (ERC)

Catalan Republican Left

Formed in 1931, immediately before the declaration of the Second Republic, ERC was an alliance of left-leaning regionalist groupings. It was led by the charismatic Francesc Macià (p53) until his death in 1933, when he was replaced by Lluis Companys, the man largely responsible for ERC's creation. Despite its talk of independence, ERC was content to settle for the devolution granted by the Republic, under which it dominated Catalan politics and ran the regional government. It was suppressed by the Franco regime and, although it re-emerged thereafter, was unable to regain its former strength (p149).
See also: *Frente Popular* (p76)

have involved modernising outdated equipment, but in the absence of a true tax reform there was no money to do so. Inevitably, this aggravated the dissatisfaction caused by the other changes, and by rumours that promotion was now dependent on pro-Republican views. In August 1932 a group of right-wing officers led by General Sanjurjo attempted a coup, but it was quickly suppressed by loyal troops.

The coup attempt came while the government was struggling to pass legislation not only on Catalan devolution but also on an even more controversial issue. Although the need for **land reform** was recognised in principle by all the government parties, its details were another matter. In the summer of 1932 discussions had reached deadlock, but the coup attempt gave them renewed impetus, and measures were agreed soon after. Unfortunately they were badly flawed.

Part of the problem was that Socialist support had to be bought by allowing estates owned by the aristocracy to be expropriated.

As a vindictive reaction against the coup's suspected supporters, the move set an unhappy precedent (p73). It was also a meaningless gesture since, while estate owners were eligible for compensation, the government had no funds with which to pay them. In addition, the understandable emphasis on the plight of landless labourers in the South meant that the problems of northern smallholders were largely ignored. And, most important of all, the extent of reform was modest in the extreme.

The land reform fiasco turned discontent on the left of the political spectrum into a major problem for the government (p75). Throughout 1932 it repeatedly had to dispatch the security forces to deal with those who attempted, in a long-standing anarchist tradition, to take land redistribution into their own hands (p48). The clashes reached a tragic

reforma agraria

land reform

While referring, as elsewhere, to changes in the pattern of landownership and to landholding in general, in Spain land reform is especially associated with the break-up of the large estates (*latifundios*) commonly found in poorer parts of the country's centre and south, many of which were notoriously underused for agricultural purposes. As a result, land reform became an extremely emotive issue for both wings of the workers' movement, as well as a particular aim of many '**regenerationists**' (p40).
See also: *colectivización* (p85)

climax in January 1933 at the Andalusian hamlet of Casas Viejas, when 25 villagers were shot dead after they had killed several Civil Guards.

Azaña's coalition was fatally weakened, and the Socialists increasingly distanced themselves from it under pressure from their left (p75). With utter hypocrisy, the Right – which previously had criticised it for being too mild in dealing with such outbreaks – also used the incident to berate the government as authoritarian. Lerroux, sensing he was aboard a sinking ship, joined in their attacks. In November, unable to command a majority in Parliament, Azaña resigned and a general election was called. Abandoned by the Republican Right, the Socialists and the Radicals, the Left Republicans fell victim to the electoral system, which effectively ensured that only the two largest groupings in each provincial constituency could win seats. They were decimated, Azaña's own party obtaining just five seats. The reforming years were over.

The rise of the Right

The main feature of the 1933 election was a strong swing to the Right. This reflected the extent to which the government's various reforms, and above all its religious legislation, had provoked a fierce backlash among the more traditionalist sections of Spanish society. As a result, the parties which now took over the Republic's government were concerned to undo the work of their predecessors. Indeed, there was widespread suspicion that the largest party wished to overthrow the Republic itself.

In 1931 the Spanish Right barely existed as a political force. Primo de Rivera's single party (p61) had melted away with its creator. The old 'dynastic' parties had withered under his rule, a process completed by the discredit of their *raison d'être*, the monarchy. Nor was the Church the bulwark it had been. The Papacy's depression-inspired concern with social issues sat uneasily with the reactionary views of the Right. Within Spain many parish priests, finding that their own financial circumstances were precarious, were sympathetic to social reform. When the head of the Spanish Church, Cardinal Segura, viciously attacked the newly proclaimed Republic, and was banned from the country as a result, the support he received from Catholics was lukewarm.

This decline in the Right's fortunes was irrevocably changed by the adoption of the new Constitution, whose strongly anticlerical provisions (p69) alienated all shades of Catholic opinion and gave a target against which conservatives could campaign. Further steps in the same direction, including a ban on the Jesuits, only increased their indignation and resolve. For the first time, the Right was able to mobilise supporters *en masse* at rallies over large areas of the country, something which only the workers' parties had previously managed, and then only in particular urban areas.

The catalyst for this transformation was a new political organisation, the **CEDA**, intended by its leader, José-María Gil-Robles, to become a mass party capable of defeating the Left in a free election. Its philosophy was also new to the Spanish Right, reflecting as it did the Christian Social ideas now in favour with the Vatican. These ideas were based on respect for the Church's teaching but also emphasised the state's role in providing for the less well-off. However, the CEDA also had other features that made it the object of deep distrust among its opponents.

Confederación Española de Derechas Autónomas (CEDA)

Confederation of the Right

An alliance of various right-wing parties, the most important of which was José-María Gil-Robles' People's Action (*Acción Popular*), the CEDA was set up in 1933. Under Gil-Robles' leadership it grew rapidly, and topped the poll at the next year's general election. However, the dubious compatibility of its ideas with democracy made even conservative Republicans distrustful. As a result it was excluded from power until October 1934, when its admission to government sparked off an attempted left-wing revolution (p76). Defeated at the 1936 election, the CEDA disintegrated once Civil War broke out later that year.

Part of the problem was Gil-Robles' refusal to make clear his attitude to the Republican form of government. His own fervent monarchism, and the fact that he had rich backers hostile to the Republic, were well-known. Yet he refused to say whether he wanted to restore the monarchy, declaring his policy to be one of 'adapting to circumstances' (*accidentalismo*). Even more worryingly, he displayed open sympathy with developments in Austria, where his fellow Christian Socials had imposed a virtual dictatorship. The government's alarm at the CEDA's rise is thus understandable, but its clumsy over-reaction in attempting to have the party banned and its meetings broken up only increased the CEDA's appeal to those unhappy with the reforms.

By 1933 their ranks included employers resentful at the extension of labour regulation (p69), and much of the middle-class, concerned that even limited land reform might herald a threat to their own property. By no means all were particularly conservative; many were convinced Republicans, and suspicious of the Church. Their unease, along with the antagonism evoked in Castile by Catalan devolution, was picked up by the sensitive antennae of Lerroux, who swiftly positioned his Radicals to exploit it by ratting on his government colleagues (p71).

For the 1933 election the Radicals and CEDA formed an alliance which also included smaller right-wing groups, notably the Agrarians, who enjoyed strong support among the smallholders of Old Castile. With the help of the electoral system (p71) the alliance won a solid parliamentary majority. The CEDA was the biggest winner of all, and became the largest single party. However, President Alcalá Zamora shared the widespread suspicions of its intentions, and declined to appoint Gil-Robles as Prime Minister. As a result, during its second phase the Republic was run by weak coalitions of centre parties, headed usually by a Radical, and with the CEDA's parliamentary support.

Known to the Left as the 'two black years' (*bienio negro*), from the colour associated with the Church, this period saw a concerted attempt to reverse the Azaña government's policies, in particular its anticlerical legislation. Thus, as well as repealing some social measures, such as wage regulation, and some aspects of land reform, the Radicals also reintroduced government support for the clergy's salaries – an ironical decision, given that the Church was one of their traditional bogeys (p50).

Regionalism was also anathema to the CEDA's fierce Spanish nationalism, and became another target for their joint programme of counter-reform. In the Basque

Country that involved blocking proposals put forward by the Basque Nationalist Party, which had previously been a firm supporter of the Right. The CEDA's social policies were very similar to its own (p44), but now, on the promise of devolution from a future government of the Left, it began campaigning alongside its traditional Socialist enemies against its former allies. And in Catalonia, too, the Right was driven onto the defensive.

The old Regionalist League (p44) had recovered some of its former strength in 1933, but at the subsequent regional election it was again crushed by the more radical ERC (p70), this time for good. Emboldened by its triumph, the regional government moved to help one of its key constituencies, the small tenant farmers who had been hit by the effects of economic depression. The Smallholdings Act (*Ley de Cultivos*) was designed to give them greater security by bolstering their rights *vis-à-vis* landowners, but the implications for property rights in general alarmed both the Catalan *bourgeoisie* and the Madrid government, which referred the Act to the Constitutional Court. By doing so it turned a class issue into something much more emotive; a national conflict between Spain and Catalonia. When the Court threw out the Act in autumn 1934, the ERC reacted in correspondingly heated terms.

The ERC's anger was directed chiefly at the Radicals, who had already been weakened by the defection of a faction, led by deputy leader Martínez Barrio, which objected to the party's U-turn on religious policy. Sensing an opportunity, Gil-Robles brought the government down, and made the CEDA's entry into its successor the price of his continuing support. It was a fateful decision, being used by the Left to justify an attempted revolution (p76). That in turn set off a spiral of increasingly undemocratic behaviour on both sides of the political spectrum, which ended in war.

Already Lerroux had set a bad example. Pardoning former Primo supporters banned from politics by the Azaña government could be interpreted as a gesture of reconciliation: his amnesty for those involved in the 1932 coup attempt could not (p70). But the new, CEDA-dominated administration's reaction to the 1934 'revolution' plumbed new depths of vindictiveness and bias. Thousands of ordinary workers were put on trial, many for relatively minor offences, while the left-wing press was censored and Catalan autonomy suspended. Efforts were even made to implicate Azaña in the rising, when in fact he had tried to calm the situation. Yet the many, and manifestly well-founded claims of Army brutality were not even investigated.

The CEDA's performance in other areas of government was initially less partisan. In some – public works, the status of leaseholders, provision of low-cost rented housing – its Christian Social ideas inspired policies that were little different from those of the Azaña era. However, as the effects of depression, and Gil-Robles' insistence on maintaining military spending, made budget cuts inevitable his party's line hardened, with education suffering badly. But it was above all the complete reversal of land policy, which now blatantly favoured big landowners, that made the CEDA look downright reactionary. Indeed, Gil-Robles' promotion of extreme right-wing generals, and his talk of a 'revolution' to return Spain to its roots, gave weight to the Left's argument that it did not merit treatment as a democratic party.

For some on the Right, though, the CEDA was too cautious. Nominally they were **monarchists** but, for most, the real issue was not so much the Republic's lack of a king

monarquistas

monarchists

While technically it also included **Carlistas** (p12), the term 'monarchists' was usually understood to mean those who supported the abolition of the Second Republic and the restoration of Alfonso XIII (*alfonsistas*). For the most part strongly Catholic, some supported the **CEDA** (p72), while others joined the smaller, more reactionary Spanish Renewal (*Renovación Española*); later they all gravitated towards the 'Nationalist Bloc' set up by José Calvo Sotelo. During the Franco era monarchists were among the regime's most prominent supporters (pp100–1), but they also formed part of the 'legal' opposition (p116).
See also: ***familias*** (p100), ***aperturistas*** (p118)

as its reformist nature. Their feelings lacked a vehicle until, in May 1934, the charismatic José Calvo Sotelo returned from exile (p62). He gave the far Right a new impetus with his vicious verbal attacks not just on the Republic, but on Gil-Robles for 'treacherously' propping it up. Like his contacts with seditious generals, they made the undemocratic nature of his intentions plain to all, supporters and opponents.

Gil-Robles' plans were now approaching fulfilment. The four-year moratorium imposed by the Constitution on amendments to its text would soon be up, and he could move to repeal Article 26. But his moment never came. In late 1935 Lerroux's political career was ended by financial scandal; without him, the Radicals fragmented and the government fell. Again, President Alcalá refused to countenance a CEDA-led administration, and called an election for February 1936. In total, the Right obtained more votes than in 1933. But its parliamentary strength was decimated by the electoral system, since the enmity between Gil-Robles and Calvo Sotelo prevented the necessary close cooperation between the parties (p71). For the Radicals, such technicalities were irrelevant: in common with the rest of the centre, their support in the country simply vanished.

The reunification of the Left

In 1936 the Right's opponents reaped the reward of standing as a united bloc, in contrast to their fragmentation in 1933. That had been caused by the workers' disillusion with Republican reforms, and its increasingly radical expression. The process of radicalisation was accelerated by the election of a right-wing government, and culminated in an attempted revolution. Its failure, and the government's brutal reaction to it, opened the way for a reunification of the Left as a whole.

In the changing pattern of relations within the Left the Socialists played a crucial role. Given the absence of an anarchist party (p48), they were the only means by which the Left's working-class support was represented in the Parliament, which had become the centre of political life. They were also the link between the workers' movement as a whole and the Republicans, with whom anarchists mainly refused to talk. The main channel for such contacts was the Basque Socialist leader Indalecio Prieto, one of those who attended the signing of the San Sebastian Pact (p63). Thereafter he persuaded the PSOE to drop its policy of non-cooperation with middle-class parties (p47) – overcoming the reservations of party leader Julián Besteiro and others – and to join the Republic's Provisional Government (p68).

While he argued that the Republic would bring in the reforms the PSOE had always seen as the prerequisite for a revolution (p47), Prieto's real reasons for cooperating with it were pragmatic; that the alternative was much worse. Pragmatism also weighed heavily with the Socialist movement's trade union wing, the UGT (p59), which found that state-sponsored labour regulation brought the same advantages as under the Primo regime (p59), only in greater measure; civil service jobs for union officials, and the title as well as the functions of Labour Minister for the UGT leader, Francisco Largo Caballero. As a bonus, it was able to secure a further rise in membership by offering workers access to – often favourable – arbitration procedures.

Such access remained the preserve of the UGT because Spain's other large labour organisation, the anarcho-syndicalist CNT (p49), continued to boycott arbitration. Its attitude was dictated by the traditional anarchist view that all governments, dictatorial or democratic, were equally bad (p48). Even so, amidst the euphoria of 1931 many anarchists forgot their disdain for '*bourgeois*' elections and voted, mainly for the PSOE. In the same year a group of prominent anarcho-syndicalists led by Angel Pestaña issued a manifesto in which they argued against an immediate revolution. But 'the thirty' and their supporters (the '*treintistas*') were overwhelmingly defeated, and expelled from the CNT.

For the next two years, anarchism was in thrall to its terrorist tradition, represented by the Iberian Anarchist Federation (p60). Attacks on property were common, often accompanied by waves of political strikes; Barcelona, Seville and Saragossa were especially affected. With the government's failure to legislate an effective programme of land reform, the focus of violence shifted to the countryside (p70). In 1932 the Alto Llobregat area of Catalonia was briefly 'liberated' from government control. Andalusia was another hotbed, with the tragic incident at Casas Viejas merely the worst of many (p71).

Its attitude hardened by the government's tough response to such activities, in 1933 the CNT urged its followers 'Don't vote', an injunction most were happy to obey. In theory, the right-wing government their abstention helped to elect was meant to provoke a spontaneous revolution. In practice, its effect on most anarchists was another bout of the periodic disillusion to which their movement had always been prone (p48).

In the meantime, the failure of land reform had affected Socialists as well, provoking the PSOE to leave the government. The UGT, terrified of losing rural members to the CNT, changed its line even more dramatically. Abandoning his habitual caution, Largo Caballero began to talk of an imminent workers' revolution. After the Right's election victory he set up a semi-secret Workers' Alliance (*Alianza Obrera*), with the aim of uniting militants from both wings of the workers' movement under UGT leadership. He also stepped up his inflammatory rhetoric, warning that he would regard the CEDA's admission to government as a fascist takeover. When it occurred (p73), he was forced to back his words with deeds.

Largo Caballero's call for a 'revolutionary strike' was catastrophic. Dispirited anarchists mainly ignored it, with particularly damaging effects in Catalonia. There, the ERC regional government had also boxed itself into a corner with intemperate attacks on the Madrid authorities (p73), and was dragged along in Largo's wake. The regional premier, Lluis Companys, reluctantly declared Catalonia a free Republic within federal Spain, but few workers rallied to his support and, even worse, the Catalan police controled by his own party helped to crush those who did. 'Free' Catalonia survived less than a day; in most of Spain the uprising was over even more quickly.

Only in Asturias did the 'October revolution' get off the ground. There anarchists, and Communists, who were well represented among the local miners, backed Largo's Alliance. For a week they controlled the coalfield area, and even when the government sent in hardened units of the Moroccan army, the miners put up determined resistance which ended only after several thousand had been killed or wounded. Their resistance gave the Left a powerful symbol. But it derived more concrete benefit from the government's over-reaction to events (p73), which not only drew workers together but also unleashed a wave of sympathy for them among Left Republicans (p68).

The 1934 uprising thus provided a foundation on which to rebuild the unity of 1931, a process initiated by Azaña. Founding a new party, 'Republican Left', he toured the country speaking in favour a renewed alliance. He found a willing ally in Prieto, who swung chastened Socialists behind the notion of a '**Popular Front**' to fight the 1936 election. Its programme was simple; resumption of reforms, release of imprisoned strikers and an amnesty for those involved in the 'October revolution'. On that platform the Front won a narrow lead in votes, which was converted by the electoral system (p71) into a large parliamentary majority.

Although the Front as a whole was broader than the alliance that had formed the 1931 Provisional Government (p68), its Republican component was markedly depleted. Its real strength lay in the working-class support which the CNT had, unprecedentedly, helped to mobilise by calling on its supporters to vote. But, as before, that backing was represented almost exclusively by the PSOE. It was therefore disastrous that pressure from Largo Caballero prevented his party from entering the new government.

Without the Socialists it looked like a minority administration, its only parliamen-

---

Frente Popular
....

Popular Front

Based on the notion of a broad alliance of all progressive forces to oppose fascism, or the far Right in general, the Spanish Popular Front (or 'People's Front') was formed in late 1935. It was made up of: middle-class Republican parties – the **Left Republicans** (p68) and Martínez Barrio's dissident Radicals (p73), renamed Republican Union; regionalist parties – the Catalan **ERC** (p70) and the Basque **PNV** (p45); and elements of the workers' movement – the Socialist **PSOE**, the **Communist Party** (p86) and the 'Syndicalist Party' founded by the rebel anarcho-syndicalist, Angel Pestaña (p75). Once the Civil War started it was extended by the inclusion of the anarcho-syndicalist **CNT** (p49) and FAI (p60).

tary base being that of the Republican MPs, whose meagre numbers actually over-represented their popular support. Even worse, its main law and order instrument was the Assault Guards (*Guardias de Asalto*). Set up in 1931 because of doubts about the existing security forces' loyalty to the Republic, they had since fallen under the control of the Socialists, becoming a sort of party militia. As a result, a succession of weak cabinets were constantly attacked by the Right as unrepresentative and partisan.

The new government provided grounds for such charges by following the bad example of their right-wing predecessors (p73). The 'revolutionaries' of 1934 were not just pardoned but feted, and press censorship was aimed almost exclusively at the conservative press. As well as allowing such actions Azaña succumbed to the mood of hysteria, talking of radical reform in terms calculated to alarm even moderate conservatives. But he remained the Republicans' greatest asset, and when they appointed him President in place of the officious Alcalá Zamora they only worsened their plight. Day-to-day government was left in the charge of Santiago Casares Quiroga (p68), who was quite inadequate for the task.

By this time, in any case, the government was no longer in control of events. Admittedly Catalan autonomy was restored (p76), and work began on similar devolution for Basques and also Galicians; even land reform (p70) was reintroduced and pursued with some vigour. But the real force for change on the land now was the seizure of estates by farmworkers convinced that the Front's victory meant that revolution had come. The Socialists made little attempt to disabuse them. In the cities, too, politics was becoming a spiral of street violence between organised gangs, including those of the openly fascist Falange (p82). Their appearance indicated how the division into two camps apparent in 1933 had been widened and polarised.

On the Left this could be seen in the growing strength of the Communists, to whom the Socialist youth organisation defected *en bloc*. Largo Caballero was speaking of revolution in fierier terms than ever; on May Day he presided over a massive parade whose banners demanded a workers' government and lauded the Soviet Red Army. Meanwhile, on the Right, Gil-Robles' gradualist strategy (p72) was in ruins; his own party's youth wing defected to the Falange and his leader's mantle passed to the more extremist Calvo Sotelo (p74), who had plans in place for a military-backed coup. On 13 July 1936 they were pre-empted when Calvo Sotelo was murdered by Assault Guards avenging a colleague killed by the Falange. It was the spark that set the country alight.

Exhibit 5.1: Programme of the CEDA (1933)

Extracts from the first two sections

I. RELIGIÓN

1.ª La Confederación Española de Derechas Autónomas declara que en el orden político-religioso no puede ni quiere tener otro programa que el que representa la incorporación al suyo de toda la doctrina de la Iglesia católica sobre este punto. Las reivindicaciones de carácter religioso deben ocupar, y ocuparán siempre, el primer lugar de su programa, de su propaganda y de su acción. [. . .]

2.ª C.E.D.A. formula su más enérgica protesta contra el laicismo del Estado y contra las leyes de excepción y de la persecución de que se ha hecho víctima la Iglesia católica en España. [. . .]

3.ª La C.E.D.A. [. . .] se atendrá siempre a las normas que en cada momento dicte para España la Jerarquía eclesiástica en el orden político-religioso.

II. RÉGIMEN POLÍTICO GENERAL

[. . .]

3.ª Se ha de organizar la representación nacional de modo que las Cortes reflejen el verdadero sentir del pueblo español, tanto en los estados de opinión política manifestados por los individuos, cuanto en la organización corporativa que responda al carácter orgánico de la sociedad.

4.ª Robustecimiento del Poder ejecutivo, en la medida que sea necesario, para que desenvuelva eficazmente la función que le corresponde dentro de la organización fundamental del Estado. [. . .]

Source: Artola, M. (1991) *Partidos y programas políticos 1808–1936: Tomo II.* Madrid: Alianza.

Exhibit 5.2: The '1934 Revolution' in Asturias (1934)

Statement issued by one of the 'provisional revolutionary committees' established in the province

COMITÉ REVOLUCIONARIO DE ALIANZA OBRERA Y CAMPESINA DE ASTURIAS A TODOS LOS TRABAJADORES

Compañeros: Ante la marcha victoriosa de nuestra revolución, ya gloriosa, los enemigos de los intereses de nuestra clase utilizan todas sus malas artes e intentan desmoralizar a los trabajadores asturianos que en magnífico esfuerzo se han colocado a la cabeza de la Revolución proletaria española.

Mientras en el resto de las provincias se dan noticias de que en Asturias está sofocado el movimiento, el Gobierno contrarrevolucionario dice en sus proclamas

continued

a los trabajadores de nuestra región que en el resto de España no ocurre nada y nos invita a entregarnos a nuestros verdugos.

Hoy podemos decir que la base aérea de León ha caído en poder de los obreros revolucionarios leoneses y que éstos se disponen a enviarnos fuerzas en nuestra ayuda. Contra la voluntad indomable del proletariado asturiano, nada podrán las fuerzas del fascismo.

Estamos dispuestos, antes de ser vencidos, a vender cara nuestra existencia. Tras nosotros, el enemigo sólo encontrará un montón de ruinas. Por cada uno de los nuestros que caiga por la metralla de los aviones, haremos justicia con los centenares de rehenes que tenemos prisioneros.

Sépanlo nuestros enemigos. ¡Camaradas: un último esfuerzo por el triunfo de la revolución! ¡Viva la revolución obrera y campesina!

Source: Ruiz, D. (1975) *Asturias contemporánea (1808–1936).* Madrid: Siglo XXI.

Topics

■ What does the CEDA appear to regard as the ultimate political authority (Exhibit 5.1)? Does its view have any precedents in modern Spanish history?

■ What sort of political regime does the CEDA appear to want? What does it have in mind when it refers to the 'verdadero sentir del pueblo español'? Do its views in this respect presage any future developments?

■ What sense does Exhibit 5.2 give of the political climate in Spain in 1934?

■ What, if anything, do the views expressed there have in common with those of the CEDA?

■ Was the Republic doomed to failure?

■ Why were the various Republican parties so easily marginalised over the course of the Republic?

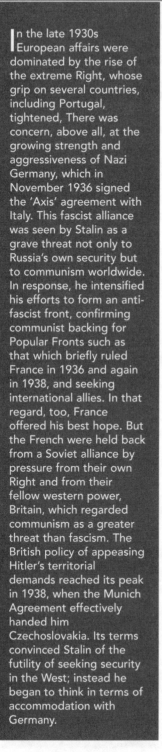

An unequal struggle (1936–1939)

In July 1936 Spain was shaken yet again by a military revolt. This time, however, the uprising met with fierce opposition, and triggered off a three-year civil war. The conflict's course reflected a shifting balance of advantage, as the initial edge afforded the Republic's defenders by superior popular support was first eroded and then reversed by their own divisions and the rebels' growing cohesion. Foreign intervention from various sources also played a decisive part. For, while it helped to stiffen the Republican authorities' resistance, it crucially enabled the insurgents to survive the failure of their coup attempt. It also contributed to their grinding progress to victory, which went hand-in-hand with the rise to supreme power of General Franco.

The creation of 'Nationalist Spain'

The 1936 uprising was the result of planning by both soldiers and civilians. But circumstances dictated that it was essentially an old-style military declaration – and one with no clear leader. Like most such coups it failed, but the rebels were rescued by a new factor in such situations; outside intervention. Thanks to this help the Nationalists, as they had become known, were soon in control of a large part of Spain, in which they established what amounted to a separate state.

In the increasingly tense and polarised conditions of 1936 (p77), various right-wing groups abandoned all notion of regaining power by democratic means and began conspiring to overthrow the Republic's government. Notable by its absence was the party that had spearheaded the Right's recent political rise, since the ambivalent attitude of the CEDA's leader, José-María Gil-Robles (p72), made him as suspect to the plotters as to democrats. Instead, the principal civilian conspirator was José Calvo Sotelo, who had the backing of most monarchists (p74), including many with considerable wealth and influence. But as a political force they were heavily dependent on their leader, and were effectively neutralised by his assassination (p77).

Also involved in the plot were the **Traditionalists**, the heirs of the old Carlist movement. Unlike Alfonso's supporters, they could call on an element of mass support in the Carlist heartland of Navarre where, well before war broke out, drilling of Traditionalist volunteers (*requetés*) was under way. While they represented an important fighting resource for the rebels, in other respects the Traditionalists' value to the uprising was limited; outside Navarre the extreme reactionary nature of their ideas was as likely to frighten off supporters as attract them.

The **Falange** party's main assets were its charismatic leader, José Antonio Primo de Rivera, and the street-fighting experience of its student gangs (p77). But at the February election it had failed to win a single seat, and despite having grown since, its popular backing remained tiny. Moreover, it was an uneasy alliance between the well-off young (*señoritos*) and a limited number of the workers and peasants to which its leader's romanticised brand of fascism was intended to appeal. Doubts concerning the compatibility of this new approach with the traditional conservatism of the Right in general led to the young Primo only agreeing to join the conspirators at the last minute.

Given the weakness and diversity of these civilian elements, the uprising became in essence a matter for disgruntled generals among whom each had its sympathisers, even the Falange. Along with a desire for minimal political interference in Army affairs, the military plotters shared two grievances against the Republic. One was the collapse of law and order, for which they held it responsible. The other was a nebulous but powerful conviction that it was destroying a 'true Spain' whose foundation was not 'artificial' democracy but respect for authority, and which made no concessions to equally 'artificial' regionalist claims. Their beliefs led the rebellion's leaders to style their enterprise a 'National Movement', and in the war that followed their side became known as Nationalists (*nacionales*).

The rebels' nominal head was General Sanjurjo, who had been exiled in Lisbon since the failure of his 1932 coup attempt (p70). But even before his death in an air crash on 20 July 1936, age meant that his authority was far from uncontested. Thereafter a number of generals harboured ambitions to replace him, the most obvious candidates being Emilio Mola, who had been responsible for organising the uprising inside Spain, and Francisco Franco, whose task was to assume command in Morocco (p58), where he had served with great distinction. The issue was a touchy one and, given that all the generals expected a quick victory, they tacitly agreed to shelve any decision until it had been achieved.

Their expectations were shattered as soon as the revolt got under way, prematurely, on 17 July in Morocco, and one day later, as planned, elsewhere. In terms of popular backing it suffered from the fact that most barracks were located in towns, while mass support for the Right was concentrated in the northern countryside, above all in Old Castile (p34) where the coup met with little resistance. In other regions its success was limited to a few larger cities where individual commanders acted decisively and rode their luck, most spectacularly General Queipo de Llano in Seville. Elsewhere, and crucially in Madrid and Barcelona, the revolt was crushed (p84).

Even within the armed forces support was patchy. The paramilitary Civil Guard proved much less enthusiastic than anticipated, while the bulk of the fledgling Air Force remained loyal to the government. Within the Army itself reactions were mixed, though most of the lower ranks – mainly conscripts drawn from the social groups which were most solidly behind the Popular Front government elected earlier in the year – were hostile. In Morocco, the elite troops of the Army of Africa rebelled and quickly established control, but since the naval uprising had been a complete failure, and those officers who did attempt to rebel were overwhelmed, there was no immediate way the North African forces could be brought into action in mainland Spain.

As a result, the coup's leaders were staring defeat in the face, until they were saved by the first outside intervention of the war. Both Hitler and Mussolini responded to Franco's pleas by sending airforce units to Morocco to airlift his troops across the Straits of Gibraltar to Andalusia. There they linked up with Queipo de Llano's forces to advance on Madrid from the south-west, while other columns under Mola's command approached the capital from the north. Whereas Mola's inexperienced soldiers and Traditionalist militiamen were halted with relative ease, the battle-hardened Army of Africa advanced inexorably through Extremadura, so that soon all rebel-held territory was joined in a single 'zone' stretching in an arc from Cadiz to the Pyrenees.

At this point the problems of coordinating action on several fronts spurred the Nationalist generals into establishing a single command structure. Franco's control of the Moroccan Army now gave him an unanswerable claim to primacy, and at a meeting in Salamanca on 21 September the generals appointed him to be their Supreme Commander (*Generalísimo*). They also gave him the title of 'Head of the State', for the duration of the war as they thought, although this restriction was omitted from the official announcement on 1 October (p90). For the rebels' purpose was more then military. They were claiming, above all to foreign observers (p88), that the territory they had overrun had the same status as the legitimate Spanish state, whose resistance had turned out to be stronger than expected.

The Republicans and their divisions

From the moment of the uprising, the term 'Republicans' was used to denote all those involved in resisting it. This involved not only the old Republican parties but also their allies in the workers' movement. Indeed, the workers bore the brunt of the war effort although they were sharply divided on what the war was about, and how it should be fought. The Communists played a key role in the debate, which, while it gave them a growing influence, eventually became the main reason why the Republicans' initial unity inexorably crumbled.

Despite persistent rumours of a right-wing plot, the July uprising caught the government off-guard and almost entirely unprepared. The Republicans – in the pre-war sense – of which the government was made up were demoralised by the course of events since the Popular Front's election victory (pp76–7), as was evident in their reactions to the coup. Casares Quiroga, the weak and ailing Prime Minister (p77), simply resigned; his successor, the more conservative Martínez Barrio (p76), sought to negotiate with the rebels; it was only when he was replaced by José Giral that the government decided to resist.

While its supposed guardians dithered, the Republic was saved by three factors. The first was the indecisiveness shown by the insurgents in a number of centres, the second the loyalty of many Army and Civil Guard commanders (p83), without which their rebel colleagues might well have succeeded. The third was a massive display of opposition to the coup from ordinary Spaniards, especially urban workers, who took to the streets and demanded that the government give them arms to defend it, as Giral eventually agreed to do. His action allowed the hasty formation of **militia** units by the various workers' organisations, which in several places, including Madrid and Barcelona, played an important part in suppressing the rising.

Spontaneous resistance to the coup was part of a wider phenomenon: the belief among many on the Left that it offered an unparalleled opportunity to stage their own revolution. Their conviction had a variety of effects, including a wave of violence directed against the rich and, especially, against the Church buildings and its personnel. This reaction was largely the work of 'mavericks' (*incontrolados*) acting on their own initiative, and soon died down. Altogether more important was the open debating of revolutionary ideas as to how the country should be run, ideas shared at least in part by some leading figures not just in the anarcho-syndicalist CNT (p49), but also in the Socialist trade union, the UGT (p59).

In a number of towns and cities revolutionary committees (*juntas revolucionarias*), composed of workers' representatives, were set up to administer public services instead of, or alongside the official authorities. At the same time, widespread and often successful attempts were made to **collectivise** economic activity. The advocates of immediate revolution also insisted that the militias were not merely an emergency recourse, but should form the basis of the Republic's defence in the longer war now looming.

It was the militias' ineffectiveness against Franco's experienced regulars (p84) that highlighted the practical problems of these revolutionary policies, and crystallised a very different view of the war among other sectors of the Left. To much of the Socialist Party (PSOE), and even the leadership of the CNT and UGT, the war was not an opportunity, but a mortal threat both to the '*bourgeois*' Republic and to workers. That view, which had also underlain the formation of the Popular Front (p76), now led to its revival in strengthened form when, in September 1936, a new government was formed.

The new Prime Minister was the UGT leader Largo Caballero (p75), the figure best placed to unite both sections of the workers' movement. Socialists also filled the majority of cabinet posts. The middle-class parties were reduced to two ministers, although Azaña (p68) remained the Republic's President and figurehead. Two posts also went to the **Communists** and to the Front's regionalist

---

milicia

militia

Groups of volunteers raised to defend the interests of a particular group or party, militias were a feature of Spanish politics from the first half of the nineteenth century (p10). During the Civil War they fought on both sides, but for the Republicans the term acquired special overtones. It implied the absence of conventional military hierarchy and discipline, both within units and in their relations with others and with the overall Republican command; in that sense it was associated with **anarchist** influence (p48).

---

colectivización

collectivisation

In Soviet Russia, collectivisation brought to mind the imposition of large-scale, centrally-controlled units of production. In Spain it was associated with **anarchist** ideas of work on a small scale, involving autonomy and participative management, and consequently opposed by the **Communist Party** (p86). During the early phase of the Civil War it was implemented in some parts of the Republican zone, both on the land, as a sort of spontaneous **land reform** (p70), and in commerce and industry, especially by supporters of the anarcho-syndicalist **CNT** (p49).

Partido Comunista de España (PCE)

Spanish Communist Party

Founded in 1921 by dissidents from the Socialist **PSOE** (p47) and anarcho-syndicalist **CNT** (p49), the PCE has never operated throughout the whole of Spain, communism being represented in Catalonia by the Catalan United Socialist Party (PSUC). It was banned under the Primo dictatorship and achieved little success during the Second Republic. Strictly obedient to Soviet instructions, in 1936 it reversed its refusal to cooperate with 'bourgeois' parties and backed the **Popular Front** (p76). During the Civil War it acquired significant influence on the Republican side, but the tactics it used to do so alienated many of those who belonged to other parties on the Left. The PCE played a leading part in opposition to the Franco regime (p114), but after 1975 proved unable to capitalise on the prestige that its action had brought (p129). Since 1986 it has been the dominant partner in the United Left alliance (p143).

See also: **Comisiones Obreras** (p114); **consenso** (p129)

members, the Catalan ERC and the PNV, whose support was sealed by granting Basque devolution. A month later the CNT and, astonishingly, the Iberian Anarchist Federation (p60), abjured their principles and also accepted cabinet posts, so that the government now included representatives from all sections of the Republic's support.

The most significant aspect of these changes was the inclusion of the PCE. At the start of 1936 it had been little more than a sect, but since then two factors had greatly increased its importance. One was the fact that, as Franco's column bore down on Madrid (p84), the Soviet Union – unlike the Western Powers (p88) – came to the Republic's aid. From the autumn of 1936 it sent large quantities of tanks and planes, and – through the international communist movement – recruited most of the volunteers who formed the International Brigades (*brigadistas*). These reinforcements played an important part, first, in the successful defence of Madrid and then in defeating two further assaults on the capital at the battles of the Jarama and Guadalajara. The crucial intermediary between the Republican authorities' and the source of this precious support was the PCE.

However, the PCE's ascent also reflected another change; the adoption of pragmatic policies in response to Stalin's decision that the overriding priority was to defeat the Right. Suddenly, the Communists became fervent opponents of revolutionary activity that might alienate middle-class support. As the only force on the government side solidly behind such moderation, they attracted support from those whose enthusiasm for the Republic did not extend to wanting their own property to be collectivised. Their approach also brought them significant influence among the Republican leadership, not least because it was broadly shared by the PSOE's majority faction, led by Indalecio Prieto (pp74–5).

Together, the PSOE and the PCE were responsible for the new government's efforts to bring revolutionary enthusiasm under control in the interests of the war effort. Law and order was imposed, where necessary by force. The revolutionary committees were disbanded, agricultural collectives suppressed, and industry made increasingly subject to central planning and control. Most controversially, the government moved to integrate the militias – whose weaknesses were again highlighted by the fall of Malaga in early 1937 – into a new People's Army (*Ejército Popular*), organised on the more conventional lines favoured by the Communists.

Resentment at these steps was widespread, above all in Barcelona where the revolutionaries were especially strong. Conscious that it could not defy them, the regional government had agreed to run the city in tandem with an Anti-Fascist Militia Committee. In May 1937 the third major force in regional politics, the Communist-dominated PSUC (p86), moved to disband the Committee. Its action was resisted by the POUM, a communist splinter group with anarcho-syndicalist leanings, and by grass-roots anarchists. After several days of confused street fighting the revolutionaries were completely defeated, and pragmatic policies were imposed in Catalonia, too.

Their proponents used the disorder in Barcelona as an excuse for Juan Negrín, a Socialist close to Prieto, to replace Largo Caballero as Prime Minister. Under Negrín's leadership resistance continued for another two years, despite the loss of the vital northern industrial areas over the summer of 1937. On several occasions, most notably in the battles of Teruel (winter 1937/38) and the Ebro (autumn 1938), the People's Army even managed significant local advances. However, it could not reverse the general pattern of defeats, in which the collapse of Republican unity played a key part.

While the Barcelona clashes were not the start of that process, they did accelerate it markedly. First of all, by fatally undermining Catalan enthusiasm for the Republic, not only among workers but also among a middle-class alarmed at the regional government's manifest inability to control events. Crucially, also, Largo's removal prompted the CNT and FAI representatives to withdraw from the government, further weakening its credibility among workers. That same step also added to growing suspicion of the party that, along with Prieto, had engineered it; the PCE.

Doubts had already been aroused by the party's constant efforts to increase its influence, particularly within the People's Army, and by the ruthless nature of its methods. Now the first revelations about Stalin's rule in Russia were mirrored by the Communist secret police's murderous pursuit of the defeated POUM, and other opponents. Another favoured PCE tactic was to mount scurrilous attacks on opponents in their own press, one of which drove Prieto out of government after he attempted to resist PCE influence. As with the resort to terror tactics, the move was ultimately self-defeating, even though accompanied by the CNT's return to government, since Prieto's departure inevitably alienated much of his substantial support within the PSOE.

The chief charge against Prieto was defeatism; like PSOE leader Besteiro (p75), he had questioned the point of continuing with increasingly hopeless resistance. Quite apart from the fact that the Nationalist leadership had no intention of negotiating (p91), though, they timed their public musings badly, at a time when the Czech crisis seemed, at last, to offer the prospect of Western aid. To encourage it the Republican government disbanded the International Brigades, hoping to quell British fears of Communist influence; the last volunteers left in November 1938. By then, however, the Munich agreement had dashed hopes of an anti-fascist alliance, and also hastened the ending of Soviet support. Now the Republic really was lost.

Its end came tragically with another, pathetic Army uprising. The revolt was led by

Colonel Casado, a soldier who had stayed loyal in 1936 and now commanded what remained of the People's Army, Communist interference in which he deeply resented. He was also convinced, quite wrongly, that the sole barrier to a negotiated end to the fighting was the PCE's presence in Negrín's government. He therefore attempted to overthrow it, but succeeded only in sparking off six days of street fighting in Madrid, at the end of which the capital lay undefended. The war was over, as a triumphant Nationalist communiqué announced on 1 April 1939.

Franco's triumph

Although it was signed by a number of generals, the announcement was issued in one name alone: that of General Franco. It was a graphic illustration of the importance he had assumed during the war's progress. Of course, there were several reasons for the Nationalists' victory. Franco's leadership was only one of these, but it was crucial in determining the nature of his side's triumph, and in linking it indissolubly to his own person.

To some extent victory was due to factors beyond the Nationalists' control, such as their opponents' divisions, and the stunted economic development of Spain's main industrial region, Catalonia, that rendered its factories ill-suited for conversion to munitions production. Nor could they claim credit for the realities of economic and political geography that left the arms-producing industries of the North an easy prey, and placed Spain's main food-producing areas in their hands from the war's outset. The rather fortunate capture of Seville (p83) was also vital, as it gave the rebels control of the poor southern areas where the Left had solid support, and collectivisation would have been received as a boon rather than a threat (p86).

Above all, there was the balance of foreign intervention, which was clearly in the Nationalists' favour even before 1938, when France ceased to ignore smuggling across the Pyrenean frontier and Soviet supplies tailed off (p87). Once Hitler and Mussolini had thrown their support behind the insurgency (p83) they were determined to avoid the propaganda setback its defeat would have meant. Indeed, their common interest in a Nationalist victory helped prompt their formal alliance of November 1936. Thereafter both sent substantial aid to Franco's troops, virtually unhindered by the **Non-Intervention Pact** they had signed with the Western Powers.

Pacto de No Intervención

Non-Intervention Pact

Signed in 1936 by Britain, France, Germany and Italy, the Pact was an agreement to refrain from intervening in the Civil War. Its legal basis was questionable – since it effectively accepted the Nationalists' spurious claim to be given equal treatment with the Republican government (p84) – and its practice was downright fraudulent. It was respected by the two Western Powers, thus denying the Republic French aid and impeding supplies to it from third countries. However, since Britain was determined to stay out of conflict, in Spain or elsewhere, the Pact did virtually nothing to prevent Hitler and Mussolini from supplying the Nationalists as they wished.

In quantitative terms, the greater contribution came from Italy. The Italians had supplied most of the Spanish Air Force's existing machines, and now they provided further supplies and back-up to the Nationalists, while denying vital spare parts to the Republicans. Mussolini also committed substantial numbers of ground troops, including armoured units, although they turned out to be of limited value; while they led the capture of Malaga they failed badly at Guadalajara (p86). Hitler's support was more limited in quantity but of higher quality, consisting of elite air units, including that responsible for the bombing of **Guernica**.

Aid from the Axis powers was crucial in establishing Nationalist military superiority,

> ### *Guernica* (Basque: *Gernika*)
> #### Guernica
> Because of its associations with their **traditional privileges** or 'old laws' (p13), Guernica is of enormous symbolic importance to Basques. In 1937, during the Nationalist northern offensive, it was the target of a bombing raid by the German Condor Legion which caused heavy civilian casualties, tactics which were to be perfected in the Second World War. The Basque Statute of Autonomy was signed there in 1979 (p133).

above all in the air. Ultimately, though, the war was won on the ground, and there the rebels' success in building up an effective Army was vital. The limited response to their initial coup (p83) left them no more advanced in that respect than the Republicans. Even so, the Nationalists had significant assets in the greater experience of their leaders, especially in Morocco, and the Army of Africa itself; they also had the benefit of German and Italian advice. Above all, the nature of their uprising and the support it had received meant that there was minimal resistance to the imposition of standard military practices in training and action; the Traditionalist and Falange militias (p82) were integrated into a single Nationalist Army without any of the problems experienced on the other side.

As well as its primary role at the front, the rebel Army also served as the chief instrument of organised terror within the Nationalist zone. From an early stage these tactics were associated particularly with Franco. One of the most notorious mass executions occurred at Badajoz during his initial march on Madrid, and once he was established as effective ruler of rebel-held Spain, such killings and other forms of brutality were routinely used against known or suspected government supporters. As a result there was little of the uncertainty that wracked Republican Spain, where the better-off were constantly suspected of mere 'geographic loyalty', and rumours abounded of a 'fifth column' of traitors within.

Franco's insistence on stamping out opposition in captured areas before proceeding to a further offensive was one reason why, in strictly military terms, the war lasted longer than necessary. Several times, too, Franco chose tactical options that almost certainly prolonged it. Most glaringly, having defeated the Republicans' Teruel offensive, he ignored the obvious course of a direct attack on Catalonia and instead advanced on Valencia through the difficult terrain of the Maestrazgo district. But such moves were not errors. They were part of a deliberate strategy of attrition (*desgaste*), designed – like the use of terror – quite literally to eliminate his opponents.

Imposition of this approach, which was unmistakably his own, was a mark of Franco's new status as the Nationalists' undisputed leader. The emergence of such a figurehead was assisted by the military ethos of the insurgency, with its emphasis on hierarchy and obedience. And Franco's elevation to the role in October 1936 (p84) was partly due to the disappearance of all other contenders in the space of a year; following the deaths of Calvo Sotelo (p82) and Sanjurjo (p83), José Antonio Primo de Rivera (p82) died in a Republican prison in late 1936, and Mola (p83) was killed in another air crash the following summer. But Franco himself also manoeuvred to ensure his pre-eminence, halting his march on Madrid to relieve the rebel garrison besieged in the fortress (*alcázar*) at Toledo, and then exploiting the feat to bolster his own prestige.

Moreover, once installed as effective ruler of Nationalist Spain, Franco worked single-mindedly to consolidate his position, which rested on three pillars. The first was his tremendous standing within the Army (p83). The second was a new political organ-isation, whose creation reflected his conviction that the main reason for Spain's decline lay in the fractious squabbling of party politics. Determined to avoid any such develop-ment in his fief, he decreed the merger of the two largest parties among his support, the Falange and the Traditionalists (p82). All other political organisations he outlawed forthwith.

The merged party was to be known as the *Falange Española Tradicionalista y de las JONS*, a clumsy title that betrayed the incompatibility between Traditionalism and the modernising, socially-minded ideas of the Falange. Franco quickly crushed the resul-tant discontent, imprisoning José Antonio's successor as Falange leader, Manuel Hedilla. But such methods soon became unnecessary. Membership of the new single party – still known colloquially as the Falange – was a requirement for public office in the Nationalist zone, not to mention an invaluable badge of loyalty. New recruits flocked to it to secure their material interests, and their sheer numbers drowned out dissent from purists, whether Traditionalists or Falangists.

The new Falange was to some extent modeled on the parties created by Mussolini and Hitler, and performed some of the same functions. With its members spread throughout society in the Nationalist zone, it enabled the authorities there to exercise close control over the population's behaviour. It was also used to promote, through relentless propaganda, a fascist-style leadership cult. Yet the Falange never exercised the control over other institutions, notably the Army, typical of true fascist parties. Nor did Franco assume its leadership, a task he left to his brother-in-law and faithful subor-dinate, Ramón Serrano Suñer. Instead, his status as *Caudillo*, the nation's hero and predestined leader, rested ultimately on the backing of a very different organisation, the third pillar of his authority.

Outside the Basque Country and, to a lesser extent, Catalonia, the Catholic Church solidly backed the Nationalist cause from the outset. Even the more sympathetic lower clergy had been alienated by the Republic's religious legislation (p69), and by anticler-ical violence once war broke out (p85). Franco, for his part, was a firm believer of the traditional school, and regarded the Church as one of the foundations of the 'true Spain' he sought to restore. To that end he quickly set about re-establishing its social role, especially by handing it control over education.

In return, the Church threw its moral authority enthusiastically behind him and the cult of his leadership. Spanish bishops gave their blessing to the elaborate and deliberately old-fashioned ceremonies which became a feature of public life in the Nationalist zone, and which appeared to give Franco the status of a saint. The clergy also sanctioned and promoted his notion of the war as a 'crusade', consciously evoking the country's reconquest from the Moors (pp1–2) – and conveniently overlooking Franco's use of Muslim Moroccan troops, especially in terrorising civilians. The idea was a powerful one in the context of civil war, submerging the inevitable divided loyalties under the powerful appeal of patriotism.

But while the 'crusade' notion fostered growing unity among Nationalists, it also had deeply divisive implications, both for the present and the future. It implied unmistakably that the Nationalists' opponents were not truly Spaniards at all, and not merely foreign but inherently hostile to 'true Spain'. Indeed, in Franco's eyes the Republicans embodied an 'anti-Spain' which must be utterly defeated, if not annihilated; at no time would he countenance negotiations with its representatives. His view of them was encapsulated in an extraordinary measure he decreed as the war drew to a close. This 'Political Responsibilities Act' effectively declared all those who had served the Republic – Spain's legitimate government – in any capacity to be guilty of treason. It set the tone for the much of what was to follow.

Exhibit 6.1: The Communist view of the War (1936)

Extract from manifesto issued by the PCE in December

[. . .S]i queremos ganar la guerra, no basta ya la improvisación de nuestras Milicias, ni el heroísmo que nuestras fuerzas armadas han demostrado en tantas batallas, sino que es preciso transformar éstas en un gran ejército popular, dotado de la disciplina y de los medios técnicos que exige la guerra, una guerra como ésta que se nos impone contra ejércitos imperialistas bien pertrechados por sus respectivos países. Por esto, la realización de la consigna de crear un ejército popular, férreamente disciplinado, obediente a los mandos y con sólida estructura, consigna lanzada desde los primeros días por nuestro Partido, es hoy de una necesidad imperiosa si queremos ganar rápidamente la guerra. [. . .] Urge acabar con las fuerzas dispersas, con las Milicias sindicales, de partido, regionales, etc., que si en los momentos iniciales de la lucha fueron la forma obligada para encuadrar rápidamente las fuerzas armadas que hubieron de improvisarse para batir al fascismo, ahora que tenemos enfrente no sólo moros, legionarios, requetés y falangistas, sino un ejército orgánico, formado por tropas alemanas, italianas, portuguesas, ya no bastan, pues, para vencer a este ejército, también nosotros necesitamos un ejército regular, superior al enemigo en armamento, en disciplina, en moral y en combatividad.

Source: Vázquez, M. & Valero, J. (1978) *La Guerra Civil en Madrid*. Madrid: Tebas.

Exhibit 6.2: The Church and the Nationalist uprising (1937)

Extract from a pastoral letter issued jointly by the country's bishops

Demos ahora un esbozo del carácter del movimiento llamado "nacional".
Creemos justa esta denominación. Primero, por su espíritu; porque la nación
española está disociada, en su inmensa mayoría, de una situación estatal que no
supo encarnar sus profundas necesidades y aspiraciones; y el movimiento fue
aceptado como una esperanza en toda la nación; en las regiones no liberadas
sólo espera romper la coraza de las fuerzas comunistas que le oprimen. Es
también nacional por su objetivo, por cuanto tiende a salvar y sostener para lo
futuro las esencias de un pueblo organizado en un Estado que sepa continuar
dignamente su historia. [. . .]

El movimiento ha fortalecido el sentido de patria, contra el exotismo de las
fuerzas que le son contrarias. La patria implica una paternidad; es el ambiente
moral, como de una familia dilatada, en que logra el ciudadano su desarrollo
total; y el Movimiento Nacional ha determinado una corriente de amor que se ha
concentrado alrededor del nombre y de la sustancia histórica de España, con
aversión de los elementos forasteros que nos acarrearon su ruina. Y como el amor
patrio, cuando se ha sonbrenaturalizado por el amor de Jesucristo, nuestro Díos y
Señor, toca las cumbres de la caridad cristiana, hemos visto una explosión de
verdadera caridad que ha tenido su expresión máxima en la sangre de millares de
españoles que le han dado al grito de "¡Viva España!", "¡Viva Cristo Rey!"

Source: Aguirre Prado, L. (1964) *La Iglesia y la Guerra Española*. Madrid: Servicio
Informativo Español.

Topics
FOR DISCUSSION

■ What are the key points of the PCE manifesto (Exhibit 6.1)?

■ How does the way they are expressed compare with earlier left-wing documents of this kind, in content and in style (cf Exhibits 2.1, 3.2, 5.2)?

■ What themes of Nationalist propaganda are reflected in Exhibit 6.2?

■ How would you interpret the notion of 'charity' described in the final lines?

■ Could the Republicans have won the Civil War? Would they have been better off without Soviet aid?

■ What were the bases of popular support for the Nationalists, initially and as the war progressed?

CHAPTER 7

Back to the future (1939–1959)

From 1939 to 1945 Europe outside the Iberian Peninsula was embroiled in World War II. Initially, its course favoured the fascist Axis powers, Germany and Italy. However, in 1942 the balance of forces changed decisively, with the intervention of the United States and Hitler's attack on Russia. Thereafter the Allies slowly but surely turned the tables, and in 1945 achieved complete victory. Almost immediately the Soviets imposed Communist rule in Eastern Europe, and by 1949 the Cold War between the two superpowers had begun, giving rise to new security fears in western Europe. Economically, though, the region had begun a remarkable recovery, greatly helped by US aid under the Marshall Plan. Indeed, it now formed part of an American-dominated western economy, whose foundations were laid at the 1944 Bretton Woods Conference, which established the World Bank and the International Monetary Fund. Along with the Organisation for European Economic Cooperation (later to become the OECD), and the links that culminated in the formation of the European Economic Community in 1957, these bodies provided a framework for steady growth throughout western Europe.

General Franco's victory in 1939 ushered in a period of 36 years during which Spain's history was determined ultimately by his own distinctive attitudes. Yet, even so, the nature of his rule underwent significant changes. Thus, while in the early 1940s his regime flaunted its fascist side, by the 1950s it was attempting to present a democratic face to the outside world. Nevertheless, one thing remained constant throughout both decades: the regime sought its inspiration in the past, be it the Civil War period or an earlier one. For a long time the regime's survival was threatened by the isolation from the contemporary world which, in various senses, that implied. Only when it was relaxed was Franco able to entrench his rule. But, at the same time, he was brought up against the harsh realities of modern international relations, especially the economic ones.

The New State

The form of government imposed by Franco throughout Spain after his triumph in the Civil War was essentially a continuation of arrangements in the Nationalist zone during the conflict. The name he gave it, the 'New State', emphasised its affinity with fascism, as did the special status it gave to the Falange. Although to a large extent a reflection of Franco's own ideas, its economic policy also had fascist overtones. By the late 1940s it had brought the regime to the verge of collapse.

The wartime character of the new regime was evident from the very top down. The unity of command established in 1936 (p84) was retained, with Franco acting as Head of State, Head of Government and – last but far from least – Supreme Commander of the Armed Forces. Moreover, his pronouncements made quite plain that the legitimacy of his rule – its ultimate justification – derived not from any constitution or hereditary rights, but quite simply from his victory over the Republic. Hence the constant glorification of the original 1936 'uprising' (*alzamiento*) and the importance attached to 18 July, the date associated with it (p83).

Nor did the cessation of hostilities mark the end of Franco's 'crusade' against those he regarded not just as his enemies but as Spain's (p91). Rather it provided an opportunity to strike at those of them who previously had been beyond his reach, in the government zone. Initially, his revenge took the form of savage violence; tens of thousands of Republican sympathisers were shot, and many more sentenced to prison sentences, which were often lengthy. And, right to the end of his life, the survivors suffered systematic discrimination in access to state benefits and employment.

More generally, the policies of **Franco's regime** favoured those sections of society that had supported the 1936 revolt, in particular large landowners and financiers. Conversely, industrial workers saw their trade unions banned along with other basic freedoms, including those of association and expression, and their wages held down. Franco's other *bête noire* – regionalists – also suffered. Devolution was revoked, and stern measures taken to stamp out any notion of regional distinctiveness. But while Navarre and Alava, which had largely backed him, were allowed to retain the financial privileges agreed in 1876 (p32), the 'rebel' provinces of Guipuzcoa and Vizcaya had theirs abolished.

Another relic of wartime was the continuing high profile of the Armed Forces, especially the Army. In part that was due to the high level of repression. But their role went considerably further; indeed, the new regime flaunted its military character, contrasting its 'virility' with the alleged feebleness of its civilian predecessors. Military men consistently made up a large part of Franco's cabinet (*Consejo de Ministros*), in the early years often filling up to half the portfolios. In the administration, both central and local, their presence was equally marked, and officers even took up key posts in business. Military courts, too, were given wide jurisdiction to deal with civil offences.

Bizarrely, Franco's own preferred designation for the reactionary dictatorship he had imposed was the 'New State'. At first sight an odd choice, coming from such an arch-conser-

---

franquismo

Franco era; Franco regime; Franco's political philosophy

As well as the period during which General Franco ruled, from 1939 to 1975, the Spanish term is used to mean his regime and the ideas that underlay it. Its main features in that sense were: his own supreme authority; an authoritarian, traditionalist concept of Spain based on an idealised image of its past; and an aggressive nationalism, directed less against external enemies than against his opponents, real and imagined, inside Spain.

vative as the dictator, it was easily understood in terms of the world situation. For its overtones were clearly fascist, and up to 1941 the fascist Axis leaders who had supported his own campaigns seemed set to win the World War. Anxious to place himself in the victors' camp, Franco made the fascist salute obligatory in Spain, and developed a keen interest in the notion of a Spanish 'race' along Nazi lines.

Franco also played up Spain's indigenous version of fascism, the Falange. Within the larger single party into which Franco had merged it – also called the Falange, for short (p90) – it had been bent to his will during the war, and now the dictator felt confident enough to give it a prominent role in his regime. Thus the Falange emblem – an arrow and bundle of rods, or fasces – was displayed at the entrance to every town and village, and its anthem 'Face the Sun' (*Cara al sol*) sung at official occasions and school assemblies. The party's founder, José Antonio Primo de Rivera (p82), acquired martyr status; his motto, 'Spain; One, Great, Free' was adopted by Franco. The blue fascist-style shirts worn by Falange members became a common sight, and a 'Blue Division' was sent to fight alongside the Nazis in Russia.

The Falange also took on roles typical of a fascist-style party, most obviously by controlling of the government propaganda machine. Directed from 1939 to 1941 by the poet Dionisio Ridruejo, the 'Spanish Goebbels', it ran numerous newspapers and radio stations whose unvarying themes were the regime's triumphs and the evils of its foes at home and abroad, allegedly linked in a conspiracy of communists, freemasons – and Jews. The Falange was also in charge of the strict censorship to which all other media organs were subjected. Meanwhile its network of subsidiary organisations, including the Women's Section (*Sección Femenina*), disseminated the regime's message throughout Spanish society, while also providing the means of snuffing out any sign of dissent.

The Falange also had a government role, as the second main source of ministers in Franco's early cabinets after the military. But its main powerbase lay in the **government-controlled trade unions** and their central 'Syndical Organisation'. Established by the 1938 Labour Charter (*Fuero del Trabajo*), these were the only form of industrial organisation allowed by law, since all independent action by workers in common, including collective bargaining, was banned. As well as their control function, the unions also provided a degree of job security through the system of employment tribunals (*Magistraturas de Trabajo*) they ran, which were in some ways

---

sindicatos verticales

government-controlled trade unions

Based on the ideas of the **Falange** (p82), which rejected the 'horizontal' notion of class underlying the workers' movement, the 'vertical' unions included all those who worked in a particular industry – managers, workers and even employers. Their importance to the **Franco regime** was reflected in the term it used to describe its own philosophical basis in the 1940s: National Syndicalism (*nacional-sindicalismo*). In practice they acted as a means of government control over workers. From the 1960s on they were increasingly infiltrated by opponents of the regime (p14), and were dissolved shortly after Franco's death. See also: ***democracia orgánica*** (p99)

reminiscent of arrangements under the Primo regime and the Republic (pp59, 69). They were also behind the introduction of a mild form of social insurance.

All these social measures reflected the influence of the Falange's fascist ideas, which could be seen also in the economic field. There, the regime' strategy of autarky (*autarquía*) – running the economy in isolation from the outside world – was to some extent dictated by the World War. That it was also in part a deliberate choice was shown by Franco's refusal of US loans when they were first offered. Autarky had the attraction of being associated with Nazi Germany, and of corresponding to Franco's delusion that Spain was well-endowed with resources, and hence naturally rich. But perhaps above all, for a simple soldier self-sufficiency was a matter of national pride. Hardship – especially when borne chiefly by his enemies – was greatly preferable to dependence.

In its efforts to achieve self-sufficiency, the regime intervened in the economy on a massive scale. Spain's already high tariff barriers were raised still further, as were restrictions on foreign investment. Movement of persons both in and out of the country was strictly controlled. Wages, and some prices, were set by official decree; rationing was introduced. Business activity, in particular the establishment of new firms, was subject to a mass of regulations. And the promotion of new industry became chiefly a matter for government, the concern of another Falange stronghold, set up in 1941: the National Industry Agency (*Instituto Nacional de Industria*). Coming on top of all the damage wrought by the Civil War, the effects were disastrous.

Production failed to reach pre-war levels, themselves low by European standards. Rampant black-marketeering (*estraperlo*) brought quick riches to a few while millions scraped a bare existence. Deaths from starvation and malnutrition were commonplace, so that the early 1940s became known as the 'hungry years' (*años de hambre*). Conditions in the cities were so hard that Spain experienced a phenomenon unparalleled in modern Europe: a return to the land. This was further encouraged by a National Land Settlement Agency (*Instituto Nacional de Colonización*), in a desperate attempt to increase food production by re-cultivating marginal areas.

This was a plan more typical of the Third World, in which the UN officially classified Spain towards the decade's end. In any event, it failed to solve the country's grave problems; for several years a genuine famine was kept at bay only by shipments of wheat from Argentina, sent on favourable financial terms. The need for such charity laid bare the abject failure of autarky. But its origin was equally revealing. For, since the defeat of fascism, Peron's Argentina was one of very few countries favourably disposed to Spain. Most of the world seemed happy to see his regime starved into submission (p102). The New State, with its strongly fascist overtones, had become a millstone round Franco's neck.

Politics without parties

Franco began to downplay the fascist side of his regime as soon as it became clear that the western democracies were going to prevail in the World War. At the same time, he had begun to introduce elements of what he called democracy. It was a cosmetic exercise. Certainly politics existed, in the sense of a struggle for influence, but it continued to be played out, as before, between groups with no democratic basis. The only changes that took place involved the balance of power between them.

Franco distanced himself from fascism in a variety of ways after 1942, and more rapidly after 1945. Thus, the raised-arm salute was dropped, as was the name 'New State'. The Falange representation in government was cut, and its presence in public life generally reduced (p97). Its social measures, too, were watered down. In Labour Tribunals (p97) the dice were loaded increasingly in the employers' favour. And although land settlement measures (p98) included a system of fixed rents, it was large landowners who gained most from the project as a whole. Other aspects of the Falange's social programme were simply abandoned, to the disgust of the party old guard (*camisas viejas*).

The regime's first concession to the forms of democracy also came in 1942, when Franco issued a 'Creation of Parliament Act' re-instituting the Spanish Parliament (*Cortes*). However, as the Act's title implied, the new, single chamber assembly bore little relation to previous bodies, or the principles on which they had been based. The new Parliament was partly appointed by Franco himself, and partly indirectly elected by institutions under the regime's control, such as the trade unions and local authorities. Up to a half of the representatives (*procuradores*) were government-employed civil servants. In any case, they were given only advisory powers; their real function was to play the part of Franco's rubber stamp, and they performed it faithfully.

Then, in 1945, Franco unveiled his Spaniards' Charter (*Fuero de los Españoles*). In it he disavowed his own previous description of his regime as 'totalitarian'; instead he used a new term, **'organic democracy'**. But the reference to democracy was misleading. The Charter did nothing to prevent continuing discrimination against, and repression of former Republican supporters (p96), and it consolidated censorship and denial of basic rights; Spaniards had the 'right' to express their views, provided they were in agreement with those of the regime! In particular, the ban on political parties was confirmed.

Yet although overt political activity was banned, jockeying for power and influence continued behind the scenes. Indeed, Franco subtly encouraged it, as it allowed him to play interests off against each other and thereby protect his own authority. Never formally organised, these interests nonetheless formed loose groupings that, at least initially, corresponded to the various elements that had supported the 1936 rising. Their existence, though officially unmentionable, was an open

---

democracia orgánica

'organic' democracy

Adopted by the Franco regime in 1945 as a description of its philosophy, 'organic' democracy – as opposed to the 'inorganic', liberal variety – was based on the theory that individuals' interests were best represented, indirectly and collectively, through bodies that were well-established in society. Such natural 'organs' included the **government-controlled trade unions** (p97), professional associations, the Church and, latterly, the family (represented by its male 'head'), but not political parties. The notion bore some resemblance to the ideas of the Austrian Right in the 1930s (p72); as then, it was a cover for dictatorship.

> ### *familias*
> ─────────────────────────────
> ### clans
> ─────────────────────────────
> Lacking in any official status or
> formal organisation, the Franco
> regime's clans were loose
> groupings among its supporters
> who shared broadly the same
> aims or interests, and who
> competed for influence within and
> over it. The main ones are usually
> considered to be: the military; the
> **Falange** (p82); the Church and its
> satellite organisations; the
> **monarchists** (p74); the
> **Traditionalists** (p82); and, latterly,
> the civil service (p104).
> See also: ***tecnócratas*** (p110)

secret, and they were commonly known as the regime's '**clans**'.

In many ways the most crucial clan was the military, including not just the three main forces but also the paramilitary Civil Guard and armed police; as before, Army officers were the key group. Indeed, the end of World War II further strengthened the military's already considerable importance (p102), bringing as it did the prospect of international action against a regime that had made no secret of its backing for the Axis. In the event, however, the only attempted invasion was a small affair by Spanish Communist volunteers, which was soon crushed. Thereafter the military's security role reverted to the suppression of occasional strikes and, at a later stage, student demonstrations.

Politically and socially, the military retained a strong influence (p96). Franco's cabinets always contained a military presence, and not merely in the ministries responsible for the forces – when he eventually relinquished the post of prime minister it was to an Admiral (p117). But in some ways the forces fared surprisingly ill; like military spending in general, officers' salaries were kept low, because their loyalty did not need to be bought. Shut off from civilian society in special living quarters and by habitual intermarriage, fed on a constant diet of regime propaganda, the officers corps and their families remained stuck in the 1930s, convinced that only Franco stood between Spain and disaster. In clan politics they only took the initiative in order to block the proposals of others.

Despite its downgrading by Franco, the Falange remained a player in the game. Falangist ministers continued to serve in government, notably José Antonio Girón de Velasco, who as Labour Minister long controlled the powerful unions (p97), and José Luis Arrese, responsible for the introduction of subsidised housing (*viviendas de protección oficial*). Its supporters also kept a strong presence in the media. Yet after 1945 the old-style, fascist-inspired Falange never enjoyed the same influence as before. Instead, it was supplanted by groups connected with traditional Spanish institutions, popular respect for which could help to bolster Franco's authority, as an association with international fascism had before.

Thus Franco's interest in a possible restoration of the monarchy strengthened the position of its many supporters among senior Army officers, large landowners and financiers. Some of these monarchists (p74) were Traditionalists (p82), but most backed the claim of ex-King Alfonso. With his death in 1941, their attention – and Franco's – focused on his exiled son, don Juan de Borbón. However, Don Juan had his own mildly liberal agenda, and was also aware of his potential symbolic value to the dictator, both domestically and internationally. His advisers had already had talks with exiled

Republicans (p102), and in 1945 he offered to assume the throne in agreement with Franco, but only as a constitutional monarch.

For the dictator, and for most influential monarchists, that was too high a price to pay for restoration; Franco's unconstitutional regime had brought them too many benefits. Moreover, as the danger of outside action against the regime receded (p102), so did Don Juan's worth as a proof of its non-fascist nature. In 1947 Franco felt confident enough to pass an Act of Succession ruling out any compromise with Don Juan. While it declared Spain to be a kingdom (*reino*), it also made Franco himself Regent for Life, effectively suspending the monarchy until his death. Moreover, it empowered him to nominate who should then ascend the throne, subordinating the principle of heredity to Franco's own authority. The Act stated that the dictator was responsible only 'to himself and to God'.

Realising that his bluff had been called, Don Juan decided on an accommodation with Franco. In 1948 he agreed that his son, Juan Carlos (p117), should be educated under the dictator's supervision. In return, the monarchists' leading paper, *Abc*, was allowed to reappear, giving them privileged if limited access to public opinion. Moreover, just as before 1947, governments contained a good proportion of ministers who sympathised with their ambitions. But they had lost their chance to exert real leverage over Franco, and their influence was increasingly usurped by representatives of an even more venerable and conservative institution.

Franco's alliance with the Church had already been immensely helpful to him during the Civil War (pp90–1), and had remained strong since. For all the fascist-style rhetoric of the New State era, the restored Church influence already apparent in the Nationalist zone had been extended and intensified. All school education was placed under its control, which for the first time reached to the universities. Social mores were governed by strict traditional principles. In 1945 a further aspect became apparent; the political role of Catholic lay organisations.

In a government reshuffle that year, the key post of Foreign Secretary went to Alberto Martín Artajo, a prominent member of the National Catholic Propaganda Association (*Asociación Católica Nacional de Propagandistas*), whose explicit purpose was to extend Church influence into the political sphere. Over the next decade the ACNP achieved considerable success, with several more leading figures becoming ministers. A second important agent of Catholic influence was the pressure group 'Catholic Action', which in 1946 set up a section to work among industrial workers, the Workers' Brotherhood (*Hermandades Obreras de Acción Católica*).

By the 1950s, the Church was clearly the most powerful influence on the regime, and the favoured term to describe its philosophy was now Catholic Nationalism (*Nacionalcatolicismo*). Ultimately however, both the Church and its satellite organisations, like the other clans, were subordinate to the authority Franco had demonstrated in 1942. At that time, after scuffles between their followers, he summarily dismissed the head of the Falange, Ramón Serrano Suñer (p90), and downgraded the Traditionalist leader General Varela. When, 14 years later, he decided on a similar 'judgement of Solomon', the fact that Education Minister Ruiz Giménez was an ACNP member did not save him from the sack along with Suñer's successor.

Nevertheless, the Church's privileged position was underlined in 1953, when a Concordat was signed between Spain and the Vatican to replace that of 1851 (p14). The agreement gave Franco the right to nominate all Spanish bishops, and implicitly guaranteed that his regime – and its leader – would continue to be bathed in an aura of religiosity. Yet on balance the new agreement was extraordinarily favourable to the Church. Spain was declared a confessional state, guided by Catholic precepts; no other religion could be practised in public; and Canon, or Church Law was integrated into the state's Civil Code. These concessions were not just a mark of Franco's religiosity, or the price of Church backing for his regime within Spain. They also reflected his continuing need for the stamp of the outside approval that 'organic' democracy had so far failed to bring.

The price of international acceptance

For some time after 1945 the Franco regime's survival was far from assured. While domestic opposition was negligible and the western Allies held back from intervention, the international isolation they imposed threatened the regime with collapse. But slowly the economic situation improved, and in the 1950s isolation was eased by the new circumstances of the Cold War. That assisted the regime to consolidate. But it also meant that Franco's options were greatly constrained, as he soon discovered.

Among Franco's opponents, the defeat of his former Axis backers in the World War raised hopes of support from the victorious allies to overthrow him. The Communist Party was sufficiently encouraged to mount an attempted invasion across the Pyrenees in 1945. It was easily defeated, however. Thereafter internal opposition virtually disappeared, crushed by repression, propaganda, and the parlous living conditions of most Spaniards (p98). Occasional – illegal – strikes occurred, as in 1947, but they were an expression of economic desperation, not political resistance.

Nor did the former Republican leaders who had fled Spain prove any more of a threat, since their chronic divisions had been aggravated by the bitterness of defeat. Because of resentment over Communist behaviour during the Civil War (p87), the government-in-exile set up under José Giral (p84) excluded the group which, despite the setback in 1945, remained best placed to organise underground resistance. It was further divided by the attempts of its leading figure, Indalecio Prieto (pp74–5), to negotiate with the right-wing leader, José María Gil-Robles (p71), now an adviser to monarchist pretender Don Juan. When he then reached an accommodation with Franco in 1948 (p101), the exiles were left in complete disarray.

By then, too, it was clear that the victorious western powers had no intention of overthrowing Franco by force. However, they did seem prepared to impose their will on him by another means; isolation. In 1946 the French closed the Pyrenean frontier, and later the same year Spain was refused admission to the newly-formed United Nations on the grounds of its tacit support for Nazi Germany. Almost all countries then followed a UN injunction to withdraw their ambassadors from Madrid, the sole exceptions being Argentina, Portugal, Switzerland and the Vatican. Another sanction that had real material effects was Spain's exclusion from the Marshall Plan, in 1947.

Even these measures failed to shake Franco; in some ways they actually helped him. For isolation gave real force to his regime's propaganda about an international conspiracy against it, just as the 1945 invasion had been grist to the mill of its anti-communism. Isolation also allowed Franco to justify, even glorify, his strategy of economic self-sufficiency, which had brought Spain to the verge of starvation. That very real threat slowly receded, thanks to continuing Argentinian food aid (p98), until eventually, with the help of a bumper harvest in 1951, it was dispelled altogether. Even so, a wave of strikes that same year was a reminder that the country's appalling economic state continued to threaten the regime's stability.

These various pressures explain the yearning for international acceptance, towards which the 1953 Concordat with the Vatican (p102) was a small but vital step. Later the same year came a much more important one, the background to which was the outbreak of the Cold War and the development of new weaponry. Long-range strikes against the Soviet bloc were now technically possible, and Spain constituted an excellent potential base for them which the US was determined to secure. Ignoring the continuing reservations of their European allies, the Americans began attempts to woo Franco. When he rejected their offer of cheap loans, they raised the stakes by offering a full-blown treaty.

Formal recognition by the world's most powerful country was too great a prize to sacrifice on the altar of self-sufficiency. In 1953 Franco signed the series of accords known as the **Defence Agreements**. Although their direct material benefits proved disappointing, that was more than compensated by the acquisition of such a powerful friend. In 1955 the advantages of the agreement were illustrated when Spain was admitted to the UN. The regime ascribed this success to the skills of its Foreign Minister, Martín Artajo (p101), though in reality the decisive factor in ensuring that the objections of a decade earlier were now overlooked was US pressure. And without the backing of the world's leading economic power, there was no question of an effective trade embargo against the regime.

Having swallowed his national pride, Franco now accepted the financial support he had previously scorned. This provided the Spanish economy with a significant boost, as did the general upswing in the world economy during the early 1950s, especially after the regime relaxed its trade restrictions slightly towards the middle of the decade. Coupled with the policy of state-promoted industrialisation (p98) – and the fact that its starting point was so low – these external factors enabled the country to enjoy a sudden burst of growth. For some years production rose at around six per cent annually, so that pre-war

> ### *Acuerdos para la Defensa*
> #### Defence Agreements (of 1953)
>
> Signed in 1953 between the Spanish and US governments, the Defence Agreements, or 'Pact of Madrid', permitted the Americans to set up and operate four military bases on Spanish soil. They were renewed on a five-yearly basis up to 1978, after which the issue was caught up in the furore surrounding Spain's entry to NATO (p141). After lengthy negotiations a further, partial renewal was agreed in 1988, under which the US retained only the naval base at Rota, near Cadiz.

levels were finally surpassed. Living standards rose appreciably, especially for a small but growing middle class.

Insofar as public satisfaction was increased, growth had a stabilising effect. But it also had other, less positive outcomes. Reversal of the drift back to the land (p98) revealed the grave lack of adequate urban housing; many poorer Spaniards were condemned to live in shanty-towns (*chabolismo*) which became a breeding-ground for discontent. Prices rose sharply, to the discomfort of workers whose wages continued to be controlled by law. Among the better-off young, prosperity awakened the desire for greater personal freedom. When the Education Minister, Ruiz Giménez, was prompted to partly relax conditions in the universities in 1956, the result was an outbreak of student unrest that cost him his job (p101).

That same year also saw the largest strike wave yet, though this time it did not elicit the usual response. Employers whose businesses were at last getting off the ground were reluctant to have them disrupted, and had the funds to meet wage demands. They found an ally in Labour Minister Girón (p100), who saw a chance to re-assert the Falange's credentials as defender of worker interests (pp97–8). In some industries the government was persuaded to concede wage rises of up to 30 per cent. This policy pacified the strikers, certainly, but for the economy as a whole the effects were disastrous.

Inflation was pushed still higher, increasing the already dangerous disparities between different sectors of the economy, and further reducing the competitiveness of Spanish goods on world markets. This was especially serious given that, as the economy took off, Spanish manufacturers had begun to demand more sophisticated plant and machinery. Yet it was precisely these capital goods that the country could not produce. The result was a soaring import bill and a widening trade gap, which Spain's exports of agricultural produce and low-grade manufactures were quite incapable of closing.

The rapidly worsening situation alarmed the country's new trading partners, of which the USA was now the most important. Worried that Spain might be unable to pay its debts, the Americans brought their influence to bear on the International Monetary Fund and the Organisation for European Economic Co-operation. The two agencies agreed to provide further substantial loans, but only in return for changes in economic policy. Spain was required to abolish the system of multiple exchange rates it had used to restrict imports, in contravention of international trade guidelines. And Franco had to take another gulp of nationalist pride, and devalue the peseta.

Franco's reaction to these developments came in 1958, in legislation ostensibly concerned with the single party which had long been a bulwark of his power (p90). Its function had changed considerably since the 1940s, when repression and propaganda were primary tasks of his governments. Now, however, their overriding concern was to run the apparatus of a modern state. In the absence of democratic politics that gave enormous influence to civil servants, who had emerged as a new 'clan' within the regime (p100) and the strongest influence within the party. Moreover, its title evoked unfortunate memories of fascism. That was now changed officially to the '**National Movement**', and all former versions (p90) were banned.

However, that was the only concession to change made by the 'Principles of the National Movement Act'. In general, it restated the regime's underlying tenets in fundamentalist terms. Admittedly, it defined Spain not just as a 'traditional, Catholic monarchy', but also as a 'social and representative' one. Yet the basis for doing so was still the organic brand of democracy dreamed up by Franco in the 1940s (p99). All legislation was required to conform to the 'spirit' of the Movement, whose National Council was given the task of checking that it did so. And the Movement itself was defined as the 'communion of Spaniards united by belief in the ideals which gave life to the Crusade' – in other words, as one side in the Civil War to which the very name harked back.

In effect, Franco was saying that, as far as he was concerned, nothing had changed. But it had. The partial integration into the world community which had helped the regime to consolidate also meant it was no longer master of its own fate. Indeed, the regime had already tacitly acknowledged this fact: in 1956, by quietly surrendering the Moroccan protectorate that was Spain's last claim to 'greatness', in the imperial sense dear to Franco (p58); and, a year later, in changing its economic tack at America's behest. When the mild changes introduced at that time failed to produce the desired effect, Spain came under renewed US pressure. Eisenhower's Madrid visit of 1959 was lauded by the regime as a signal of acceptance into the US-dominated western economic order. It failed to see that the celebrated embrace with which the American president greeted his fellow general could equally be interpreted as a bear-hug.

Movimiento Nacional

National Movement

First used as a self-description by the insurgent side in the Civil War (p83), 'National Movement' was adopted in 1958 by the **Franco regime** (p96) as the official designation of the sole political organisation permitted under its rule, replacing the original name *Falange Española Tradicionalista y de las Juntas de Ofensiva Nacional Sindicalista* (p90). All government employees, including military officers, were required to be members. It was assured representation in government – its secretary-general was automatically a minister – and in Parliament, of which its own National Council functioned as an unofficial upper house. The Movement controlled important sectors of Spanish life, in particular the media and the **trade unions** (p97), in both of which old-style **Falangists** (p82) retained some influence. As a whole, however, it was dominated by bureaucrats, many of the **technocrat** type (p110). It was officially dissolved on 1 April 1977.

Exhibit 7.1: 'The Principles of the National Movement Act' (1958)

The second last of Franco's 'Basic Laws' (final article omitted)

Yo Franciso Franco Bahamonde, Caudillo de España,

Consciente de mi responsabilidad ante Díos y ante la Historia, en presencia de las Cortes del Reino, promulgo como Principios del movimiento Nacional, entendido como comunión de los españoles en los ideales que dieron vida a la Cruzada, los siguientes:

I

España es una unidad de destino en lo universal. El servicio a la unidad, grandeza y libertad de la Patria es deber sagrado y tarea colectiva de todos los españoles.

II

La Nación española considera como timbre de honor el acatamiento a la Ley de Díos, según la doctrina de la Santa Iglesia Católica, Apostólica y Romana, única verdadera y fe inseperable de la conciencia nacional, que inspirará su legislación.

III

España, raíz de una gran familia de pueblos, con los que se siente indisolublemente hermanada, aspira a la instauración de la justicia y de la paz entre las naciones.

IV

La unidad entre los hombres y las tierras de España es intangible. La integridad de la Patria y su independencia son exigencias supremas de la comunidad nacional. Los Ejércitos de España, garantía de su seguridad y expresión de las virtudes heroicas de nuestro pueblo, deberán poseer la fortaleza necesaria para el mejor servicio de la Patria.

V

La comunidad nacional se funda en el hombre, como portador de valores eternos, y en la familia, como base de la vida social; pero los intereses individuales y colectivos han de estar subordinados siempre al bien común de la Nación, constituida por las generaciones pasadas, presentes y futuras. La Ley ampara por igual al derecho de todos los españoles.

VI

Las entidades naturales de la vida social: familia, municipio y sindicato, son estructuras básicas de la comunidad nacional. Las instituciones y corporaciones de otro carácter que satisfagan exigencias sociales de interés general deberán ser amparadas para que puedan participar eficazmente en el perfeccionamiento de los fines de la comunidad nacional.

continued

VII

El pueblo español, unido en un orden de Derecho, informado por los postulados de autoridad, libertad y servicio, constituye el Estado Nacional. Su forma política es, dentro de los principios inmutables del Movimiento Nacional y de cuanto determinan la Ley de Sucesión y demás Leyes Fundamentales, la Monarquía tradicional, católica, social y representativa.

VIII

El carácter representativo del orden político es principio básico de nuestras instituciones públicas. La participación del pueblo en las tareas legislativas y en las demás funciones de interés general se llevará a cabo a través de la familia, el municipio, el sindicato y demás entidades con representación orgánica que a este fin reconozcan las leyes. Toda organización política de cualquier índole, al margen de este sistema representativo, será considerada ilegal.

Todos los españoles tendrán acceso a los cargos y funciones públicas según su mérito y capacidad.

IX

Todos los españoles tienen derecho: a una justicia independiente, que será gratuita para aquellos que carezcan de medios económicos; a una educación general y profesional, que nunca podrá dejar de recibirse por falta de medios materiales; a los beneficios de la asistencia y seguridad sociales, y a una equitativa distribución de la renta nacional y de las carga fiscales. El ideal cristiano de la justicia social, reflejado en el Fuero de Trabajo, inspirará la política y las leyes.

X

Se reconoce al trabajo como origen de jerarquía, deber y honor de los españoles, y a la propiedad privada, en todas sus formas, como derecho condicionado a su función social. La iniciativa privada, fundamento de la actividad económica, deberá ser estimulada, encauzada, y, en su caso, suplida por la acción del Estado

XI

La Empresa, asociación de hombres y medios ordenados a la producción, constituye una comunidad de intereses y una unidad de propósitos. Las relaciones entre los elementos de aquélla deben basarse en la justicia y en la recíproca lealtad, y los valores económicos estarán subordinados a los de orden humano y social. [. . .]

Topics

■ To which institutions does Exhibit 7.1 refer, explicitly and implicitly? What roles are they assigned by the Act?

■ What attitudes does the Act reflect towards
(a) liberal democracy,
(b) capitalism, and
(c) regionalism?

■ What evidence is there of a desire to improve relations with the outside world?

■ What similarities and differences does the Act suggest between Franco's ideas and those of earlier representatives of the Spanish Right (cf. Exhibits 2.2, 3.1, 4.1, 5.2, 6.2)?

■ How new was the 'New State', in Spanish terms? Which aspects of it were retained after the designation itself was dropped in the later 1940s?

■ What significant changes occurred in Spain, and in the Franco regime itself, between 1939 and 1959?

CHAPTER 8

The bottle half-uncorked (1959–1975)

The 1960s represented a period of economic growth. It was underpinned by the network of trans-Atlantic institutions set up in the 1940s and extended in 1961 by the creation of the Organisation for Economic Cooperation and Development (OECD). In western Europe a further support was the European Community, as the EEC became in 1967; six years later it acquired three new members, including Britain. The decade also saw a trend in favour of social and personal freedom which, with the liberalising decisions of the Second Vatican Council, even affected the Catholic Church. In 1968 the pressure for change boiled over in widespread protests, especially among the young, who were heavily influenced by new interpretations of Marxist ideas. Change was also reflected in a so-called eurocommunism that rejected the authority of the Soviet Union. The uncertainty caused by these events was heightened by others. In 1971 the western system of fixed exchange rates collapsed; in 1973 came the first 'oil shock', a massive price increase imposed by the producer countries. And in 1974 came a different kind of shock, when the Portuguese dictatorship was toppled by army officers close to the country's Communist Party, the only one in southern Europe not to have gone 'eurocommunist'.

At the end of the 1950s the Franco regime was faced with a choice. It could bow to American pressure for radical changes in its economic policies, or it could risk a return to the conditions of the early 1950s. Not even Franco was prepared to contemplate that. Instead, he entrusted his regime's fate to a group of its supporters who felt that the changes were actually in its interest. And, to a degree, events proved them right. The spectacular economic development brought by the new policies did indeed increase Spaniards' material satisfaction. But it also triggered changes that fomented opposition among certain groups, and a more general, if muted dissatisfaction, which some within the regime sought to counter by relaxing its authoritarian nature. As their leader neared his end, he made clear his intention that they should not succeed.

Uneven development

For some of its supporters, the grave situation faced by the Franco regime in the late 1950s was not a crisis but an opportunity. They believed that economic change could and should be managed, in order to equip the regime for survival in the contemporary world. Their ideas formed the basis of Spain's astonishing economic development in the 1960s. However, that success also triggered off substantial social changes which were barely compatible with the regime's snail-paced political evolution.

The domestic impetus behind the new course originated within the civil service elite, which by now had become very influential (p104). Some of these **technocrats** were members of, or associated with the **Opus Dei** organisation, which believed that the survival of a conservative, Catholic regime could only be assured by satisfying the popular desire for better living standards, the form of legitimation (p96) usual in modern capitalist societies. The necessary economic growth, they believed, was best achieved by allowing market forces free rein through the ending of government intervention in the economy (p98). By contrast, they favoured continued strong control over society, to prevent it going along the liberal, secular road it had taken elsewhere in the West.

The technocrats' influence dated from 1957, when some of the group's leading figures were brought into government to oversee changes in economic policy. When the inadequacy of those changes gave rise to US pressure for more (p105), they were able to persuade Franco to give them a virtually free hand over economic strategy. The U-turn is now usually associated with 1959, the year in which most of the measures making up the 'Stabilisation Plan' were enacted. The Plan is often seen as being essentially an exercise in cutting intervention and red tape. But, though some deregulation did occur, it was neither new – most price controls were abolished in 1956 – nor by any means complete. As a result, when Franco died, by modern western standards his government was still playing a large economic role.

tecnócratas

technocrats

Perhaps better described as 'professional experts', the technocrats were the highly-trained specialists, mainly in economics and finance, who acquired decisive influence in the late 1950s. Many were under the influence of the **Opus Dei**, including Mariano Navarro Rubio, appointed Finance Minister in 1957, and Alberto Ullastres, who took over the Trade portfolio at the same time. Other leading technocrats were Gregorio López Bravo, Minister for Industry and subsequently Foreign Minister, and Laureano López Rodó, another Opus member, who co-ordinated the 1959 measures known as the 'Stabilisation Plan' and the various subsequent Development Plans.

In the event, two other aspects of the technocrats' strategy proved to be more crucial. One was a standard package of deflationary measures (*medidas de ajuste*), introduced in agreement with the OECD and International Monetary Fund, to which Spain was admitted in 1960. Wages were frozen and public spending reduced. The result was a sharp slowdown in the economy, with severe effects on employment and earnings. But the package achieved its aims of bringing down inflation, eliminating many uncompetitive firms and forcing the survivors to become more efficient.

The final plank in the technocrats' strategy was the one most resisted by Franco, since it involved finally abandoning any idea of autarky (p98). The opening-up (*apertura*) of Spain's economy that followed had two key aspects. On the one hand, controls on inward investment were relaxed. Foreign capital was now permitted to acquire a controlling stake in companies in all but the most politically sensitive industries, such as defence. On the other hand, restrictions on the movement of persons were eased. Tourism, previously grudgingly accepted, was promoted, while Spaniards were allowed, even encouraged, to seek work outside the country.

The effects were dramatic. Investment poured into the country, attracted by low production costs and the helpful industrial relations framework – in plain English, the absence of normal trade union freedoms. Spain launched, at last, a full-blooded process of industrialisation which now affected not only Catalonia and the Basque Country, but also Madrid and its rapidly growing satellite towns, as well as a number of other regional centres, notably Valladolid. At the same time tourism took off, so that within a few years Spain became the world's leading provider of beach holidays. The result of these twin stimuli was the period of very rapid growth which brought the word 'boom' into the Spanish language, and marked the beginning of what became known as the 'development years' (*años de desarrollo*).

> ### *Opus Dei*
> #### Opus Dei
> Founded in 1928 by the Aragonese priest José María Escrivá de Balaguer, Opus Dei (Latin: 'God's Work') is a lay organisation dedicated to preserving conservative Catholic principles in the face of economic modernisation. Under the Franco regime the Opus, as it is frequently known, acquired considerable power, its members and sympathisers filling many top ministerial and administrative posts from 1957 on. Although its political influence was dented by the 1969 Matesa scandal (p118) and, more severely, by Franco's death, the Opus continues to be strongly represented in business, finance and higher education; several leading figures in the **People's Party** (p152) are believed to be members. See also: *inmovilistas* (p119)

Nor was it just growth that was achieved. Soaring receipts from tourism, combined with the remittance payments (*remesas*) sent by emigrants to their families at home, were more than sufficient to make up for Spain's trade deficit, and so soothe the concerns of its trading partners (p104). Emigration also solved the problem of unemployment inherent in such massive structural change; in effect, it was simply exported. And remittances helped ensure that although wage-earners paid the vast bulk of taxes, the material benefits of growth were felt almost throughout society, at least in the rapidly expanding cities.

To a degree, rising prosperity had the effect envisaged by the technocrats. Television sets and cars might not necessarily turn workers into enthusiastic supporters of the regime, but they often meant that the resigned resentment of its early years transmuted into apathy. Such indifference was constantly fed by the official media, with its comparisons between 'Franco's peace' and the 'anarchy' that had allegedly preceded it. To those who, for the first time, had significant material possessions to lose, it could seem a powerful argument, especially if they were too young to have their own memories of how 'peace' had been achieved (p91).

But development also had other effects. The decline of agriculture, and the attraction of city jobs, led to depopulation of the countryside on a massive scale (*éxodo rural*). Even in Francoist Spain urban life brought a wider range of experience, especially for the young, many of whom were increasingly resentful of the constraints imposed by strict Catholic morality (p101). Not only that; tourism and emigration meant that more and more Spaniards were coming into contact with the outside world. They became aware that life in other western countries bore no resemblance to the regime's propaganda; instead it seemed to involve not only higher living standards but also greater personal freedom – and more fun.

These trends contributed to the growth of opposition in the 1960s (p113). It was kept in check by the repression directed by the hard-line General Alonso Vega as Interior Minister, which the technocrats – and Franco – regarded as the natural complement to their economic liberalisation. Harder to deal with, since it could not be crushed by the security forces, was the widespread discontent to be found at a lower level, representing a potential breeding ground of future protest. It was this threat which led some within the regime to propose a form of liberalisation that went beyond the economic sphere (*aperturismo*).

In most cases such liberalisers were also motivated by dislike of the technocrats. Thus one proposal came from José Solís Ruiz, Secretary-General of the National Movement (p105). An old-style Falangist (p82) deeply distrustful of the new course, liberalisation for him meant making the government-run unions attractive to workers in the face of competition from illegal alternatives (p114). To do so he proposed the free election of union representatives, and even a limited right to strike. His ideas were blocked, but some leading civil servants opposed to the technocrats were more successful. Their principal representative was the Minister of Information, Manuel Fraga Iribarne, author of the 1966 Press Act.

The Fraga Act, as it became known, brought big changes in the regime's control over the media, including the abolition of 'prior' censorship, i.e. the requirement for editors to get material approved in advance of publication. Instead they now had to judge for themselves what would, and would not, prove acceptable. For those who guessed wrongly, the Act retained harsh punishments, in the form of suspensions and fines. It was also insidious, imposing as it did a form of self-censorship. But its application by Fraga's Ministry was relaxed enough to allow a number of mildly critical journals to appear.

---

leyes básicas (del franquismo)

(Franco regime's) basic laws

In the absence of a constitution, the basic ground rules of government under the **Franco regime** (p96) were set out in legislation passed over a period of almost 30 years. The first of these basic laws were decrees issued in the Nationalist zone during the Civil War, in particular those by which Franco was installed as Head of State and Government (p84), and the 1938 Labour Charter (p97). There followed the 1942 Creation of Parliament Act (p99), the Spaniards' Charter of 1945 (p99), and the 1947 Act of Succession (p101). The most important of the basic laws were the Principles of the National Movement Act, passed in 1958 (p105), and the 1967 'Organic Law of the State'.

For the first time in 30 years a form of public debate was possible. However, it confined itself to economics; political criticism was still strictly taboo.

Some political relaxation was also apparent in the last of the regime's **basic laws** promulgated in 1967. As well as a degree of religious freedom – for the first time since 1939 faiths other than Catholicism could be practised publicly – this 'Organic Law of the State' (LOE) also provided for parliamentary elections. In fact, though, they were as big a sham as earlier aspects of 'organic' democracy (p99). The electorate was restricted to – male – heads of households; the elected representatives remained a small minority in Parliament, most of which continued to be appointed; and the elections were subject to strict control by the authorities, to ensure that only approved candidates were successful.

The LOE was thus proof of how Spain's political evolution continued to lag far behind its economic development. That had not gone unnoticed by her neighbours who, less compliant than their American allies (p103), had rejected her application to join the European Economic Community in 1962 – specifically on the grounds that she was not a democracy. The decision was a severe blow to the technocrats, who knew that continuing growth could only be assured by access to wider European markets. The gap between political and economic development also had the more immediate drawback of stimulating opposition of various sorts within Spain itself.

The emergence of opposition

Overt opposition to the regime had never been completely eliminated; indeed, the 1950s had seen several waves of strikes. But it was only in the next decade that unrest among industrial workers became persistent and widespread. The 1960s also saw an upsurge of opposition from regionalists and, ironically, from the institution which had been the regime's chief support: the Church. Although it rarely turned to anything stronger, by the end of the decade wide sections of Franco's core support were feeling discontent.

As a reaction to earlier industrial unrest, in 1958 the regime decided to allow a degree of collective bargaining over pay, on the condition that the negotiations would take place under the wing of its own trade unions (p97). In doing so it unwittingly gave a spur to a process that was already under way; infiltration of the unions by organisations set up by workers themselves in defiance of the regime. At first these **Workers' Commissions** operated locally, but in the 1960s they established a nation-wide network, which greatly increased their capacity for effective action.

At the same time, economic growth was changing the status of workers and their own expectations. Skill shortages in key industries greatly increased their bargaining power. Successful businesses, especially those engaged in export, wanted quick solutions to labour problems, and therefore preferred to deal with representatives who could deliver their members' agreement – which increasingly meant the Commissions. Moreover, rising wages meant that many workers now had a small financial cushion, and so were readier to undertake strike action if their demands were not met. All these factors strengthened both the workers' militancy and the Commissions themselves.

Comisiones Obreras (CCOO)

Workers' Commissions

The Workers' Commissions were illegal associations of workers, created to give employees an alternative form of representation to the Franco regime's own **tightly-controlled unions** (p97). The first was set up in 1957. Initially created by separate local initiatives, the Commissions soon came together to form a nationwide underground organisation. Their founders were inspired by widely varying political views; including liberal Catholic ideas (p116), but in the 1960s the Commissions fell under the influence of the **Communist Party** (p86). In the late 1970s they grew dramatically to become Spain's largest labour organisation. Although their appeal was later constrained by their militancy and their Communist ties, they nonetheless remained strong.

By the mid-1950s the Commissions were effectively under the control of the Communist Party, whose ideas were well-suited to underground operation – and whose objective was to bring down the regime. This contributed to a change in the nature of industrial action, which increasingly focused on political issues. The regime itself also helped the process along, since strikes were routinely suppressed by the security forces, often brutally, and frequently turned into battles of attrition. This violence bred resentment, and from there it was only a step to political protest. By the time Franco realised the danger and attempted to crack down on the Commissions (p118) they were far too well established, and could no longer be rooted out of his own union apparatus.

Neither of the two main strands of the pre-Civil War workers' movement took any significant part in these developments. The anarcho-syndicalists (p48) had been virtually eliminated by repression in the regime's early years. But the Socialists' abstention from infiltrating the official unions was a deliberate choice, prompted by fears that they would be accused of collaborating as they had done under the earlier Primo dictatorship (p59). Ironically, industrial strife reached its highest levels in the Basque Country, a traditional Socialist stronghold. But that was due to other developments since Franco came to power.

Despite Franco's clampdown on regionalism (p96), at first the Basque regionalist movement had not attempted to oppose his regime. It shared some of his conservative ideas (p45), and its supporters often benefited economically from his rule. Moreover, his attempts to stamp out the Basque language meant little in the urban areas, where it had long disappeared. And regionalism's core, the banned Basque Nationalist Party, showed little appetite for organising resistance.

The situation was changed irrevocably by the economic growth which began in the 1950s, and accelerated in the next decade (p111). It brought a second wave of industrialisation to the region, which penetrated beyond the Bilbao area into the countryside of Guipuzcoa. There it caused enormous social upheaval in the tightly-knit rural communities that were the last major stronghold of the Basque language, whose future now looked bleak indeed. They now became the main recruiting ground for **ETA** – a new and very different regionalist organisation.

One of ETA's aims was to protect the language, which was achieved effectively by the establishment of clandestine Basque-language schools (*ikastolak*). But its fundamental desire was to strike back at the regime, which led it to get involved in industrial action and – a new departure for Basque regionalists – to establish close links with Spanish workers' organisations of the Left. The conjunction of appeals to national and class solidarity proved a potent mixture, and led to repeated waves of strikes in the region. In response, the regime imposed states of siege and exception, during which indiscriminate brutality by the security forces was the order of the day.

The government's reaction backfired completely, merely serving to bear out ETA's contention that the Basque Country was 'occupied' by a hostile Spanish state. This sense of national conflict was intensified after ETA turned to violence in 1968. From then on its attacks on the security forces, and their persistent over-reaction, fostered the notion of a 'war' in which ETA acted as the Basque 'army'. Moreover, its links with the Left meant that national sentiment was not only deepened but also extended to new sections of Basque society. By the end of the decade it had become the standard-bearer of a radicalised and immeasurably strengthened movement.

The situation in Catalonia was less dramatic, but no less serious for the regime. The business community (p43), the historical core of regionalism, was alienated by Franco's removal of self-government, by his simplistic economic policies (p98) and by the isolation from Europe to which his political ones led (p113). Moreover, much of the middle-class deeply resented his attempt to stamp out the Catalan culture, to which they felt strong ties.

Culture certainly formed the initial focus of early underground activities in the region, but, as in other cases, the severity with which the regime cracked down on them broadened the scope of protest. A group led by Jordi Pujol (p149) began the work of 'nation-building' (*fer país*), a long-term strategy of establishing contacts throughout Catalan society and building a consensus on its future once the regime eventually came to an end. By the end of the 1960s virtually all opinion in Catalonia was agreed, not just that democracy had to come, but that it must bring devolution with it.

In both the Basque Country and Catalonia, as in the past, these regionalist protests

---

Euskadi ta Askatasuna (ETA)

Basque homeland and liberty

Formed in 1959 by younger members of the **PNV** (p45) to oppose the Franco regime's assault on Basque culture, ETA later adopted a vague form of 'revolutionary' socialism to go with its demand for Basque independence. In 1968 it turned to violence, which was directed initially against the security forces and others closely linked to the dictatorship. In 1974 it split into 'military' and 'politico-military' branches, the second of which disappeared in 1982 (p147). After Franco's death, and despite the granting of Basque autonomy, ETA refused to moderate its demands or abandon violence. It became a significant danger to stability, both in its own right and as the potential excuse for a coup (p133). In the early 1990s it had appeared to be on the verge of defeat, but was revived by revelations about a government-sponsored dirty war carried out against it in the 1980s (p151). See also: **Herri Batasuna** (p147); **caso GAL** (p151)

received backing from the local clergy. Altogether more surprising was the critical stance increasingly adopted by the Spanish Church in general towards the regime. When the Bishops criticised the 1959 Stabilisation Plan (p110) for paying too little attention to the weakest in society, they showed which way the wind was blowing. In the next decade it became a gale.

Part of the cause of the Bishop's intervention lay in the Second Vatican Council, which aligned the Church world-wide with demands for human rights and against authoritarian regimes. To Franco this line was as unacceptable as it was inexplicable; he refused to allow one of the Pope's pronouncements to be read in Spain – on the grounds that it was heretical. But despite his powers under the 1953 Concordat (p103), he was unable to prevent the Vatican filling senior positions in the Spanish Church with men whose rejection of his regime was more or less explicit.

Among the lower clergy such attitudes were already common. By the 1960s, references to the Civil War no longer cut much ice with younger Spanish clerics. They were more concerned with issues affecting their parishes in the present, such as the lack of basic freedoms and, in many areas still, abject poverty. Many became involved in more-or-less clandestine political and industrial activity, through the legal Catholic workers organisations, the HOAC (p101) and its offshoot, the Catholic Young Workers (*Juventudes Obreras Católicas*), or by joining the Workers' Commissions. The Vatican Council and its aftermath meant that these activities enjoyed the support of their superiors.

Meanwhile, lay Catholics led by the former Education Minister, Joaquín Ruiz Giménez (p104), had established an informal Christian Democrat grouping. Taking advantage of the relaxation of censorship in 1966 (p112) it brought out the journal *Cuadernos para el Diálogo*, which became an important arena for debate. Along with two other mildly critical groups – the monarchists led by José María Gil-Robles (p102), and the so-called Social Democrats set up by a former propaganda chief, Dionisio Ridruejo (p97) – it was tolerated by the regime. Together they termed themselves a 'democratic' opposition, to emphasise that they would have nothing to do with Communists.

These groups were often accused of being Franco's stooges, and they undoubtedly played into his hands in some ways. By sticking to the unspoken limits of their criticism, they allowed him to claim that his regime accommodated dissent. And they sometimes gave the regime's propaganda machine a soft target, as when in 1962 they met in Munich and publicly urged the EEC to reject Spain's application to join (p113). The official media had a field day condemning the treachery of what they dubbed the 'Munich conspiracy' (*Conturbernio de Munich*). But, at the same time, the 'legal' opposition's existence and criticisms, both widely known, helped to sustain a growing sense of dissatisfaction among what had once been the bedrock of the regime's support, the middle-classes.

Middle-class discontent took many forms. The most visible was student protest, which intensified after a number of dissident academics, including the popular Professor Enrique Tierno Galván, were dismissed in 1965 for criticising the regime; it got a further boost from the events of 1968. More generally, the better-off young were increasingly unhappy at being denied the personal freedoms enjoyed by their peers abroad. Not a few joined the PCE, usually because it was the only group organising serious underground opposition, rather than for any great belief in its ideas. Finally, exclusion from Europe in another sense – economic – led some business leaders to conclude that there must be political change of some sort. However, like the vast majority of the population, they had tacitly accepted that this was impossible while the dictator lived.

The regime's death throes

In 1970, as his regime entered its fifth decade, Franco was 78. Clearly his death could not be far away, and he had begun making arrangements for it, determined that it should not be a prelude to significant change. In response, his opponents also prepared for outright confrontation. That, in turn encouraged his hard-line supporters to dig in deeper. With the regime, quite literally, in its death throes, those who hoped for some form of gradual relaxation were left with little influence.

By the late 1960s Franco had long since ceased to determine the day-to-day operation of his regime. Indeed, his 'arms-length' approach to government, exemplified by lengthy shooting holidays with cronies, was common knowledge. But his ultimate authority, which continued to rest essentially on his personal standing (p96), remained uncontested. His forthcoming disappearance thus posed a two-fold threat to his regime, and Franco himself was well aware of the need to make preparations for a world without him (*posfranquismo*).

The planning began in earnest with the 1967 'Organic Law of the State' (p113), which established that the new King would be essentially a figurehead without real power, a Head of State but not of Government. Two years later, Franco at last formally settled the question of who would ascend the throne on his death (p101). In reality, his choice had been clear ever since his 1948 agreement with the legitimate heir Don Juan (p100), whose son had thereafter been carefully groomed by Franco as future King. Prince Juan Carlos, for his part, had given every indication that he knew what was expected of him, to the extent that he had become publicly estranged from his less compliant father. Nevertheless, Franco did not intend him to have any option.

It was for this reason that, also in 1969, the dictator appointed as deputy Prime Minister his trusted servant Admiral Luis Carrero Blanco, a die-hard conservative who had allied himself with the technocrats and their patron, the Opus Dei (p111). Carrero was clearly earmarked to succeed Franco as Head of Government, a position from which he would be able to exercise a tight control over the King. Admittedly, Juan Carlos would have powers of his own in some areas, such as military affairs or designation of the prime minister and other senior figures. But Franco made sure they were subject to ratification by bodies stuffed full of his own appointees: the Parliament (p99), the National Council of the Movement (p105) and, particularly, the Council of the Kingdom (*Consejo del Reino*), a committee whose powers were greatly extended in 1967. The dictator's confidence in these arrangements was reflected in his famous assurance that he had left everything 'all tied up' (*atado y bien atado*).

Franco's determination that his regime should continue unchanged (*continuismo*) was also evident in his reaction to an outbreak of bickering in its ranks, caused by various proposals for mild liberalisation (p112). They had been bitterly opposed by the regime's most conservative supporters. In 1969 a leading **liberaliser**, Manuel Fraga (p112), retaliated by leaking details of a business scandal, the so-called Matesa affair (*caso Matesa*), involving a number of prominent conservatives. As in the past, Franco used the opportunity to exert his authority (p101), sacking both Fraga and National Movement leader, José Solís Ruiz. But this time his judgement was also a clear blow to the liberalisers, among whom, at the time, Solís was counted (p112).

The new government marked a return to the strategy of 1959 (p110). Several leading technocrats (p111) were recalled or promoted, their task being to revive the economic growth whose slowdown had led to business dissatisfaction and an increase in industrial conflict. At the same time, Carrero Blanco – who, in practice now headed the cabinet – was joined by several other hard-liners, with the intention of cracking down on the emerging opposition. Specifically, efforts to stamp out the Workers' Commissions (p114) were intensified. The union's premises were raided and shut down, many activists arrested and a number, including its leader Marcelino Camacho, given long prison terms.

At the same time, a major anti-ETA offensive was launched, and numerous suspected activists arrested. In 1970 sixteen of them were tried by a military court in Burgos; five were sentenced to death. Franco's decision to commute their sentences to life imprisonment did little to still domestic and international outrage, caused as much by the nature of the proceedings as the verdicts. In particular they provided another target for Church criticism of the regime (p116), which had already become more outspoken with the Pope's appointment of Cardinal Enrique y Tarancón as Bishop of Toledo and head of the Spanish clergy.

But it was in the Basque Country itself that the results were most dramatic. Pro-ETA demonstrations multiplied, in which workers increasingly joined as, following a brief recovery in 1971/72, the economy faltered once again. The resultant clashes with the security forces only heightened public support for ETA, giving a major boost to its activities. Bank robberies, kidnappings and attacks on the security forces all increased. Most spectacularly, in December 1973 ETA struck a major blow to Franco's plans when it assassinated Carrero Blanco, who had finally been appointed prime minister just six months before, by blowing up his official car on a busy Madrid street.

By now Franco's health was deteriorating visibly, and his opponents in general had begun to make preparations for his demise.

aperturistas
....
liberalisers

Never formally organised, the liberalisers favoured making some concessions to genuine democracy without abandoning the basic authoritarian conservatism of the **Franco regime** (p96). Unlike the so-called democratic opposition (p116) they were members of, or close to the regime, and were to be found in several of its **clans** (p100); their ranks included public servants, **Falangists** (p82) and businessmen.

They were furthest advanced in Catalonia, where the high degree of consensus already achieved (p115) had made it possible to set up a clandestine Assembly, which included representatives of virtually all opinion in the region. Elsewhere, however, such cooperation proved impossible. The problem was the Communist PCE, which had by far the strongest underground organisation of any opposition group, but was distrusted by the others for its ambivalent role during the Civil War (p87).

In an attempt to overcome such reservations, the PCE's leader, Santiago Carrillo, announced his party's conversion to the Eurocommunist ideas pioneered by its Italian counterpart. The move was partly successful. In July 1974 the PCE established a Committee for Democracy (*Junta Democrática*), in which it was joined not only by the Workers' Commissions already under its influence (p114), but also by groups ranging from liberal monarchists to the People's Socialist Party (*Partido Socialista Popular*) set up by Professor Tierno Galván (p116).

However, Carrillo's gesture failed to overcome Socialist suspicions, even though control of the PSOE (p47) was wrested from its ageing leadership in 1974, at a party conference held in the French town of Suresnes. Its new leaders were keenly aware that Socialist organisation within Spain had been badly neglected (p114), and had no desire to be swallowed up by the better-placed PCE. In June 1975 they formed a 'Platform of Democratic Convergence' together with the Basque PNV, the 'legal' Christian Democrats led by Ruiz Giménez (p116) and a number of smaller groups. On one thing, however, Platform and Committee were agreed. Given that the regime showed no willingness to change, there could be no question of compromising with Franco's appointed successors (p128).

These various forms of opposition served to entrench attitudes among the regime's **die-hards**, especially the military officers who were ETA's main target. All the greater was their fury at a speech by Carlos Arias Navarro, Carrero's successor as PM, on 12 February 1974. For Arias appeared to promise a degree of liberalisation, floating the idea of a 'Statute of Associations' that would allow some sort of political debate, albeit within strict limits. But the 'spirit of 12 February' did not last. Its promoter was a colourless figure with none of Carrero's prestige within the regime. Nor was he helped by the April coup in Portugal, which sent a shiver through all its supporters. Soon the die-hards were firmly back in charge.

The first indication came with the dismissal in October of Pío Cabanillas, Fraga's successor as Information Minister (p118). He had largely persevered with the more relaxed censorship policies of his predecessor, the most visible result being the appearance of pornography on Spanish bookstalls.

> ### *inmovilistas*
> #### die-hards
>
> United by their fierce opposition to any relaxation of authoritarian rule after Franco's death, the die-hards formed a loose alliance of convenience in the last years of his regime. They included a number of old-style **Falangists** (p82), such as long-time Labour Minister Girón de Velasco (p100) and the one-time **liberaliser** Solís Ruiz (p112), some **technocrats** close to **Opus Dei** (p111), the openly Fascist Blas Piñar, who set up his own 'New Force' party, and many Army officers.

Ultraconservatives were outraged – as was Franco. Then, in December, the die-hards' renewed ascendancy was confirmed when the eagerly-awaited draft of Arias' Statute was finally published. It provided that 'associations' would have to be approved by the National Council of the Movement, a clear sign that no real dissent was to be permitted.

Cabanillas' sacking removed the last liberaliser from government. It provoked several others, leading administrators with links to the financial and intellectual communities, to resign in despair. Events in 1975 seemed to justify their fears of outright conflict. When Bishop Añoveros of Bilbao spoke out in favour of Basque nationalist aspirations, he was placed under house arrest, leading to a stand-off with the Vatican. Industrial unrest reached new heights as Spain was hit by the effects of the 1973 oil shock, and ETA's violence continued unabated. In August, in another triumph for the hard-liners, an Anti-Terrorist Act introduced mandatory death sentences for political killings. A month later, two ETA activists and one from the left-wing FRAP group were executed under its terms. When Franco finally died on 20 November, the chances of a tranquil handover of power looked minimal.

Exhibit 8.1: Manuel Fraga's early political philosophy (1968)

Extract from one of the leading liberaliser's best-known works

[. . .] En [las Cortes] se han procurado conjugar las más valiosas enseñanzas de nuestra tradición multisecular con las exigencias debidas al mundo en que vivimos y a la realidad política actual de nuestra nación.

Por eso, cuando esta realidad política lo aconsejaba, se han introducido algunas modificaciones en el sentido de un mayor perfeccionamiento en el mecanismo representativo, uniendo en este alto Cuerpo representativo junto a la representación de los productores la de los consumidores, a través de la Familia, que es la célula básica del consumo en la economía moderna.

Este perfeccionamiento no es, por otra parte, sino un eslabón más en la cadena de mejoras que nos permite un Régimen siempre abierto y previsor de unas instituciones que sirvan fielmente al imperativo de los tiempos. Este realismo político que ha impulsado los pasos del nuevo estado, ha producido ya resultados que a la vista de todos están. Entre ellos son de citar la nueva Ley de Prensa e Imprenta y, sobre todo, la Ley Orgánica del Estado, con toda la serie de perfeccionamientos que prevén los más variados órdenes de nuestra vida política tales como las leyes sobre la Libertad Religiosa, el mundo sindical, el procedimiento electoral, el Régimen Local, así como la reforma de algunas de las Instituciones fundamentales de nuestro Estado [. . .].

Source: Fraga Iribarne, M. (1968) *Horizonte español*. Madrid: Héroes.

Exhibit 8.2: The regime promotes itself (1969)

Opening of a typical work issued by the regime's propaganda service

EL MILAGRO DE FRANCO

A lo largo de este año español, tan español que va de 18 de julio a 18 de julio, [. . .], Francisco Franco, que desde aquella inolvidable jornada burgalesa del día primero de octubre de 1936 -con un sol dorado y con toda España metida en las calles de la pequeña ciudad, pequeño rincón de aquella Patria tan dura, tan pequeña también y tan llena de esperanzas- rige con pulso sereno nuestros destinos nacionales, cumplió sus primeros setenta y seis años. La gran aventura de su vida, puesta desde adolescente al servicio de España, siempre en los lugares de mayor riesgo y la mayor responsabilidad, encontró en este aniversario un eco unánime de felicitación popular. Incluso en grandes sectores de la Prensa extranjera, por regla general y constante histórica, tan atrabiliaria a la hora de juzgar a los hombres de España y, por supuesto, a España misma, bajo cualquier signo que la presida, se inició una conversión de frente -entrañable an algunos, admirativa en muchos, fría, pero objetiva, en otros- respecto a este veterano general y estadista que ha dado a los españoles la paz más larga que conoce su Historia y también su tranco político más lleno de realizaciones, prosperidad y posibilidades de futuro. [. . .]

Source: Servicio Informativo Español (1969) *Crónica de un año de España*. Madrid.

Topics

■ How could Fraga's work (Exhibit 8.1) be understood as an argument in favour of change in the Franco regime as it then existed?

■ What role did the family play in most Francoist thinking? What role is it assigned by Fraga in this text?

■ What arguments, explicit and implicit, does Exhibit 8.2 use to glorify Franco? What connotations would the word *milagro* in the title have had?

■ Who would have read such a text in 1969? How credible would it have been to most Spaniards?

■ Who benefited from the 'boom' of the 1960s, and how?

■ To judge by much of what one reads and hears nowadays, opposition to Franco's regime was very widespread towards the end of his rule. How is that impression to be reconciled with the regime's survival until 1975?

A delicate operation (1975–1982)

In the second half of the 1970s the economies of Western Europe experienced major problems, aggravated by a further 'oil shock' in 1979. As one way to recapture the dynamism of previous decades, the countries of the European Community – and in particular its economic locomotive, Germany – began to consider expanding the EC to take in the relatively undeveloped economies of Southern Europe. They wanted also to ensure that stable democratic regimes emerged from the processes of change in the region which began with the overthrow of right-wing dictatorships in Greece and Portugal during 1974, in the latter case under Communist leadership. Contrary to western, especially American, fears, that turned out to mark the furthest leftward swing of the political pendulum that had begun in the previous decade. Now it moved steadily back towards the Right, accelerated by the election of aggressively free-market, anti-communist governments in Britain and America in 1979. Later that year the ascendancy of the 'New Right' was given a further boost by the Soviet invasion of Afghanistan and the renewal of the Cold War. The only challenge it faced came after the election of a Socialist government in France which was pledged to resist the trend to free market economic policies.

Like Primo's departure 45 years before, Franco's death in November 1975 left Spain emerging from dictatorship at a time of economic recession. This time, though, the international political environment was much more helpful. Ironically, the delicate process was eased most of all by the fact that Franco's regime was a much sturdier edifice than Primo's, and did not immediately collapse. Consequently change, when it came, was initiated from within the old regime, enabling its structures to be dismantled without provoking the wrath of extreme conservatives. That, in turn, made it possible to begin constructing a new system in cooperation with the left-wing opposition. Only then was the operation threatened by an attempted coup, whose failure provided the renewed impetus required to conclude successfully Spain's transition to democracy.

The Right outmanoeuvred

So long awaited, with apprehension and hope, Franco's death proved rather an anticlimax. The arrangements he had put in place swung into operation and power remained firmly in the hands of the hard-line conservatives who had exercised it in the dictator's last years. Although pressures for change were building up, there seemed to be no way of releasing them while Franco's institutions remained intact. Yet that was precisely what happened from mid-1976 on.

The dictator's plan for the survival of his regime (*continuismo*) was triggered immediately on his death, beginning with the coronation of his chosen successor. In his investiture speech, the newly crowned Juan Carlos I spoke of a desire not just for 'opening up' (*apertura*) but for 'democratisation'. With the King's encouragement, the first cabinet of his reign included several leading liberalisers, notably Manuel Fraga Iribarne (p112). But his, and their, room for manoeuvre remained tightly circumscribed by the hold exercised by Franco's die-hard supporters (p119) over a range of key institutions, including the Parliament (p113), central and local administration, the National Movement (p105), the judiciary, and the armed forces.

As a result, Juan Carlos had little option but to retain Franco's appointee, Carlos Arias Navarro, as Prime Minister (p119). His reputation as a liberaliser was a telling insight into the thinking of the die-hards who still held most of the reins of power. For his notions of a distinctively Spanish democracy (*democracia a la española*) were firmly based on the 'organic' variety devised by his former master (p99), for whom he retained an unswerving admiration. But the fact that he held them at all suggested that, unlike the die-hards, he had some inkling of the pressures on him.

To a large extent the pressures were the delayed result of the 1973 oil shock. Its initial impact on Spain had been muffled by the economic progress resulting from development in the 1960s. In spite of Spain's extreme dependency on foreign oil, the government was preoccupied with the political rather than the economic situation. Now it reaped the whirlwind. Recession in western Europe shut off the safety-valve which, for a decade and a half, had released pressure on Spain's labour market; emigration ceased, and those who had left to work abroad began flooding back to their homes in Spain (p111). Unemployment rose steeply, as did prices, fanning the opposition's campaign of industrial unrest (p128).

Nor was the opposition alone in demanding change. An alarmed business community lobbied for political concessions to reduce industrial tensions in the short term and, looking further ahead, to allow access to the benefits of EC membership (p117). Externally, the Community itself was anxious for Spain to fulfil the conditions to join, while the Americans were desperate to prevent a repeat of the Communist takeover in Portugal. Both pressed for significant political reform and discreetly supported those who favoured it.

Largely as a result, Arias took some hesitant steps in that direction. Along with a pardon for some political prisoners and a vague commitment to future reforms, he announced the removal of restrictions on the press. And, although officially political parties remained banned, in practice they were permitted to begin operation. These moves provoked strong opposition from the most extreme die-hards, who hankered after a return to full-blooded dictatorship (*nostálgicos*), especially the military officers among them (*el búnker*). Throughout the first half of 1976 they blocked all moves towards further change as pressure, domestic and external, steadily built up.

Something had to give, and in June it did. When Parliament rejected the central plank in Arias's strategy of minimalist reform – his proposals to legalise political parties under strict conditions – he resigned. Here, clearly, was a chance to break the deadlock. Hopes were high that Juan Carlos would appoint someone with the moral authority and drive to push through real changes. Hence the disappointment and astonishment when, on 1 July, he named a senior Francoist bureaucrat with no liberalising track-record. That, though, was a prime attraction to the King's adviser, Torcuato Fernández Miranda, an enigmatic figure who had given long and loyal service to Franco, but now played a key role in persuading the institutions left by his old boss to dismantle themselves.

No one was better qualified than Adolfo Suárez to implement that strategy – first of all, because he had been secretary-general of the National Movement (p105). On the one hand, that gave him credibility with the reactionaries, on the other a deep knowledge not just of the workings of Franco's institutions but also the personal histories of their members. Secondly, he had served as head of the state-run television service, and understood like no other Spanish politician how the medium could be used to influence opinion. And, finally, unlike most of the regime's grey functionaries, he was telegenic, and too young to evoke negative memories of the Civil War and its aftermath (p96).

Suárez's appointment marked the real start of Spain's transition to democracy (*transición democrática*). The key to the operation was that change should be initiated without opposition help, partly because its promoters wanted to keep a firm grip on power, and partly because such support would alert the reactionaries. To carry it out Suárez relied on a group of close allies, former Francoist bureaucrats like himself, who wanted limited, controlled change in order to avoid anything more drastic. The most prominent – Rodolfo Martín Villa, Fernando Abril Martorell and Leopoldo Calvo Sotelo – took up key posts in his cabinet; a number of other ministers were drawn from an informal Christian Democrat grouping known as '*Tácito*', whose ranks included both liberalisers and members of the 'legal' opposition tolerated by Franco (p116).

With his team in place, Suárez seized the initiative. Within a month of taking office he announced extensions of various basic liberties, notably freedom of assembly and association. This action reduced the potential for high-profile clashes between opposition demonstrations and the police, as did a further amnesty for political prisoners. Having halted, at least temporarily, the spiral of rising tension, and the consequent hardening of attitudes among both opposition and reactionaries, Suárez made his key move, and announced plans for political liberalisation.

His Political Reform Bill (*Proyecto de Ley de Reforma Política*) was published in September. It proposed a new, two-chamber Parliament which, unlike the existing house (p113), would be fully elected. Parties would be legalised, subject to approval by the government. Beyond that, the proposals were deliberately vague. There was no mention of a new constitution: on the contrary, the old regime's basic laws (p112) would remain in force. The fact that Suárez repeatedly had recourse to the extensive decree powers they conferred on him seemed a further sign that major change was not in the offing.

Even so, his plans evoked the reactionaries' fury. The King's role as Supreme Commander of the Armed Forces, and the military connections he had built up during his long apprenticeship, were crucial in keeping them under control. Admittedly the Army Minister, General De Santiago y Díaz de Mendívil, resigned in protest. But that allowed Suárez to replace him with Lieutenant-General Gutiérrez Mellado, a committed democrat who immediately set about bringing the Army under control by a shrewd combination of discipline and administrative reforms.

With military opposition defused, the next hurdle was the old, Francoist Parliament. Here the crucial players were Suárez and Fernández Miranda, who occupied the key post of Speaker (*presidente*). Their methods were a combination of procedural manipulation and arm-twisting of individual representatives (*procuradores*), backed up by judicious references to the pressures for change from outside Spain. The final vote, held on 18 November, was a testimony to their skills: the Political Reform Act was passed by 425 votes to 59.

Suárez's next obstacle was self-imposed. In order to pre-empt charges that his proposals lacked democratic legitimacy, he had scheduled a national referendum for 15 December. This time it was his media knowledge and skills that were decisive. Shamelessly manipulating coverage by the state television service, and employing his own charisma to the full, he won another overwhelming victory. Over three-quarters of the electorate voted, and 94 per cent were in favour. Attention now switched to the general election which, under the terms of his own Act, Suárez had to call no later than 30 June 1977.

In preparation for the election in February he legalised most of the opposition parties. However, in the case of the Spanish Communist Party (PCE) the Supreme Court, still dominated by Franco's appointees, overruled him, as the Reform Act allowed it to do. It was a crucial moment. At that time the PCE was seen as the strongest opposition force (p128), and without its participation the election would be meaningless. On the other hand, by legalising the PCE the government risked provoking a coup by military reactionaries. Suárez faced them down, with the King's support (p131), and legalised the PCE by decree. However, while that solved one problem, it aggravated another, since it ensured even tougher competition for Suárez in the forthcoming election. And as yet he had no party of his own, and no time to create one. His solution was to hijack an existing party.

The *Centro Democrático* was one of the innumerable groupings set up in the wake of the Reform Act. Its leader, José María Areilza, was a prominent Francoist who had broken with the dictatorship. Conservative, but unambiguously democratic, it had swallowed up several similar mini-parties and looked well-placed to appeal to middle-class voters. But with virtually no organisation outside Madrid it had little prospect of tapping this potential, which was also limited by Areilza's age and pompous style. When Suárez offered to jump aboard, bringing not just his own growing prestige but also his contacts in the recently wound-up Movement (p105), Areilza's lieutenants summarily ditched their leader and gratefully accepted Suárez as his replacement.

A number of the Prime Minister's own allies also took up senior positions in the hurriedly renamed **Centre Democratic Union** (p127) just in time for the election campaign. Once again, Suárez showed himself both skilled and ruthless in exploiting his advantages: civil service back-up, the Movement's country-wide apparatus and, as before, TV exposure. In the poll on 15 June his new party exceeded all outside expectations by winning the largest share of the vote, outpolling not just the barely organised

Right, which performed abysmally (p133), but also the historic parties of the Left (pp128–9). Reconfirmed in his position as Prime Minister, this time by parliamentary vote, Suárez was left standing atop the ruins to which, in under a year, he had reduced Franco's seemingly impenetrable defences.

The Left tamed

The 1977 election results endorsed Suárez's strategy. But they also left him no alternative to continuing down the tricky path of reform, while tackling various other pressing problems. Furthermore, they meant that he could no longer, as up to now, govern virtually alone. Instead he was forced to seek support from the leaders of the left-wing opposition who, for their own reasons, were also anxious to work together. Out of their cooperation came the transition's legal foundation – a new constitution.

While the UCD was the undisputed winner of the 1977 election, and formed a government on its own, it had no overall majority, and won fewer votes than the left-wing opposition as a whole. Having started down the

> ### Unión de Centro Democrático (UCD)
> ....
> ### Centre Democratic Union
>
> Formed to fight the 1977 general election, the UCD was a 'centre' party in the sense that its leadership included both opponents and servants of the Franco regime. In addition to one faction composed of the latter, whose support for transition was essentially pragmatic, the UCD comprised three main ideological groupings: Christian Democrats, liberals and moderate Social Democrats. Once the **1978 Constitution** (p130) was approved the divisions between them became unbridgeable, and the party crumbled and was dissolved shortly after its defeat at the 1982 election (p134). Its leader, Adolfo Suárez (p125), attempted to construct a successor, the Social and Democratic Centre, but without success.
> See also: **Partido Popular** (p152)

road to change it was clear that Suárez could not stop now, and it was generally agreed that the next step should be a new Constitution. And that was by no means the only challenge facing the Prime Minister, since near-crises had emerged on two other fronts.

The first crisis was the law and order situation. After splitting into two branches, ETA (p115) had not just continued, but stepped up its violence; in the autumn of 1977 the 'military' wing launched a new and more ferocious campaign. Nor were the problems confined to the Basque Country. From December 1976, a shadowy left-wing group, GRAPO, carried out a string of kidnappings, while in January 1977 far-right gunmen shot dead five labour lawyers in the Atocha district of Madrid.

The second crisis was caused by the further deterioration of the economy (p124). Strikes continued at a very high level, and during 1977 inflation rose to 25 per cent. Industries which had grown up in the 1960s boom, and grown accustomed to working under a dictatorship, were ill-equipped to deal with recession, especially now that their employees enjoyed normal trade union freedoms. Major restructuring was clearly necessary (p140) – and that would inevitably provoke even more unrest among workers.

Some guarantee of industrial peace was thus essential for stability, and this, combined with the failure of the Right at the polls, forced Suárez to seek the parliamentary support he needed on his Left – that is, from the Socialists and Communists, who between them had received the vast majority of left-wing votes in June. Luckily for Suárez, both parties were now in a mood for compromise, far removed from the one in which they had entered the transition period.

Back in 1975 the entire opposition (p119) had been in favour of making a 'clean break with the past' (*ruptura*). Admittedly, its components disagreed as to what exactly that meant. For some it implied merely political and, perhaps, social reform; the farther Left also wanted radical economic changes, such as far-reaching nationalisation and state-directed redistribution of wealth. But there was general agreement that those associated with the Franco regime should play no part in creating its replacement. The unanimity was such that the two umbrella groups which had coalesced around the Communist and Socialist parties joined forces, under the name of 'Democratic Coordination' (known popularly as the *Platajunta*).

The limited extent of change during the first half of 1976 (p124) hardened the opposition's line still more. In the absence of any political forum, its main tactic was industrial action, to which many workers were in any case being pushed by economic circumstances (p124). The resultant strikes repeatedly erupted into violent confrontations with the security forces, especially in the Basque Country, where left-wingers and nationalists continued to make common cause (p115).

One clash in Vitoria during March, which led to five workers being shot and killed, illustrated the dilemma facing the Left's leaders. They were well aware that, contrary to American nightmares, the situation was quite unlike that before the 1974 left-wing revolution in Portugal, where large sections of the Army had gone communist. In Spain the armed forces remained solidly conservative, if not reactionary, and any attempt to force change against their will would have involved a bloodbath, for which no one else had any stomach. Hence the alacrity with which the Left grasped at the chance for negotiated change when Suárez offered it.

Within weeks of his appointment both Felipe González, head of the Socialist PSOE and Enrique Tierno Galván, leader of the small but influential People's Socialist Party (*Partido Popular Socialista*), had agreed to meet the PM for exploratory talks. Even PCE leader Santiago Carrillo had informal contacts with him. When Suárez's proposals for political reform were published (p125), those Christian Democrats who had joined the opposition front (p119) supported them, oblivious of the fact that – like the left-wing leaders' actions – they were incompatible with any notion of a 'clean break'.

Yet at the end of October, the opposition leaders publicly reaffirmed that a clean break was their goal. When Suárez submitted his proposals to a referendum, they called on voters to abstain. The fact that less than a quarter of the electorate heeded their advice (p126) indicated how far that position had lost credibility. Moreover, the referendum campaign had made painfully clear how effectively Suárez could exploit his privileged access to TV. Even though they would have their own election broadcasts before the upcoming election, his opponents were well aware that the government's control of news coverage would still give it a head start.

Their fears were confirmed by the results (pp126–7), which also abruptly changed the balance of power within the different parties that made up the opposition. Up to then the PCE had been regarded as its strongest component, especially given its strong links with the Workers' Commissions (p114) which had been so prominent in organising industrial protest. In contrast, the Socialist union, the UGT (p59), had been relatively cautious in its calls for action, since like the PSOE, it had not had sufficient time to rebuild its organisational bases, which had been neglected during the dictatorship (p114). Nonetheless, the Socialists easily outpolled the PCE to become the second largest party in Parliament.

The results showed that voters preferred younger faces, such as those of Suárez and González, and moderate policies; they were clearly in no mood to relive the conflicts of the Republic and Civil War. The Left's leaders were also aware that talk of radical change increased the already significant danger of a right-wing coup should they ever manage to win power. González and Carrillo decided to cut their losses. Abandoning the lost cause of a 'clean break' to the far-left splinter groups, they began to talk in terms of a 'democratic' or 'agreed break' (*ruptura democrática/pactada*) and offered to give Suárez the informal support he needed in return for a say in the next phase of change.

Since 1975 there had already been signs of a willingness to **compromise**, on both Right and Left, that was new to Spanish politics: they included the Church's decision not to back an official Christian Democrat Party, with its inevitable echoes of the CEDA (p72), and the Communist Party's recognition of the monarchy. By the late summer of 1977 that new openness had become the transition's *leitmotiv*. Its first fruit came in October, when the two left-wing parties signed the 'Moncloa Pacts' with the government. The terms, whereby they agreed to persuade their associated unions to tone down industrial action, indicated that they knew the weakness of their position. They delivered on their promise, and as a result inflation was brought down to a more manageable level, and the pressure on Suárez considerably eased. In return they received a promise to create more jobs – which predictably went unkept.

The pay-off for the Left's leaders, if not their grassroots supporters, came in the drafting of a Constitution. For Suárez abandoned his original intention of having the text drafted by government lawyers, and instead handed over the task to Parliament, where proposals could only be passed with the Left's approval. As a result, the document finally agreed at the end of 1978 was significantly less conservative than many of the PM's

---

consenso

(spirit of) compromise

In many ways compromise is the standard stuff of democracy, but the extent to which it was displayed by politicians during the transitional period was remarkably different from the intransigence that had so long characterised Spanish politics. Its protagonists were the **UCD** (p127) government and the leaders of the **Socialist** (p47) and **Communist Parties** (p86). They were supported to varying degrees by the main trades union federations, the **UGT** (p59) and **the Workers' Commissions** (p114), and the employers. Its main fruits were the process known as 'social concertation'. This produced a series of agreements on economic policy which began with the Moncloa Pacts, and the **1978 Constitution** (p130).

Constitución del 78

1978 Constitution

Officially the 1978 Constitution was the work of the parliament elected in June 1977, which became in effect a constituent assembly (*Cortes constituyentes*). It was based on the draft produced by a seven-man committee (*ponencia*) known as the 'fathers of the Constitution'. In line with the prevailing **spirit of compromise** (p129) there were three representatives of the governing **UCD** (p127) and one each for the **Socialists**, the **Communists**, the right-wing **People's Alliance** (p133) and the Catalan regionalist **CiU** (p149). Their text was agreed with only minor amendments, and the final version was overwhelmingly approved in a referendum on 6 December 1978, except in the Basque Country, where the result was ambiguous (p132).

See also: **Estado de las Autonomías** (p132)

supporters would have wished. Nonetheless, it was widely hailed as a triumph.

The 1978 Constitution, which in a formal sense brought the transition to a close, settled several conflicts that had bedevilled Spanish politics for a century and more. The Socialists presented only token objections to the monarchy, happy to accept that Juan Carlos' performance in the role (pp124–5) had saved them from having to take an awkward decision. Religion caused more controversy, as both the main left-wing parties adamantly opposed granting any special status to the Catholic Church. But eventually they agreed to recognise it as a 'social reality', which was enough to satisfy most conservative opinion. The Constitution also included ingenious provisions to deal with regionalism (pp131–2).

The main error that was made in drafting the Constitution, which went unnoticed at the time, was to assume that the electoral system made it impossible for a single party to win an overall parliamentary majority (p143). For the moment, though, that assumption proved correct. In fact, the first election held under the new Constitution, in March 1979, produced results very similar to those of 1977. Suárez's party, the UCD, again won most seats, while falling well short of an overall majority. Once again the Left, especially the PCE, had to take on board its electoral weakness. All seemed set for a continuation of the compromise course of the past eighteen months. But it was not to be.

Compromise had been a successful strategy for one very particular set of circumstances. However, that moment had passed, and, with the Constitution agreed, politics returned to everyday bread-and-butter issues. Some related to the country's economy, whose serious problems were aggravated by the second oil shock in 1979. Others, symbolised by the possibility of legalising divorce, concerned the type of society that Spain should now become. Many involved fundamental clashes of interest and beliefs that could not be resolved by compromise, but instead needed a strong government able to give a firm lead. And that was precisely what Spain lacked.

The problem was not so much that the UCD had no parliamentary majority; since despite complaints from their own rank and file, for whom democracy had brought few material benefits, the Left's leaders still held back from toppling it for fear of a coup. The problem was UCD's make-up. In essence, it was an alliance of convenience between groups which had nothing in common beyond the desire to bring about a smooth transition (p127). With that achieved, at least on paper, it had no purpose or cohesion.

As a result, the UCD was wracked by a succession of disputes, especially over divorce, and because of the rivalry between the powerful 'barons' who headed its factions, and resented Suárez's reliance on a small group of his closest advisers (p125). Although the events have never been fully clarified, it seems to have been these key figures in the party who forced the Prime Minister's surprise resignation in late 1980. In the event, by ditching its greatest asset the party merely hastened its own demise (p134). Meanwhile, however, the uncertainty triggered by Suárez's abrupt departure gave an opportunity to those who found that even his brand of transition was far too radical, and who had no interest whatsoever in compromise.

Crisis and recovery

It was during the investiture of Suárez's successor that military reactionaries attempted a coup. Although this was a shock, it was hardly a surprise, having been on the cards since the transition's start. And the factor most likely to provoke it – regionalist agitation of various sorts – had been growing in importance for some time. Happily, though, the coup was easily put down, and its failure gave a new impetus to the process of reform, hastening the change of government that was so clearly required.

Ever since 1975 the military's propensity for rebellion (*golpismo*) had hovered over Spanish politics. Several times the King's influence was crucial in keeping the Army in check, notably when the PCE was legalised (p126). Some officers made no attempt to hide their far-right sympathies, and more than once the Defence Minister, Gutiérrez Mellado (p126), was the target of abuse. In 1979 and 1980 several plots were uncovered, the biggest known as 'Operation Galaxia'. Although they reflected general Army dissatisfaction at the course of events, these activities were above all a reaction to the revival of the regionalist feeling that their ex-leader had attempted to stamp out.

In the end it was the spectacular failure of Franco's efforts (p115) that left Suárez with no option but to concede a measure of self-government to Catalonia and the Basque Country. By 1976 feelings in these regions were so strong that its denial would undoubtedly derail plans for a smooth transition (p125). This view was shared by the leaders of the left-wing opposition, whose activists in the two regions backed devolution. They were thus happy to let Suárez lay the groundwork for it, while at the same time conducting discussions on the Constitution. As a result, by the end of 1977 what amounted to provisional regional governments (*entes preautonómicos*) had been set up in both regions.

The Catalan body was headed by Josep Tarradellas, a popular moderate regionalist who Suárez had brought back from exile for the task. The presence of a Catalan on the committee drafting the constitution (p130) made it possible for its views to be fed into that process. The final text, with its provisions for a **regionalised form of government**, received massive approval in Catalonia. Thereafter devolution negotiations with the central government were smoothed by the consensus already established on the path to be followed (p115). A Statute of Autonomy was duly approved without major

Estado de las Autonomías
regionalised form of government

Neither completely centralised nor genuinely federal, the territorial structure of the government established by the **1978 Constitution** (p130) is based on units known as Autonomous Communities (*autonomías/comunidades autónomas*), the boundaries and powers of which were left to be established in individual 'Statutes of Autonomy'. The three 'historic nationalities' of the Basque Country, Catalonia and Galicia were allowed immediate access to extensive devolution. Other regions could only follow this fast track (*vía rápida*) if they met demanding requirements to demonstrate popular support. Otherwise they had to follow the slow route (*vía lenta*) which involved immediate low-level devolution, with the opportunity for upgrade after five years. As a result, devolution turned out to be more of a process (*proceso autonómico*) than a structure (p146).

problems. This restored the *Generalitat*, as the regional government was again to be known (p69), and invested it with extensive powers, including education and policing.

In the Basque Country, lack of representation on the constitutional working party was just one, relatively minor problem. This was because the regionalists there insisted that self-government was a matter for Basques alone to decide, and that no Spanish constitution could deny them the right to choose independence if they so wished. As far as ETA (p115) was concerned, even talking about devolution was taboo. The non-violent PNV (p45), by contrast, was willing to do that, especially as its triumph at the recent election allowed it to pose as the Basques' representative *vis-à-vis* Madrid. However, it refused to back the Constitution, either in Parliament or at the subsequent referendum (p130).

The plebiscite's results in the region complicated the situation still further. For, although there was a majority of 'Yes' votes, widespread abstention meant that they constituted only a minority of the Basque electorate. ETA immediately claimed that the Basques had 'rejected the Constitution', and used that as a justification for its continuing campaign of violence (p127). The message was repeated incessantly by People's Unity (HB), the political wing set up by ETA's 'military' branch (p147), which in the 1979 election took nearly a sixth of Basque votes on a platform of complete separation from Spain.

Although it once again topped the poll, the PNV took fright and started emphasising that it shared the same separatist goal. It also implied repeatedly that so long as independence was denied, violence, if not justified, was at least understandable. In reality HB's vote, like the frequent and large pro-ETA demonstrations, reflected lingering respect for the armed organisation's resistance to Franco (p115), and the resentment felt against the excesses of the security forces in dealing with anyone suspected of connections with it. But that was easily overlooked, inside and outside the Basque Country. With the left-wing opposition also demanding wide-ranging devolution, the pressure on Suárez was immense.

As a result, the PNV was able to win major concessions. The Basque Statute of Autonomy, known as the Statute of Guernica (p89), included all the powers granted to

Catalonia as well as the tax-collecting powers suppressed by Franco (p32). Like its Catalan equivalent, the Statute was approved by referendum in October 1979. In February 1980 the PNV won a convincing victory in the first regional election, and immediately formed a government. It then showed less interest in using its devolved powers than in complaining that they were not greater, and that Navarre had been excluded from the Basque 'Autonomous Community'. The PNV's tendency to portray every issue as a confrontation between the Basques and Madrid both fed on and fed ETA's continuing 'armed struggle', which in 1980 claimed more victims than ever before.

In Catalonia, the first election was unexpectedly won by a new regionalist party, Convergence and Union (p149). The new Catalan Prime Minister, Jordi Pujol, wasted no time in using his new powers. Yet the effects were similar to those in the Basque Country. In the central government's view, some of Pujol's measures exceeded Catalonia's competences as defined jointly by the Constitution and its Statute. Conversely, Pujol claimed that some Madrid laws infringed his region's constitutional rights, a complaint shared by the Basque PNV. Both sides repeatedly appealed to the Constitutional Court (*Tribunal Constitucional*) charged with ruling in such disputes, adding to the impression of conflict between the regions and Madrid.

These developments caused growing concern in the Army and Civil Guard, whose officers tended to be Spanish nationalists, and as such ETA's main targets. It was deepened when Andalusian politicians attempted to obtain the same sort of wide-ranging devolution as the Basques and Catalans. The process prescribed in the Constitution for such cases (p132) proved to be unsatisfactory, and while it dragged on other regions joined in the clamour for extensive self-government. The fact that talk of Spain's imminent disintegration was no longer limited to military circles was one of the arguments used by the extreme reactionary officers plotting for a coup; as a sop to military feeling, the new Constitution made the forces responsible for Spain's 'territorial integrity'.

Along with the government's incapacity to maintain law and order, the other justification they offered was that they represented a mood of popular disillusion (*desencanto*). And indeed, many Spaniards were disappointed that reform had not protected them from the effects of economic recession (p130). But the vast majority clearly wanted more change, not less; the only significant party saying the opposite was Manuel Fraga's People's Alliance, which in both elections to date had performed dismally.

However, some officers either could not or would not see that the times had changed. In the climate of uncertainty created in early 1981 by the mysterious resignation of Prime Minister Adolfo Suárez (p131) they decided to act. Their **attempted coup** was spectacular, but quickly crushed. Reaction to it underlined just how bogus was their claim to represent public opinion. Spontaneous mass demonstrations in favour of democracy were held all round Spain. The Madrid march was headed by politicians ranging from Fraga to PCE leader Santiago Carrillo. Disillusion, insofar as it had existed, was banished.

The coup attempt led the new Prime Minister, Leopoldo Calvo Sotelo, and the main opposition parties to rekindle the spirit of compromise (p129), in order to bring the

---

(intentona de golpe del) 23-F

1981 coup attempt

The attempted coup of 23 February 1981 only got off the ground in Valencia, where tanks under the command of General Milans del Bosch appeared on the streets, and in Madrid, where civil guards led by Lieutenant-Colonel Antonio Tejero stormed the Congress of Deputies – the lower house of Parliament – and held at gunpoint MPs attending Leopoldo Calvo Sotelo's investiture as Prime Minister. Prompt action by loyal troops, and the unambiguous opposition of King Juan Carlos, ensured that order was soon restored in both cities.

---

regional issue under control and so calm Army fears. In the summer they agreed a timetable for resolution of the Andalusian dilemma, but also that no more regions would be granted such extensive devolution. In addition, they agreed legislation stipulating that, whatever the Autonomy Statutes might say, the Madrid Parliament could always overrule regional laws if it wished. That decision sparked off furious Basque and Catalan protests (pp147–8), and another appeal to the Constitutional Court. But it also countered hysteria about the country falling apart.

Otherwise Calvo's government was completely hamstrung by the progressive disintegration of his UCD party (p127), and his only other significant initiative was to take Spain into NATO. That, too, was partly designed to ease military tensions, by providing the forces with new tasks to keep them occupied. But NATO entry was decidedly not a product of compromise; it was eventually imposed over Parliament's head. The Left objected bitterly. Sensing that the danger of another coup was slight, and that the UCD was close to complete collapse, its leaders had decided to go for the kill.

Of the two major left-wing parties the PSOE was now indisputably the UCD's main challenger, having maintained its wide lead over the PCE at the 1979 election. Yet its failure to do better persuaded the PSOE leader Felipe González that it must moderate its image. At the party's conference in May he proposed removing all references to Marxism from its internal rules. When he was outvoted he resigned, a tactical manoeuvre to show that his opponents – left-wingers and party traditionalists – had no alternative strategy or leader. Over the summer his henchman, Alfonso Guerra, took a firm grip on the party apparatus. At a special conference in September the changes were approved, and González overwhelmingly re-elected. His authority had been paraded publicly, making him look like the strong leader the country needed.

González's personal standing was an important card in the election that could not be long delayed. Another was the PSOE's anti-NATO campaign, very effective in a country where, thanks to its links with Latin America and the memory of 1898 (p35), anti-US feeling extended across the political spectrum. The Socialists' overall strategy was to ride the wave of enthusiasm for further social and economic change that had been unleashed by the coup attempt, portraying itself as the only political force capable of delivering such reform. It was a huge success. In the election eventually held on 28 October 1982 the PSOE won a sweeping victory, giving it the overall majority the UCD had always lacked; the former government party itself was reduced to a rump. More importantly, no voice of any consequence questioned the Socialists' right to assume power. The transition had been completed in the minds of the electorate as well as on paper.

Exhibit 9.1: King Juan Carlos addresses Parliament (1977)

Speech at the opening session of the Parliament elected in June 1977

[. . .] Hace poco más de un año y medio, en mi primer mensaje como Rey de España, afirmé que asumía la Corona con pleno sentido de mi responsabilidad y consciente de la honrosa obligación que supone el cumplimiento de las Leyes y el respeto de la tradición. Se iniciaba una nueva etapa en la Historia de España que había de basarse, ante todo, en una sincera voluntad de concordia nacional y que debía recoger las demandas de evolución que el desarrollo de la cultura, el cambio generacional y el crecimiento material de los tiempos actuales exigían de forma ineludible, como garantía del ejercicio de todas las libertades. Para conseguirlo, propuse como empresa comunitaria la participación de todos en nuestra vida política, pues creo firmemente que la grandeza y fortaleza de la Patria tiene que asentarse en la voluntad manifiesta de cuantos la integramos. [. . .]

La ley nos obliga a todos por igual. Pero lo decisivo es que nadie pueda sentirse marginado. El éxito del camino que empezamos dependerá en buena medida de que en la participación no haya exclusiones. Con la presencia en estas Cortes de los partidos que a través del voto representan a los españoles, damos un paso importante en esa dirección y debemos disponernos con nobleza a confiar en quienes han sido elegidos para dar testimonio de sus ideas y de sus ilusiones. [. . .]

Además de estos objetivos, el país tiene pendiente muchos problemas concretos sobre los que el pueblo español espera la acción directa de sus representantes. El primero es crear el marco legal adecuado para las nuevas relaciones sociales, en el orden constitucional, el regional o en el de la comunicación humana.

La Corona desea -y cree interpretar las aspiraciones de las Cortes- una Constitución que dé cabida a todas las peculiaridades de nuestro pueblo y que garantice sus derechos históricos y actuales.

Desea el reconocimiento de la diversa realidad de nuestras comunidades regionales y comparte en este sentido cuantas aspiraciones no debiliten, sino enriquezcan y hagan más robusta la unidad indiscutible de España. [. . .]

Source: Presidencia del Gobierno (1977) *Mensajes de la Corona.* Madrid: Colección Informe, núm. 15.

Exhibit 9.2: Tejero's manifesto (1981)

Statement issued by the leader of the Civil guards who stormed parliament during the 1981 coup attempt

Españoles: las unidades del Ejército y de la Guardia Civil que desde ayer están ocupando el Congreso de los Diputados a las órdenes del general Milans del Bosch, [. . .] no tienen otro deseo que el bien de España y de su pueblo.

No admiten más que un Gobierno que instaure una verdadera democracia. No admiten las autonomías separatistas y quieren una España descentralizada, pero no rota. No admiten la impunidad de los asesinos terroristas, contra los que es preciso aplicar todo el rigor de la ley. No pueden aceptar una situación en la que el prestigio de España disminuye día al día; no admiten la inseguridad ciudadana que nos impide vivir en paz.

Aceptan y respetan al Rey, al que quieren ver al frente de los destinos de la Patria, respaldado por sus Fuerzas Armadas. En suma, quieren la unidad de España, la paz, orden y seguridad. ¡Viva España!

Source: *El País* (4 March 1981).

Topics
FOR DISCUSSION

■ How does the view of the monarchy's role presented by King Juan Carlos (Exhibit 9.1) compare with that of Cánovas (Exhibit 2.2)?

■ Which institutions does he refer to, either directly or indirectly, as having a role to play in the country's future development?

■ What aspects of Spain's historical experience appear to have prompted his remarks?

■ Judging by Tejero's manifesto (Exhibit 9.2), where does, or should, ultimate authority lie in Spain? What role does it appear to ascribe to the monarchy?

■ How did Spain's situation in 1975 resemble that in 1936? Why did events turn out so differently?

■ Could the strategy of *ruptura* ever have been practicable? If so, under what circumstances?

CHAPTER 10

By 1982 the alternative economic policies pursued by the French socialist government had clearly failed, thus reinforcing the New Right's domination. As well as free market economics, its main feature was fierce anti-Communism, which laid renewed stress on the role of NATO and led to a revival of the arms race. Partly as a result, the Communist bloc crumbled in 1989, with the emergence of new states, including the three Baltic Republics, and the discredit of its underlying ideology. Meanwhile, the western economies experienced a strong recovery, concentrated in the financial sector and other services. It encouraged the EC's members – 12 in number after the enlargements of 1982 and 1986 – to plan for further integration, by setting up a European Monetary System within which their currencies were effectively pegged. In 1992 they signed the Maastricht Treaty which, as well as converting the EC into the EU, established a timetable for achieving Economic and Monetary Union by the end of the century, and economic targets for countries wishing to join. The strict budgetary discipline required by these convergence criteria served to deepen the recession that, throughout the West, was undermining the New Right, and boosting the advocates of a return to the political Centre.

Back to the mainstream (1982–1996)

By 1982 Spain had closed much of the gap on its neighbours in terms of political development. The task facing the newly elected Socialist government was to resume the economic and social modernisation held back during the Franco era and largely ignored in the transition. In the view of most Spaniards that meant joining fully in the process of European integration. The Socialists' success in achieving that aim helped them keep a tight grip on power during the 1980s. In the following decade, however, it was loosened for various reasons, some derived from their own behaviour in power, some due to changing regionalist tensions. They also now faced a serious conservative challenger, in a party whose self-conscious move towards the Centre both helped it to win power and confirmed Spain's position in the mainstream of European developments.

Into Europe

Europe – more precisely, the European Community – was the focus of the Socialist government's attention. Its leaders were convinced that Spain must join the EC, and that it must first be properly prepared to do so. The initial benefits of accession, in 1986, more than lived up to expectations, completely overshadowing the hidden costs in terms of broader foreign policy. But by the 1990s they had worn off, leaving Spain in economic difficulties just as the next phase of European integration was starting.

Hardly anyone in Spain questioned the fundamental importance of EC membership. The Franco regime had recognised it by applying for admission (p113), and even amidst other pressures the UCD government of the transition era had found time to submit a new application. On the Left, suspicions that the Community was an agent of multinational business were outweighed by the knowledge that workers in the EC were better off, and the hope that entry would kill off the old reactionary Right. And throughout society there was a vague but powerful yearning to see the country accepted by its neighbours as an equal.

Spain's new rulers were among the most enthusiastic pro-Europeans (*europeístas*). But they were also acutely aware that her claim to equal status was undermined by glaring economic weakness. The shaky foundations of development in the 1960s had left the country more vulnerable than her neighbours to the turbulences of the following decade, so that by 1982 her situation relative to the rest of western Europe was no better than in 1960. Indeed, given the increased pace of change it was probably worse. As the third industrial revolution got under way Spain had not fully emerged from the first, its economy still dependent on a manufacturing sector within which old-style smokestack industries were heavily over-represented.

The González government had long since accepted the view that the only way Spain could catch up was through exposure to competition within the EC. But there was the rub. For even the strictly controlled opening of her economy since 1959 had laid bare its lack of international competitiveness (p127). If the cure were not to prove worse than the disease, Spanish industry would have to be prepared for the shock of entry, and from their arrival in power that became the Socialists' top domestic priority. It underlay their reforms in a range of areas, particularly infrastructure and education (p143), but above all their wide-ranging programme of **industrial restructuring**.

Meanwhile a delegation led by Foreign Minister Fernando Morán and one of his senior officials, Manuel Marín, were engaged in the tortuous process of negotiating EC entry itself. The main stumbling blocks related to fisheries and French concerns about Spanish agricultural produce, but eventually they were overcome, and the Treaty of Accession (*Tratado de Adhesión*) was signed. On 1 January 1986 Spain became a fully-fledged Community member, notwithstanding the

reconversión industrial

industrial restructuring

Begun tentatively under the **UCD** government of the transition (p127), the restructuring policy aimed to shift the basis of Spanish industry from declining industries to those with better future prospects, and to encourage the creation of companies large enough to compete in international markets. The comprehensive programme which got under way after 1982 was partially successful in meeting these aims in the medium term. More immediately it had a severe negative impact on sectors such as shipbuilding and steel manufacture, with many plant closures and thousands of workers made redundant.

seven-year transition period (*período transitorio*) covering some aspects of membership which formed part of the entry fee.

Another aspect that was not mentioned in the Treaty, or even spoken aloud, related to Spain's foreign policy in general, and its attitude to NATO in particular, which her new colleagues were determined to have clarified. Their concerns went back to Adolfo Suárez's time as Prime Minister (p125), when Spain had kept its distance from US policy, notably in Latin America, and presented itself as a bridge between the West and the developing world. Such non-alignment (*tercermundismo*) was abandoned under Suárez's successor, who took Spain into NATO (p134). But the Socialists implied they would reverse the decision if elected and, although they made no immediate move to do so, Morán showed signs of reverting to the Suárez line in other respects.

In the climate of the time, that put Morán out of step with his EC counterparts, who impressed on his boss that a large, strategically important country like Spain could not be allowed to disrupt the EC's solidly pro-American line. Accepting that withdrawal from NATO was no longer an option, González decided that only endorsement in a referendum would allow to him pull off such a brazen U-turn. Voting was scheduled for 12 March 1986, and the Prime Minister set about overturning the large anti-NATO majority shown by opinion polls.

First, he persuaded his party that its previous objections had been to joining NATO, and the undemocratic way in which it was decided (p134); now that it had happened circumstances had changed, and the party's position with them; in any case, the PSOE would respect the people's choice. Next, the basic question of whether to remain in NATO was hedged round with qualifications, including a commitment to negotiate removal of the US military presence in Spain (p103). And finally González, fresh from the triumph of taking Spain into 'Europe', campaigned tirelessly for a 'Yes' vote.

The result was in doubt almost to the last. But in the end, the Prime Minister won a substantial majority, and to all intents and purposes Spain was a full NATO member. The decision marked a turning point. Within months Morán was replaced. His successor was Francisco Fernández Ordóñez who, ironically, had served under Suárez as Finance Minister. However, his mild social democratic views included no trace of anti-Americanism, and under his direction Spain's foreign policy was reoriented along unambiguously pro-Western lines. Like the NATO affair, that decision was a bitter pill for sections of González's own support (p144). But it passed largely unnoticed by most Spaniards amidst the euphoria following EC entry.

As well as a boost to national self-confidence, joining the EC also brought considerable material benefits. Over the next few years, Spain received massive financial support from the EC's Structural Funds, and with the European economy booming, private investment also poured in. For the remainder of the 1980s Spain grew faster than any other developed country. Nor was the transformation only quantitative; since growth was concentrated in the service sector, it also changed the economy's nature. By 1990 dependence on heavy industry was significantly down, and Spain was moving rapidly towards the post-industrial structure typical of the most advanced economies.

By then it was also clear that Spain's second 'boom' would soon be over. Already the government had taken some steps to insure against hard times ahead, including joining the European Monetary System in 1989. But it was reluctant to cut spending on its various expensive reform projects (pp143–4), or on the huge investments required for the high-profile events planned for the fifth centenary of the most famous date in Spanish history (p1), especially the 1992 Olympic Games in Barcelona and the Seville Expo. Not till they were over did the government adopt the austerity measures which the economic situation had been demanding for several years.

The result was that world recession hit Spain late but hard. Inflation, recently under reasonable control, took off again, and the foreign deficit soared. In 1993 the country recorded its worst economic figures for half a century, with unemployment up to over 20 per cent. During 1992 the government had twice adjusted the peseta downward within the EMS, but the cuts were insufficient to reduce the pressure on the currency. Eventually, on 'Black Thursday' (13 May 1993) Spain was forced into a devaluation larger than allowed by EMS rules – a severe setback for its aspirations to equal status with its EC partners.

If anything, though, this setback strengthened the conviction in Spain that the country must achieve entry into the forthcoming Economic and Monetary Union, whatever the cost. That meant meeting the convergence criteria set at Maastricht, an especially hard task given the state of Spain's economy. The government's strategy for fulfilling it had two main strands, the first being the Cohesion Fund set up by the EU to assist the poorer members with convergence, of which Spain would be the main beneficiary. When the richer countries tried to backpedal on their commitment, at the 1992 EU Summit in Edinburgh, González took an unusually tough line to ensure they did not.

The second and crucial strand in the government's strategy was the **Convergence Plan**. First signs were not hopeful, as Spain's relatively slow recovery from recession soon undermined the forecasts on which it was based. But it was relaunched in 1994 by Finance Minister Pedro Solbes who, ignoring protests that the Plan was aggravating the already acute unemployment situation, kept it remorselessly on course (p145). He was helped by falling international interest rates and by the fact that the conservative opposition, for all its bitter attacks on other issues (p153), fully supported his strategy. By 1995 a rapid upswing was under way and Spain was, to the surprise of many observers, a genuine candidate to join EMU as soon as it started.

Programa de Convergencia

Convergence Plan

Based on budget cuts and monetary discipline, the Convergence Plan was adopted in 1992 to meet the criteria set by the EU for entry into Economic and Monetary Union, covering currency stability, inflation, interest rates, public debt and public deficit. It was continued in its essentials by the **People's Party** (p152) elected in 1996, and EMU entry was secured the following year.

Socialism in power

The success of the Socialists' European policies not only benefited Spain. It also helped the PSOE to consolidate itself as by far the country's most powerful political force, and enabled it to push through a programme of wide-ranging reforms. These reflected the priorities of the party's leadership, which in some respects clashed with those of its traditional supporters. That led to divisions in the later 1980s, by when other, graver, consequences of the party's new-found position were emerging.

In a sense, the PSOE's high point was its 1982 election victory; never again did it win as many votes. But the party's two main rivals were unable to profit from the erosion of Socialist support; in fact, neither survived the decade in its original form. The Communists tried to capitalise on resentment at the PSOE's U-turn on NATO (p141) by turning the impromptu alliance formed to oppose it into a permanent one. Yet this United Left (IU), a lone anti-EC voice, made little headway even before 1989, when its Communist links became a veritable millstone. On the PSOE's other flank, the collapse of the UCD and the failure to construct a centrist successor (p127) left the field clear for the right-wing People's Alliance (AP). But, after rising sharply in 1982, the AP's support stagnated, prompting its transformation into the People's Party (p152).

This opposition disarray helped the Socialists to win two more general elections, in 1986 and 1989, both by comfortable majorities. But that bald statement gives little idea of their hold on power. As well as the central government they ran some two-thirds of the new regional ones (p132) and most local authorities, including nearly all of the bigger cities. What is more, their overall parliamentary majority allowed them to circumvent constitutional controls on government (p130), and to cram their own appointees into the swelling apparatus of government agencies, among them the state television monopoly, which they exploited as shamelessly as Suárez (p126). As a result, politics in the 1980s was to a large extent the internal politics of the PSOE.

The party that entered government in 1982 was no longer the mass working-class organisation of the 1930s. That PSOE had been reduced to a small hard core under Franco's rule (p114). Since his death, and above all since the party's near-split in 1979, a new PSOE had been built by a new leadership, dominated by the figure of Felipe González (p134). Although still heavily dependent for votes on the poorer sections of society, especially the expanded industrial labour force, most of its impetus and leadership now came from the middle classes that had also grown under Franco, and from lawyers and educationalists in particular.

Understandably, the party rejected the view that socialism was purely a working-class affair, as it would have been seen by the old PSOE (p47), albeit some were not averse to exploiting class resentments to win and hold support; in this González's deputy and close collaborator, Alfonso Guerra, was especially adept. Generally, though, they were less concerned with equality or redistribution than with individual liberties and economic efficiency – 'getting Spain working properly' as González put it. Together with 'Europe', their other watchword was 'modernisation'. In that they resembled the Republicans of the early 1930s, and they had in mind a similarly ambitious programme of reforms (p69).

Along with the restructuring of industry (p140), the party's main priority was education – another echo of the Republic. In their first two years in office the Socialists introduced major changes at both secondary and higher levels, although the emphasis now was on boosting skills levels rather than personal development. They also invested heavily in new infrastructure, particularly in improvements to Spain's grossly inadequate transport network. They revised the tax system to make it fairer and more efficient. They created a national health service. And they implemented extensive military reforms, helped along by Spain's entry into NATO (p134).

In all these fields, the González administration was remedying the omissions of its predecessors over the better part of a century. While its measures did not necessarily respond to the traditional world view of the workers' movement, neither did they run counter to it. But, conscious of their unhappy results in France, the PSOE government steered determinedly clear of such classic left-wing policies as the nationalisation and regulation of industry. And in two policy areas its reforms involved dismantling aspects of the Franco regime's haphazard social policy framework, whose main beneficiaries were the PSOE's own loyalest supporters.

The first such area was the elaborate system of employment regulation (p97), which made it hard for employers to shed labour, and so react quickly to changes in market conditions. Now that they faced more outside competition, that inbuilt delaying process was a distinct disadvantage; moreover, their complaints were backed up by both the EC and the OECD. In 1984 the government bowed to these pressures and, as a first step towards reducing rigidity in Spain's labour market (*flexibilización*), legalised fixed-term contracts.

The second area was social security provision in general, and state pensions in particular. Flushed with the economic success of the 1960s, the Franco regime had introduced a surprisingly generous system of social support. But it was highly bureaucratic, and assumed that boom conditions would last. Franco's successors were left to pick up the tab caused by rising unemployment, not to mention a rapidly ageing population. The problems were aggravated by the effects of industrial restructuring (p140), which left many workers with no alternative but to take early retirement. In 1985 the government decided something had to be done, and announced pension cuts.

That was too much for the Socialist trade union federation, the UGT (p59), which had expected a PSOE government to help its members, rather than assign them to the scrapheap and cut their benefits. It was also unhappy at the government's obvious intention to abandon the 'social concertation' arrangements instituted during the transition, under which unions and employers' representatives were involved in economic policy-making (p129). The UGT's respected leader Nicolás Redondo heavily criticised the pension cuts and threatened to resign his MP's seat; two years later he did so in protest at proposals for further cutbacks.

By then, the government's U-turn on NATO (p141) had driven another wedge between it and its sister union, which had not forgiven American support for Franco. Then, in 1988, the government proposed further deregulating the labour market to allow low-wage contracts for young workers. That provoked the UGT to throw in its lot with the Workers' Commissions (p114), which had been attacking González's government almost from the time it was first elected in 1982. On 14 December 1988 the two jointly staged a general strike.

For such direct action, with its almost mythical status for the Spanish workers' movement (p48), to be used against a Socialist government seemed hugely significant, especially as the turnout was impressive. González duly withdrew the offending proposals.

But he then called and won an early election in October 1989 – despite the UGT's unprecedented refusal to endorse his campaign – taking advantage of the favourable economic climate (p141). Having called the UGT's bluff, González pressed on with social cutbacks and labour market deregulation as part of his Convergence Plan (p142), ignoring two more general strikes in 1992 and 1994, and the continuing high levels of unemployment (p142).

It became clear that the party's traditional core support now wielded little clout in the PSOE. Economic change meant that the industrial workforce was shrinking. The party's membership and, above all, its office-bearers, had also come to be dominated by men and women who had been elected or appointed to public positions, and whose over-riding concern, not unnaturally, was to retain them. Formidably organised by Guerra, the PSOE became a highly cohesive electoral machine, fiercely loyal to González, its trump card. However, the party was never renowned for its original thinking (p47), and now showed few signs of fresh ideas to replace the traditional ones it had largely ditched.

Even more immediately damaging was the impression Socialists often gave of contempt for voters, symbolised by the notorious infrequency of González's appearances in Parliament. Unflattering comparisons were drawn between **felipismo**, the nature of Socialism in power, and conditions during the Franco era. One clear parallel was the prevalence of **influence-peddling** to swell party coffers. Not that the PSOE was the only culprit; all the main national and regional parties were at fault. But the Socialists held so much more power, and so had many more opportunities. And now, unlike in Franco's day, there was a free press, which gleefully revealed a succession of dubious affairs mostly involving the PSOE. The biggest was that of a bogus consultancy company, Filesa, which had been set up by prominent party figures to launder illicit income.

---

felipismo

'Felipe-ism'

Coined in the 1980s, the term *felipismo* was widely used to refer to various aspects of the **PSOE** (p47) under Felipe González's leadership. The main ones were: abandonment of the class-based attitudes traditionally associated with Spanish Socialism in favour of an emphasis on economic modernisation (p143); strong, centralised control of the party apparatus; and an approach to electioneering centred on González's charisma. More broadly, the term was applied by opponents to unsavoury aspects of government during his time in power, in particular the practice of steamrollering legislation through Parliament with minimal or no consultation (*el rodillo*), the widespread incidence of **influence-peddling** and the major scandals of the 1990s (pp150–1). See also: *caso GAL* (p151)

---

tráfico de influencias

influence-peddling

A more or less common practice in many countries, influence-peddling or favour-mongering involves the sale of public-sector jobs, contracts and other favours to individuals or businesses, in return for money or some other consideration. Its object is personal enrichment and/or the securing of funds for a political party.

Some influence-peddling was merely a matter of personal gain, as in one major case uncovered in 1990, whose protagonist was Juan Guerra. The scandal eventually obliged his brother, González's deputy, to resign from office one year later. Even so, Alfonso Guerra retained powerfully-placed supporters (*guerristas*) in the PSOE who his numerous enemies now moved to oust. Given the extent to which González had relied on Guerra – apart from anything else, he had organised every PSOE election campaign since 1982 – the feud left the PSOE in a perilous situation, especially in view of the damage caused to its public image (*desgaste*).

The situation was saved almost single-handedly by González. First, he settled the internal dispute by throwing his prestige behind Guerra's opponents, the so-called modernisers (*renovadores*). Then he called an early election for June 1993, forcing the party into a show of unity. Finally, he coordinated the campaign himself, and personally promised a crackdown on sleaze if he were re-elected. Against all predictions he was. But victory was far from the sweeping triumph of 1982; this time his party fell well short of an overall majority. To stay in power it was forced to seek outside support. Some Socialists expected González to turn to the Communists, their allies during the transition. But he chose instead to rely on regionalist support, graphically illustrating how much the PSOE had changed – and how important regionalism had become.

Regionalists, new and old

The 1978 Constitution's provisions for devolution were intended to remove the political tensions caused by regionalist feeling. In many areas they did exactly the opposite, since the existence of regional institutions naturally fostered such sentiments, giving rise to new parties all round Spain. And in the two regions where they already existed, devolution had mixed effects; while tension was indeed reduced in the Basque Country, after a difficult start, in Catalonia the opposite was true.

During 1983 the process of setting up regional governments was completed throughout mainland Spain, and the Balearic and Canary Islands. Broadly it followed the guidelines laid down in 1981 (p134), although three more regions – the Canaries, Navarre and Valencia – followed the fast track to extensive autonomy. As a result eight models of devolution were in operation; one for the ten 'slow route' regions that would have to wait five years for the chance of more powers and seven, all different, for the fast-track regions (p132). The situation was complicated further by the fact that, for obvious practical reasons, devolution of powers could not take place instantly; instead the 'transfer' of each area of responsibility to each region was subject to an individual and often long and complex process of negotiation. That was one reason why, far from being over, the devolution process (*proceso autonómico*) was only beginning.

Another reason was that devolution interacted with the strong sense of local loyalty that was virtually omnipresent in Spain. It was evident, for example, in the importance of local media, which since the demise of federal Republicanism (p28) had generally lacked a political focus. Now, though, devolution provided this, in the shape of the new regions, with their own institutions and their own flags and anthems, even in areas which did not correspond to any historical unit, and where regionalist feelings had previously been unknown. Above all, the holding of regional elections, in which parties inevitably addressed the 'people of Cantabria', or wherever, fostered the notion that those people formed a distinctive group with distinctive, shared interests. By the early 1990s there was barely a regional parliament without at least one party whose *raison d'être* was the defence of those interests.

Two of the largest parties of this new political species were to be found in Valencia and Navarre. Both fed on anxiety about the expansionist ambitions of established regionalist movements – Catalan and Basque respectively – on their doorsteps. In Navarre, especially, there were some grounds for such fears (p133), although they were exaggerated by what were essentially conservative Spanish nationalists. These regions' demands were largely satisfied by the 1983 settlement, whereas although it had a good claim to historic distinctiveness (pp2–3), Aragon received no special treatment. The Aragonese Regionalist Party (Par) exploited the anomaly to become a major player in regional politics, and the spearhead of demands for a devolution review.

Despite their own centralist tendencies the Socialists were sympathetic to change; the existing system was an administrative nightmare. But their hands were tied after the 1989 election, which left the PSOE one vote short of the overall parliamentary majority necessary to amend regional Statutes of Autonomy (p132). However, the conservative opposition was keen to neutralise what had become dangerous competition for anti-government protest votes, and agreed to support a package of measures to standardise the system and mollify the new regionalists. This reform was approved in 1994. As well as extending devolution to Ceuta and Melilla (p58), it gave all regions that wanted them the right to virtually the same level of powers; the only remaining differences were the health service, policing, and the special tax arrangements enjoyed by Navarre and the Basque Country (p32).

The extensive devolution granted to the Basques had brought no immediate reduction in tension (p133). Hopes rose briefly in September 1982, when ETA's 'politico-military' branch (p115) agreed to lay down its arms. The deal was brokered by Basque Left (*Euskadiko Ezkerra*), originally the 'poli-mils' own political wing but now an outspoken opponent of violence. Although the settlement allowed their activists to be 'reinserted' into normal society, only a minority took up the offer. Most joined the 'military' branch to form a reunited ETA as committed as ever to the 'armed struggle'.

Meanwhile, both EE and **People's Unity** (HB) had been campaigning noisily against the 1981 central legislation which curbed

> ### *Herri Batasuna (HB)*
> #### People's Unity
>
> Established in 1978 as the political wing of **ETA**'s then 'military' branch (p115), HB's programme was based on the so-called 'KAS alternative'. This demanded independence for the Basque Country, and the incorporation of Navarre. HB opposed the 1978 Constitution, and refused to recognise the validity of the Basque autonomy granted under it; its representatives embarked on a prolonged boycott of both the Spanish and the Basque Parliaments. Despite attempts to isolate HB (p148), in the mid-1990s it still commanded the support of over one-sixth of Basque voters.

regional powers (p134). The largest Basque party, the PNV, also joined in a campaign that further heightened the sense of Basque–Spanish confrontation which it had already been fomenting (p133). This strategy helped the PNV to increase its vote sharply at the 1984 regional election. But it also provoked tensions both within and outside the party, which two years later exploded into crisis.

The dispute had a number of causes, but the root of them was that the PNV's archaic ideas (p45), to which many members clung ferociously, were hopelessly out-of-tune with contemporary reality. In particular, their emphasis on the three provinces as the foundation of Basque identity constrained the new regional government's ability to exercise its powers. The outcome was a stand-off between party boss Xabier Arzalluz and the regional Prime Minister, Carlos Garaikoetxea, who resigned in 1985. The following year he set up a breakaway party, Basque Solidarity (*Eusko Alkartasuna*) and forced an early regional election.

The poll, held in November 1986, was a watershed. The PNV suffered heavy losses, mainly to the newborn EA. The combined nationalist vote, in total higher than ever, was now split between four significant groupings, since both EE and HB made gains. Its fragmentation meant that no single party was anywhere near to winning a parliamentary majority. On top of the region's already massive problems – ETA's relentless terror, and the economic effects of industrial restructuring (p140) on its heavy industry – this political crisis threatened to render it ungovernable.

In the event, it had the opposite effect. Against all expectations a coalition government was formed in early 1987 by the PNV and the PSOE's Basque section, whose relations had previously been deteriorating into bitter animosity. Now, united by a common desire for stability and a hold on power, they were forced to patch up their differences, at least in public, thus removing one cause of tension in the region. Over the next year the main cause was also mitigated, though for very different reasons.

Sensing the 1986 crisis as an opportunity, ETA stepped up its attacks, having already widened these to include agents of the regional government, whom it regarded as part of the Spanish state. Particularly affected was the regional police force, the *Ertzaintza*, whose ranks were filled overwhelmingly with nationalists, many of them PNV sympathisers. By now ETA's victims also included its own former activists who had opted for 'reinsertion', and even members of the public; in June 1987, a bomb in a Barcelona hypermarket killed 15 people. These tactics led most Basques, including nationalist voters and the PNV leadership, to turn decisively against the 'armed struggle'. In January 1988 all parties in the regional parliament, with the exception of HB, signed an agreement which condemned all violence, irrespective of its alleged motives.

The 'Ajuria Enea Pact' isolated ETA and its supporters, and greatly normalised relations among the other parties. Above all, by making the PNV drop its ambivalent attitude to violence (p133), it forced the region's key political force to adopt a less confrontational strategy. Toning down its demands for increased self-government, the party began to concentrate on using the powers had already been devolved to address the region's problems. That helped to reduce tension directly, and enabled the Basque Country to share in the economic upturn after 1986 (p141).

The PNV's new line also brought the party clear benefits. By the next regional election, in 1990, it had regained much of its lost support. By then, too, the Baltic states' independence had triggered new demands for Basques to be given the same status. The PNV was prompted to dump its Socialist partners and form an all-nationalist government with EA and EE. But the new coalition was only months old when EA backed a pro-independence campaign mounted by HB – a clear breach of the Ajuria Enea Pact, that threatened a return to adversary politics. That prospect held no appeal for the PNV, which was still reeling from its experiences in 1986, and was now closely linked with a Basque business community desperate for stable conditions. It forced EA to resign from the coalition, and renewed its Socialist alliance as the best hope for them.

In Catalonia stability did not pose a problem. Violence was limited to a few minor incidents involving a grouplet called Free Homeland (*Terra Lliure*). The only party in the region which persistently expressed dissatisfaction with the devolution granted in 1979 – Catalan Republican Left (p70) – made no real electoral impact. The regional government was run by the moderate **Convergence and Union**, which followed its surprise win in the first regional election (p133) with three more, in 1984, 1988 and 1992, all by comfortable majorities.

True to the origins of Catalan regionalism (p43), the CiU's basic concerns were regional culture and business interests. Yet Spain's entry into the EC meant that these latter were no longer quite the same. On the one hand, Catalonia was the best located of all Spanish regions to profit from closer integration and the consequent concentration of economic activity. On the other hand, removing tariff barriers against European imports also removed the main benefit to Catalan industrialists, who already believed themselves to be subsidising the national economy through their taxes, of being part of Spain.

It was no coincidence that the CiU was ready and willing to contemplate the prospect of separation. On several occasions, notably following Baltic independence, its leader Jordi Pujol speculated publicly on the possibility of independence, although he always followed up with assurances of loyalty to Spain. Such calculated ambivalence was one aspect of what came to be known as 'Pujolism'. Another was the CiU's aggressively pro-Catalan language policy, which aroused fears among the region's substantial Castilian-speaking community. Additionally Pujol, the longest-serving government leader in Europe, deliberately identified himself and his party with Catalonia, often seeming to suggest that his opponents were, in some undefined sense, not proper Catalans.

Convergència i Unió (CiU)

Convergence and Union

Formed in 1977 by the merger of Catalan Democratic Convergence, recently set up by Jordi Pujol (p133), with the older Catalan Democratic Union, the CiU quickly came to dominate internal Catalan politics, and has run the regional government alone since its creation in 1980. It has developed a new brand of regionalism, popularly known as 'Pujolism', the main features of which are: strong support for the Catalan language, an ambivalent attitude to Catalonia's position as part of Spain and, above all, Pujol's own leadership. Since 1993 the party has supported minority central governments of both Left and Right.

The largest of the rival parties was the Catalan Socialist Party (PSC), the semi-autonomous regional section of the PSOE, which at general elections regularly topped the Catalan poll. From the transition's outset it had been part of the pro-devolution consensus in the region (p115); it even defied its own Madrid leadership by proposing that Spain should be turned into a federation – the traditional stance of moderate Catalan regionalism (p44). Pujol, however, consistently portrayed the PSC as an agent of the Socialist central government. Interestingly, though, he treated the González administration itself much less harshly, rather as if they were foreign statesmen of a different political persuasion. That was perhaps another way of underlining the distinction between Catalan and Spanish affairs. But it also reflected the Catalan regionalists' traditional concern to keep at least one finger in the Spanish pie (p44).

Towards alternation

After the 1993 general election González was dependent on Pujol's parliamentary support to form a government. Naturally his backing had a price, but the main reason why the PSOE soon ran into grave difficulties derived from its own behaviour in power. As well as triggering new problems in the Basque Country, the PSOE greatly assisted the rise of the party that had finally emerged as a viable opposition to the Socialists.

The price of Pujol's backing was predictable. He feared that the levelling-up of autonomy (p147) would reduce Catalonia to being just another region, and for some time he had been eyeing enviously the fiscal privileges enjoyed by the Basques and the Navarrese (p32). Discussions soon began on devolution of more areas, including social security, but also on plans that would allow the Catalan government to retain more of the taxes it raised within its region, Spain's richest. In 1994 a trial scheme was introduced, under which the regions would be allowed to retain 15 per cent of their own tax revenues.

While that failed to satisfy Pujol, who immediately demanded 30 per cent, it alarmed the Socialist leaders of the southern regions, who seemed likely to lose out. Poor and still mainly rural, they formed the PSOE's heartland in Spain's revised electoral map. Like the party's other main support bases, the old and public sector workers, they were among the main losers from the government's Convergence Plan (p142), on which Pujol and González were fully agreed. As in the 1980s (p144), the party's policies were demoralising its own core supporters. However, it was soon to suffer more damage from developments in a quite different section of the party.

They involved accusations of corruption on a scale well beyond the influence-peddling of the 1980s (p145). A succession of public figures associated with the PSOE were shown to have profited from dubious or illegal financial deals. One such affair (*caso*) involved the Governor of Spain's Central Bank, Mariano Rubio, another Luis Roldán, the first civilian to head the Civil Guard. Additionally, some of the fortunes made during the 1980s boom were found to be the result of fraud, most spectacularly that of the banker Mario Conde. Although those concerned were unconnected with, or even hostile to the PSOE, these scandals contributed to the atmosphere of corruption in high places which González had personally promised to stamp out (p146).

Yet the most serious blemish on the PSOE's record in power was the so-called **GAL affair**. It was uncovered by Baltasar Garzón, a successful investigating magistrate (*juez*) who had been elected to Parliament as an independent on the PSOE's lists, in the belief that he would be given a wide-ranging anti-corruption brief. When he was not, he resigned to take up the investigation into suspected government involvement in a 'dirty war' against ETA in the 1980s. By the end of 1995 he had enough evidence to bring charges against a string of senior officials in the Ministry of the Interior, all Socialist appointees, and even José Barrionuevo, who had been the Minister concerned at the time, and one of González's most faithful lieutenants. Rumours abounded that the 'Mister X' behind the whole operation was the PM himself.

For months the GAL affair brought government to a virtual standstill. The effects in the Basque Country were just as serious.

> ### *caso GAL*
> ### GAL affair
>
> Uncovered – partially – in the mid-1990s, the GAL affair centred on the Anti-Terrorist Liberation Groups (*Grupos Antiterroristas de Liberación*), who a decade earlier had claimed responsibility for the killing and kidnapping of a number of Basques, in both Spain and France. Although always suspected to be part of a government-controlled 'dirty war' (*guerra sucia*) against **ETA** (p115), the groups were long shrouded in mystery, despite the conviction of two relatively junior police agents in 1988 for involvement in their activities. In 1995, however, the chain of command was traced up to cabinet level.

There ETA had been pushed onto the defensive by a series of successful police operations, and activities had taken on a note of desperation: bomb attacks on members of the public, kidnappings, and the street violence and vandalism of *Jarrai*, the youth section of its political wing, HB (p147). Such tactics reduced public sympathy even further; an end to violence had at last seemed to be in sight. The GAL affair changed all that.

Many Basques, by no means all of whom were nationalists, had always subscribed to the 'dirty war' theory; it fitted all too well with the abundant evidence that ETA suspects were tortured by the security forces. While confirmation of their suspicions came too late to revive real sympathy for ETA outside its own network of committed supporters, it inevitably gave new substance to the notion that the Basques were under attack from a hostile Spanish state. And, crucially, it came at a time when reunification of the fragmented Basque nationalist movement under the aegis of a resurgent PNV seemed a real possibility.

ETA's main opponent in the nationalist camp, the small but influential Basque Left (p147), no longer existed, having merged with the PSOE in 1993. The following year's regional election confirmed the steady decline of Basque Solidarity since its split from the PNV in 1986 (p148), and its subsequent decision to join the regional government as a very junior partner looked like a step towards reconciliation. Now, in a clear reversal of its recent moderate course (p148), the PNV began putting out feelers to HB. The obvious danger was that Basque politics would once again, as in the early 1980s, be played out as a conflict between Basques and the rest of Spain (p133). Ominously, in

1995 ETA began a new series of assassinations, choosing its victims to provoke maximum tension.

One of the first was Gregorio Ordóñez, Basque head of the opposition **People's Party**; in 1994 his party leader had escaped a Madrid car bomb. Both attacks came as the PP was trying to shed the anti-regionalist image associated with the Spanish Right in search of an accommodation with its natural political allies, the basically conservative forces of moderate regionalism in Catalonia – and the Basque Country. That was a scenario that really would marginalise ETA, especially if the PP came to power in Madrid. Ordóñez's killing, designed to provoke it into an anti-Basque outburst, confirmed that this was now a genuine possibility.

The PP grew out of the realisation by Manuel Fraga, doyen of the Spanish Right, that his Francoist past made him unelectable nationally. Accordingly he stepped down as leader of the opposition People's Alliance (p143), and in 1989 oversaw its relaunch, installing as his successor the much younger José María Aznar, and changing the party name. The new title, taken from that of the Christian Democrat group in the European Parliament, was designed to locate the PP in the mainstream of the contemporary European Right. Insofar as any clear PP policy line could be distinguished, however, it was away from the state intervention practised by the Franco regime and towards economic liberalism.

These changes enabled the PP to capitalise on the mood of self-confidence and ambition, especially among the educated, urban young – the very group that had swung most to the PSOE in 1982. It also built up a party structure under strict central control, something the Spanish Right had always lacked. Aznar himself, initially a much mocked figure, established a certain standing of his own. But even so, and with the Socialists in disarray (p146), the PP lost the 1993 general election.

Partido Popular (PP)

People's Party

Relaunched under its new name in 1989, the PP had formerly been known as the People's Alliance (AP). Although it claims to be the heir of the centrist **UCD** (p127), this right-wing party was set up in 1976 by the former Francoist minister and **liberaliser**, Manuel Fraga Iribarne (p112). Its ideas remained ill-defined, reflecting some Church and some business influence, until 1996, when having already won control of many regions and local authorities, it won the general election and formed a government.

The Socialists' ace card was their constant insinuation that the PP, despite Fraga's departure, was still Francoism by another name. Aznar knew that; he also knew that, internationally, the Right had lost its glamour – now the Centre was the place to be. In Spain the term had a special appeal because of its associations with the transition period, now regarded as a political golden age. It soon came to permeate the PP's message. However, this had the disadvantage of underlining the fact that, in policy terms, there was little to choose between the PP and the PSOE, especially as Aznar was committed to joining EMU (p142). He therefore began to concentrate his fire on the scandals overwhelming the government.

Aznar received enthusiastic assistance in this from the media, in which important changes had taken place since the 1980s. Then the Socialists had enjoyed the support of much of the press, in particular the leading daily *El País*, and also controlled the state broadcasting monopoly (p143). In 1989, however, they were forced to fulfil a long-shelved promise to allow private television stations. A year later three went on the air, the two most successful adopting a strongly anti-government line. Their negative coverage was echoed by many newspapers, especially *El Mundo*, one of several new national dailies.

This media campaign, which fed on the various influence-peddling affairs of the time (p145), really took off with the post-1993 scandal wave. It also became blatantly partisan. Several of the new media organs were run by businessmen bitterly hostile to the PSOE, and it showed; a number of *El Mundo's* revelations were themselves revealed as exaggerated or even fabricated. The PRISA group and its flagship *El País* remained broadly behind the government, and responded to the attacks with some low blows of their own. The result was an ugly atmosphere of rising tension (*crispación*).

Along with the PSOE's economic troubles (p142), the scandals took their toll. At the 1994 European election it suffered its first defeat in a nationwide poll since 1982. A year later its grip on local and regional government (p143) was broken; now the PP controlled most of Spain's regions and major cities. Pujol, the government's prop, watched these developments with growing concern. When his party suffered a mild setback in the 1995 Catalan election, he decided he could no longer afford to be linked with an unpopular administration. Later that year he withdrew his support.

González was forced to call an election for 3 March 1996. It was a nasty campaign. The PSOE again responded to allegations of corruption and abuse of power by labelling the PP as Francoist, helped by the revelation that several of its leaders were linked to the Opus Dei (p111). Its only other card was González himself who, despite his precarious situation in the GAL affair, remained enormously popular among the PSOE faithful, their loyalty cemented by the partisan nature of media coverage.

In the event the Socialists' support held up unexpectedly well; although the PP overtook them it fell well short of winning an overall majority. To form a government Aznar had to turn to the kingmaker, Pujol, and also to the Basque PNV for support. Eventually it came, showing that regionalism could also be a factor for stability. But perhaps the most significant aspect of the election aftermath was that, despite what had gone before, González hastened to congratulate the victor. As in its neighbouring states, political rhetoric and practice had been separated, and alternation in power accepted as normal. On the way to being a secular society, and on course for EMU (p142), Spain was very much back in the European mainstream.

Exhibit 10.1: Felipe González assesses Spain's situation (1987)

Extracts from a press interview

Estamos a una década de las primeras elecciones democráticas; del comienzo de los debates sobre la Constitución; de los Pactos de la Moncloa. Buena ocasión para describir el cuadro general de la situación de España.

Desde hacía más de un siglo, vivíamos en un claro aislamiento político y cultural, con miedo o rechazo a todo lo que venía de fuera, sin asimilar la pérdida del imperio colonial. España estaba enquistada en sus propias fronteras y se cocía en su propia salsa. Este aislamiento produjo períodos autoritarios, le dio una fuerza relativa mayor a las posiciones políticas de los extremos y se la quitó a las más templadas, la mayoría más amplia de nuestra sociedad. Con el aislamiento político se correspondía, también, un sistema económico cerrado, hiperproteccionista, y perdimos el tren de la primera y la segunda revolución industrial.

La década democrática ha producido una apertura al mundo sin precedentes, y un cambio sustancial en las reglas de juego del funcionamiento socioeconómico. Se ha roto el aislamiento político y nos integramos en espacios más amplios - Europa y Occidente-, y se pasa de un sistema hiperproteccionista a una eliminación de barreras arancelarias y de controles burocráticos al desarrollo de las actividades económicas, tratando de ganar competitividad interna y externa. [...]

El cambio en las reglas de juego del funcionamiento de la economía se deriva, primero, de un esfuerzo interior y, segundo, de nuestra incorporación a Europa. Empieza a notarse en España la entrada de aire fresco, de competencia, de libertad de movimiento en la economía. [...] Tenemos algunas amenazas, naturalmente; no podemos descuidar la vigilancia sobre la inflación, ni perder de vista que una balanza comercial negativa no puede sostenerse indefinidamente. Pero podemos tener la razonable esperanza de que al final de la década, España, además de un salto considerable en la competitividad y modernización del aparato productivo, siga por esa senda de crecimiento. [...]

Source: El País (8 November 1987).

Exhibit 10.2: The People's Party's inheritance (1995)

Extracts from a book written by the party's leader

El resultado de[l poder socialista] no es otro que una democracia más débil, una sociedad más débil, una economía más débil, una nación más débil. La suma de estas debilidades es *nuestro problema*.

Y nosotros queremos contribuir a su solución con una propuesta política general, que se ha ido elaborando a partir del análisis de nuestras necesidades y con la renovación de nuestras ideas.

Y digo *renovación*, porque no es cierto que vengamos de ninguna parte.

continued

Nuestro partido es joven, pero nos consideramos, con legítimo orgullo, herederos de una corriente que, con aportaciones de diverso signo, ha estado presente en la vida nacional durante más de doscientos años. La construcción del Estado liberal, a partir de la Constitución de 1812, la creación de un mercado nacional, la modernización jurídica, con obras de tanta fecundidad como nuestros venerables Códigos del XIX, han sido pilares fundamentales en la configuración de la España de hoy. El respeto a las libertades, el imperio de la Ley, la sujeción del Estado al Derecho, el protagonismo de la sociedad fueron los motores de una vasta obra, hecha con la impronta del espíritu liberal. Con demasiada frecuencia se ha querido desfigurar nuestra más reciente historia. La corriente reaccionaria ha pretendido siempre descalificar e incluso ahogar los logros modernizadores del pensamiento moderado y liberal español. Una cierta izquierda ha elaborado, por su parte, una visión maniquea de nuestra historia contemporánea, metiendo en el mismo saco todo lo que no se identificaba con sus planteamientos. Nosotros, por el contrario, reivindicamos el vigor de una opción con perfiles propios que a través de las sucesivas generaciones defendió la primacía del valor de la libertad y de la ley de un Estado sometido a èl, de una democracia en la que cupiera holgadamente la España plural y en cuyo marco se pudieran llevar adelante las reformas que demandaba una sociedad más justa. [. . .]

Source: Aznar, J.M. (1995) *España: La Segunda Transición.* Madrid: Espasa.

Topics

■ Judging by Exhibit 10.1, what does González appear to regard as the main achievements of his time in power up to 1987? To what extent do they correspond to the hopes of the Spaniards who voted for his party in 1982?

■ He criticises aspects of Spanish political behaviour in the past (*posiciones políticas de los extremos*). Who could reasonably be seen as the object of such criticism?

■ In Exhibit 10.2, Aznar portrays his party as the heirs of the Spanish liberal movement. How realistic a picture does he present of it? How credible is his claim?

■ What do Exhibits 10.1 and 10.2 tell us about the relationship between Spain's two largest political forces?

■ How would you rate Felipe González's contribution to Spain?

■ How would you rate Jordi Pujol's contribution to Catalonia? And to Spain?

Afterword

In 1997 Spain's efforts to meet the criteria for Economic and Monetary Union were crowned with success, and on 1 January 1999 it became one of the founder members of what some had begun to refer to as 'Euroland'. That step underlined just how far the country has become integrated into wider European and western developments, not just politically and economically, but also – in an important sense not touched on here – culturally. Does that mean that an appreciation of its history has become irrelevant? The answer, surely, is 'No', and not just because Spain is a recent and relatively peripheral addition to the western 'club'; the same is equally true for two countries which are at the centre of western and European events: the USA and Germany. But the fact that Spain's history has been so distinctive does perhaps make its importance that bit greater.

Thinking first of relations with the outside world, it is easy to forget that today's tourist Mecca was so cut off for so long. At the start of the nineteenth century, Spain was already a backwater. After the brief and traumatic experience of the War of Independence it became ever more detached from the outside, virtually uninvolved in trade, colonial disputes or even incipient recreational travel, being seen as an occasional destination for the more intrepid. Even the soul-searching inspired by the events of 1898 did little to increase contacts; economically, the inward turn of later 'regenerationist' thinking was paralleled by Primo's raising of the protectionist barriers first erected during the Restoration period.

During the tensest and most unhappy decade of this century Spain was briefly drawn back into European affairs, but once the Second World War was over it was again largely cut off from the developments that shaped the late-twentieth-century western community of states. Yet by the later stages of the Franco regime, for all the propaganda disseminated by the State, most Spaniards had enough contact with the outside world to know that their country was regarded as economically backward and politically unsavoury – and that both views had some foundation.

Against that background it is easier to understand Spanish attitudes since Franco's death to the outside world in general, and the rest of western Europe in particular. To an astonishing degree, the desire to be recognised as an equal partner has often seemed to override all other considerations. Thus Javier Solana, who had been a leading figure in the anti-NATO Socialist Party of the early 1980s, was appointed the organisation's Secretary-General 20 years later – to virtually general acclaim. Support for European integration, too, has been extraordinarily resilient even when, as in the early 1990s, it brought considerable material costs for many. The Communist Party's insistence on pointing out such unfortunate realities has been one of the main reasons why it has found life so much harder in Spain than in Italy since 1989.

Spanish 'Europhilia' is all the more striking when compared with attitudes in the other peripheral country which has traditionally seen 'Europe' as being somewhere else: the UK. But unlike Britain, or at least England, Spain did not have an unthinkingly accepted notion of nationhood to which European integration posed a threat. Within living memory, a country whose sense of common identity was never highly developed had experienced a civil war, followed by four decades of propaganda to the effect that a large proportion of its inhabitants were its bitter enemies. And, on the other hand, many, perhaps the majority, were deeply unhappy with the notion of Spanishness imposed by the Franco regime. Under those circumstances, being European offered, and continues to offer a way to sidestep awkward debates about Spain's essential nature.

The question of national identity bridges the external and internal aspects of Spain's contemporary situation. For the relative weakness of feelings of common Spanishness is inseparable from the strength of loyalties to particular parts and regions of the country. Given new life by the conditions of the War of Independence, they underlay Republicanism's federalist period and its extreme expression in the cantonalist movement of the 1870s. Now, in the post-Franco era, they have re-emerged with even greater vigour, which this time is being channelled in the particular form of regionalism.

Such feelings, like 'Europhilia', are both powerful and widespread, as Manuel Fraga's career illustrates. A minister under the ferociously centralist Franco regime, and a fervent critic of what he regarded as excessive devolution in the 1980s, becoming regional Prime Minister of his native Galicia seemed to be no more than a step on the way to his retirement from nationwide politics in 1989. Yet since then Fraga has displayed a strong regionalist streak, advocating a standardised administrative system that would put more responsibilities in the hands of regions in general, and doughtily defending Galicia's particular interests. More than once he has emphasised points of agreement with his Catalan equivalent, Jordi Pujol – whose own regionalist sympathies meant that he spent part of the Franco era, not in a ministerial office, but in a prison cell.

Pujol is a phenomenon in his own right who, in a sense, has single-handedly wrenched Catalan regionalism away from its historical roots. But, at the same time, his brand of regionalism is essentially a new attempt to address the problem that plagued the Regionalist League at the turn of the century: how to mobilise mass political support for the economic interests of a small, privileged group – and how to control it once mobilised. Pujol's resolution of that dilemma has depended heavily on his own personal standing, and when he goes it will re-emerge in its full force. Hence the pervasive speculation in Catalonia about the uncertainties of a forthcoming 'post-Pujol era' (*pospujolismo*), in the same way that all Spain once waited on Franco's passing.

If history still weighs heavily in Catalonia, in the Basque Country its presence is almost overpowering. For one thing, the very weakness of historical claims to Basque nationhood means that, for many nationalists, it is all the more important that they be asserted as loudly and as often as possible. The irony is that most non-nationalists have already accepted the proposition of Basques' distinctiveness, albeit not necessarily on historical grounds; the ruling People's Party is especially careful to avoid offending sensibilities in that area, at least while its parliamentary majority is so precarious.

The traditionalist aspect of Basque nationalism has been enormously important, even for ETA. In its communiqués down the years, 'revolutionary socialist' demands have sat oddly alongside those for the restoration of Basques' traditional rights. And many observers have commented on the clearly traceable links between its intransigent, irrational, violent approach to politics and the Carlist movement of the last century, from which a number of early nationalists emerged. But even more important for ETA's development, and attitudes to it, has been the Basque Country's more recent history.

For three decades now, the region has experienced one sort of trauma after another: the virtually endemic industrial conflict which formed the background to the early stages of ETA's 'armed struggle'; the often bitter debates over devolution of the decade after 1975, against a background of increased violence; the political crisis of the mid-1980s; and ETA's later evolution into a marginalised but still highly effective terrorist group. Add to that a savage industrial restructuring that threw thousands out of work and destroyed whole communities, a massive drug problem among young people and the persistent security force abuses which have killed and maimed scores, and caused less extreme harm to hundreds more – not to mention the GAL revelations of the 1990s. The contradictory impact of these various factors has been much in evidence since 1996, and will doubtless continue to be so.

There is a sense in which the GAL affair, while especially alarming because of its nature, is merely one example of a more general phenomenon that, once again, derives from Spain's particular historical experience. The apparatus of the Spanish state was constructed late in comparison to most of its neighbours – in many fields only in the

1950s, and in some not until the 1970s. It also came into being under the special circumstances of dictatorship. In 1975, the Spanish public service had little or no ethos of public accountability. Indeed, in the military and security forces the concept made no sense; there the key virtue was obedience, ultimately to a leader whose only responsibility was before God. More than two decades of democratic rule have brought some changes, but the sense that rulers and administrators occupy their positions by right and are answerable to no one has been hard to dislodge.

Another feature of contemporary Spanish government also reflects the experience of the Franco era. Dictatorships anywhere fill the administration with their own supporters. In Spain, though, the practice was already common under the façade of democratic conditions of the last century, when the successive pairs of embryonic parties – first Moderates and Progressives, later Conservatives and Liberals – used the gift of public jobs as a way of buying support. During the Socialist hegemony of the 1980s patronage recovered that function, but more often served as a means of securing party control over government, at central, regional and local level. Since the pendulum swung and the People's Party acquired a similarly strong hold on government, the same process has been visible, with the PP in turn 'colonising' large tracts of the public service and its related agencies.

The parties and the system they compose also show a strong historical imprint, their development heavily conditioned by the very limited scope for their normal activities prior to 1975. Only the PNV and, in certain areas, the PSOE ever became the sort of mass party common in most of western Europe. Not only that: for various reasons, parties as institutions were poorly regarded by unusually wide sections of opinion, including both Franco and the anarchist movement. In both these respects, Spain can be said to have anticipated developments elsewhere, towards a media-centred, personalised style of politics in which mass parties play little part, and are held in low esteem by voters. Similarly, the PP's relative lack of ideological baggage and long-standing commitments to particular interests may be one reason why it has survived the midnineties swing to the Left so much better than most of its European equivalents.

Another reason, though, is a question of timing, or rather the way in which recent history has left the political cycle in Spain completely out of step with that in western Europe as a whole. In 1982 the after-effects of the Franco regime, which included the Right's complete disarray, meant that the Left swept into power just as everywhere else the pendulum was swinging hard in the opposite direction. Then, in power, the Socialists were faced with carrying out the sort of free market reforms being undertaken throughout the West, which in Spain involved attacking welfare provisions put in place by Franco but now defended by their own traditional supporters. And, just as elsewhere the Right was eventually undermined by a reaction against neo-liberalism and a general mood of staleness, so was the PSOE, and at much the same time. Hence why, virtually since 1986, Spain's government has had a different political hue to those of nearly all of its fellow EU members.

Further reading

The following comments cannot pretend to be comprehensive. They are intended merely to offer a range of sources suitable for readers who are not specialist historians but feel ready to take the next step beyond the material provided here. A number of authors (Carr, Payne, Preston) have written so widely on the period that for reasons of space only a selection of their output can be mentioned here. There is emphatically no intention to deter readers from sampling their other works; quite the reverse, in fact.

General works

The standard academic work in English, covering most of the period in considerable detail, is Carr's massive tome (8). Much more accessible is the 'pocket version' (7) which starts with the Restoration period rather than at the outset of the liberal era. Shubert (46) provides an account that goes below the political surface, and covers more than the social history indicated by the title; he is particularly useful on the Franco era. Romero-Salvadó (45) provides an extremely up-to-date and generally readable account of twentieth-century developments. For a very different approach, concerned almost entirely with overview rather than chronological detail, try Vilar (50), in particular the later chapters, and for a Spanish view of the whole period see the book by Fusi and Palafox (16). Finally, although it was written over half a century ago, to my mind Brenan's classic (6) still provides the best introduction to pre-Civil War Spain; its topic-based arrangement and down-to-earth style allow the non-specialist reader to see the wood for the trees.

Chapter 1

Here there is very little written in English other than for specialists, although the early parts of Payne's work (36) on the military are accessible as well as enlightening. To get a feel for nineteenth-century Spain there is no better source than the novels of Galdós; one of the most famous is now available in translation (17).

Chapter 2

The articles by Harper (24) and Chandler (10), unfortunately difficult to locate, are excellent introductions to the First Republic and Restoration respectively, while Kern (32) includes a useful chapter on the operation of clientilism.

Chapter 3

For a discussion of 'regenerationist' ideas and their impact, see the articles by Harrison (25) and Ortega (34). The standard work on early Basque regionalism is by Payne (37), although Heiberg (26) offers an equally interesting view; for the Catalan variety see Balcells (1). The comparative treatments by Conversi (12) and Díez Medrano (15) offer contrasting interpretations of the differences between the two movements; both are rewarding if not light reading. Bookchin (5) provides a useful introduction to Spanish anarchism, while Geary (18) sets the Spanish labour movement in international perspective. Specifically on the PSOE, see Heywood (27), or Gillespie's detailed party history (19).

Chapter 4

The article by Ben-Ami (2) gives the best overview of the Primo dictatorship; for a more detailed account see the relevant chapters in the book by the same author (3). The relevant chapters of the works by Payne (36) and Preston (43) on the military are also useful.

Chapter 5

A considerable amount has been written on the Second Republic; given the nature of the period, treatments tend to vary significantly in their assessments. Jackson (31) and Preston (42), alone or in the international treatment written jointly with Graham (21), tend broadly to sympathise with the Left; Payne (39) with the Right, whose nature is in turn revealingly analysed by Preston (43). The article by Graham (20) analyses the crucial differences within the Socialist movement.

Chapter 6

Here both the quantity of material and the degree of partisanship is even more marked. Again, Jackson (31) and Preston and Mackenzie (44) offer eminently readable accounts from a basically Republican perspective, while the differences between the early and late editions of Thomas' work (48, 49) reflect changes in the author's own political standpoint. For an understanding of the Nationalist side, Preston's biography of Franco (41) is particularly recommended. The article by Casanova (9) offers an interesting insight into the revolutionary view of the war on the Left. Moving towards literature, Orwell's account of the 1937 Barcelona clashes (35) retains its power, while Ken Loach's film *Land and Freedom* gives an unashamedly partisan, but incredibly immediate picture of the left-wing militias. Finally, for an intriguing analysis of Britain's role in the conflict, see Moradiellos (33).

Chapters 7 and 8

Payne (38), Blaye (4), and Grugel and Rees (23), all provide analyses of the Franco regime's nature, on which Preston's massive but highly readable biography of its master

(41) is also most enlightening. The opening chapter of the same author's study of the transition (40) gives a very useful overview of the opposition forces.

Chapters 9 and 10

The transition to democracy is another much-studied topic, not least in conjunction with comparable processes elsewhere; see, for example, the work by Higley and Gunther (29). Coverdale (14), Graham (22) and Preston (40) each provide interesting accounts of the process itself, from slightly differing viewpoints. So far the period since 1982 has, naturally enough, been less widely covered, at least from a historian's perspective; that of a political scientist is included in the study by Heywood (28) of post-Franco Spain. In Spanish, the same period is covered with great thoroughness – again from a political science perspective – in the volume edited by Cotarelo (13), although readers should bear in mind the close connections of most of its authors with the Socialist party. ETA has been the subject of a number of studies; those by Clark (11) and Sullivan (47) are both highly informative, but require committed reading. The comparative studies by Conversi (12) and Díez Medrano (15) both analyse contemporary developments in the Basque and Catalan regionalist movements, while Hollyman (30) provides a useful overview of the devolution process as a whole.

List of further reading

1. Balcells, A. (1996) *Catalan Nationalism: Past and Present*. London: Macmillan.
2. Ben-Ami, S. 'The dictatorship of Primo de Rivera' in *The Journal of Contemporary History*, January 1977.
3. Ben-Ami, S. (1978) *The Origins of the Second Republic in Spain*. Oxford: Oxford University Press.
4. Blaye, E. de (1974) *Franco and the Politics of Spain*. Harmondsworth: Penguin.
5. Bookchin, M. (1977) *The Spanish Anarchists*. New York: Freelife.
6. Brenan, G. (1990) *The Spanish Labyrinth*. Cambridge: Cambridge University Press.
7. Carr, R. (1980) *Modern Spain 1875–1980*. Oxford: Oxford University Press.
8. Carr, R. (1982) *Spain 1808–1975*. Oxford: The Clarendon Press.
9. Casanova, J. 'The egalitarian dream' in *Journal of the Association of Iberian Studies*, Autumn 1989.
10. Chandler, J. 'The self-destructive nature of the Spanish Restoration' in *Iberian Studies*, Autumn 1973.
11. Clark, R. (1984) *The Basque Insurgents: 1952–1980*. Reno: University of Nevada Press.
12. Conversi, D. (1997) *The Basques, the Catalans and Spain*. London: Hurst.
13. Cotarelo, R. (ed.) (1992) *Transición política y consolidación democrática*. Madrid: Centro de Investigaciones Sociológicas.
14. Coverdale, J. (1979) *The Political Transformation of Spain after Franco*. New York: Praeger.
15. Díez Medrano, J. (1995) *Divided Nations*. Ithaca: Cornell University Press.

16. Fusi, J. P. and J. Palafox (1998) *España 1808–1996: El desafío de la modernidad*. Madrid: Espasa.
17. Galdós, B. Pérez (1988) *Fortunata and Jacinta*. London: Penguin.
18. Geary, D. (ed) (1989) *Labour and Socialist Movements in Europe before 1914*. Oxford: Berg.
19. Gillespie, R. (1989) *The Spanish Socialist Party. A History of Factionalism*. Oxford: The Clarendon Press.
20. Graham, H. 'Spanish Socialism in crisis' in *Journal of the Association of Iberian Studies*, Spring 1990.
21. Graham, H. and P. Preston (1987) *The Popular Front in Europe*. Basingstoke: Macmillan.
22. Graham, R. (1984) *Spain: Change of a Nation*. London: Michael Joseph.
23. Grugel, J. and T. Rees (1997) *Franco's Spain*. London: Arnold.
24. Harper, G. 'The birth of the first Spanish Republic' in *Iberian Studies*, 16(1&2), 1987.
25. Harrison, J. 'The regenerationist movement in Spain' in *European Studies Review*, January 1979.
26. Heiberg, M. (1989) *The Making of the Basque Nation*. Cambridge: Cambridge University Press.
27. Heywood, P. (1990) *Marxism and the Failure of Organised Socialism in Spain*. Cambridge: Cambridge University Press.
28. Heywood, P. (1995) *The Government and Politics of Spain*. London: Macmillan.
29. Higley, J. and R. Gunther (1992) *Elites and Democratic Consolidation in Latin America and Southern Europe*. Cambridge: Cambridge University Press.
30. Hollyman, J. 'The tortuous road to regional autonomy in Spain' in *Journal of the Association of Iberian Studies*, Spring 1995.
31. Jackson, G. (1965) *The Spanish Republic and the Civil War*. Princeton: Princeton University Press.
32. Kern, R. (1973) *The Caciques*. Albuquerque: University of New Mexico Press.
33. Moradiellos, E. 'The British government and the Spanish Civil War' in *International Journal of Iberian Studies*, 12/1, 1999.
34. Ortega, J. 'Aftermath of splendid disaster' in *Journal of Contemporary History*, April 1980.
35. Orwell, G. (1986) *Homage to Catalonia*. London: Secker and Warburg.
36. Payne, S. (1967) *Politics and the Military in Modern Spain*. Stanford: Stanford University Press.
37. Payne, S. (1975) *Basque Nationalism*. Reno: University of Nevada Press.
38. Payne, S. (1987) *The Franco Regime*. Madison: University of Wisconsin Press.
39. Payne, S. (1993) *Spain's First Democracy*. Madison: University of Wisconsin Press.
40. Preston, P. (1986) *The Triumph of Democracy in Spain*. London: Methuen.
41. Preston, P. (1993) *Franco*. London: HarperCollins.
42. Preston, P. (1994) *The Coming of the Spanish Civil War*. London: Routledge.
43. Preston, P. (1995) *The Politics of Revenge*. London: Routledge.

44. Preston, P. and A. Mackenzie (1996) *The Republic Besieged*. Edinburgh: Edinburgh University Press.

45. Romero-Salvadó, F. J. (1999) *Twentieth-century Spain*. London: Macmillan.

46. Shubert, A. (1990) *A Social History of Modern Spain*. London: Unwin Hyman.

47. Sullivan, J. (1988) *ETA and Basque Nationalism*. London: Routledge.

48. Thomas, H. (1961) *The Spanish Civil War*. London: Penguin.

49. Thomas, H. (1990) *The Spanish Civil War*. Harmondsworth: Penguin.

50. Vilar, P. (1977) *Spain, a Brief History*. Oxford: Pergamon.

For reference purposes

Smith, A. (1996) *Historical Dictionary of Spain*. Lanham, Michigan: Scarecrow.

Index/Glossary

A page number in **bold** indicates an insert dedicated to the entry
A page number followed by 'i' indicates a reference to the entry in an insert